This edition published October 2006
in the United Kingdom by
Ptarmigan Publishing Limited
46 New Park Street
Devizes, Wiltshire SN10 1DT

A catalogue record of this book is available from the
British Library

ISBN 1 90412 214 0

Colour origination and print management by
LPD plc London & Warwick

Printed in Great Britain by Butler and Tanner Ltd, Frome

FOREWORD

MICHEL ROUX JR

I have always been a fan of Masterchef, and even more so the new format headed by John Torode and Gregg Wallace. The production and clever editing make it compulsive viewing, it's entertaining, fun and to a certain degree educational. That is why I have always said yes when asked if I would be available to contribute.

The vast majority of my time is spent in my kitchens at Le Gavroche because I am first and foremost a chef and, in my view, cooking should not be denigrated. I am not one for prancing around like a buffoon in front of cameras trying to produce something vaguely edible in 10 minutes.

All three finalists showed that they have respect for ingredients and a love of cooking that in itself was enough to make them all winners, however that would not make good television and after all this is a competition and a winner is needed.

Much to the production team's discontent, Peter shone at almost every hurdle. His vast knowledge gleaned from his collection of cookbooks and years of practice as a home gourmet gave him the edge. Rightfully crowned as Masterchef 2006, part of his prize was to join the kitchen brigade at Le Gavroche for a month's work experience.

Within a matter of minutes, Peter was mucking in and part of the team, not an easy task when the average age in the kitchen is about 23. As a grand finale, I asked Peter to join me cooking and serving at the 'Taste of London' food festival. He approached this with his usual gusto and earned the respect of his fellow workers by giving his usual 100%. At the end of the show, having worked 18hrs a day for 5 days, I don't think I have ever seen anyone quite as happy, smiling, content and knackered.

He may just have missed his vocation in life, but I have a feeling that Peter's is about to begin.

Michel Roux Jr
Chef Patron, Le Gavroche

Acknowledgements

Thanks to the following people:

John Handley, whose faith and commitment enabled this book to reach publication.

Mark Hodson, Mark Dawson and everyone else at Ptarmigan for making a really great job of producing the book.

Jon Dudley for a cracking cover design and Adrian Turner for some seriously sexy photography that really captured the spirit of the foods I love to cook.

Thanks also to Colin Staplehurst Butchers and Terry's Fisheries, both of The Riverside in Lewes, and Bill's Produce Store also of Lewes for providing venues for photography and also many of the ingredients used in the following recipes.

Finally, thanks to John Torode and Gregg Wallace and to all those people who have offered me their congratulations and best wishes on winning Masterchef.

Throughout this book metric measurements have been used for both weight and volume, and degrees celcius for temperatures. For those of you who use other measurements, simple conversion tables can be found on page 192.

THE RECIPES

PREFACE

MasterChef Goes Large has to be one of the most gruelling televised competitions thus far created. Certainly it is a test of the contestants' cooking skills, but more than that it is a relentless test of physical, mental and emotional stamina. Unlike Big Brother or Pop Idol, the makers of MCGL assert that their show is not about thrusting unknown individuals into the limelight in order to create instant celebrities, but rather to find the best amateur cook out of those who put themselves forward to be judged. Honourable intentions indeed, and intentions that I believe were carried out to the letter by judges whose professionalism and fairness were beyond reproach. It is in the editing suite however, where many hundreds of hours of filming have to be whittled down to a series of 29-minute programmes, that those intentions may be called into question. You don't have to be a student of popular culture to understand the most basic requirement of any television programme. Whilst it may inform, educate and entertain, to succeed it must above all else secure its share of the viewing public. MCGL 2006 did well in this respect, hitting over 3 million viewers in the first week, maintaining its audience throughout six weeks of heats, and attracting close to 4 million viewers during the two weeks of semi-finals and finals. For BBC2, between 6.30pm and 7.00pm every weeknight, that is very good going.

The programme makers are very talented people, and know how to gain and maintain viewers. They took the finalists on an incredible journey from the Arctic Circle to the Tropics and arranged for us to cook at The Ritz and on the QE2, astonishing experiences that would provide material for fascinating viewing. However the truth, as it naturally occurs, can be boring, and programme makers often need to 'spice things up' by assiduous cutting and juxtaposition of words and images. Whilst the editors can justifiably claim that they can only show that which has been filmed, there is often more truth in the footage we never get to see. It is also true that accurate recordings of events may be cropped or edited so that their meanings are obscured or changed altogether.

I confess that had I been aware from the outset of the potential for unhappiness that would accompany my win, I might not have entered the competition to become MasterChef 2006. This is to take nothing away from the many genuine people I have since met who have offered me their congratulations and warmest wishes; rather to allow that those people who so forcefully expressed their disapproval of my win succeeded in making me feel wretched. It was not their fault that they believed so strongly that the judges had made the wrong decision, neither was it their fault that they had been manipulated and misled into believing that they were correct in their assessment of what they had seen. There can be no excuse for many of the unpleasant comments posted on the BBC's website and elsewhere, but those responsible may be excused for failing to comprehend how it was that they had been deliberately deceived.

I am more amused than bitter or resentful about all of this. Those who stick their heads up above the parapet must expect to get them shot at, and I remain unswervingly proud of my achievement and eternally grateful to those whose encouragement and inspiration helped me to win the title. I voluntarily entered the competition, and I accept the criticisms as well as the praise. I hope that after reading the following pages you will have a clearer view of how it was that I won the competition and also how, at the age of almost sixty, I came to enter it in the first place. Above all, though, I hope that you will gain an insight into my love of cooking and the endless possibilities that food holds for enriching the quality of our lives.

Peter Bayless May 2006

CHAPTER ONE

OUR WINNER

Our winner …Our MasterChef … is Peter.

My goodness, how astounding, I'd won. After getting through the heats and quarterfinal, then months of waiting before three weeks of almost unbelievable trials in the semis and again throughout the finals, suddenly John Torode announced that I was the winner. Only days earlier it looked like I wouldn't even make the final day, let alone win the competition.

Sunday 11th December 2005, and we had just embarked on the penultimate set of challenges in the televised competition to become MasterChef 2006. We were due a mere 36 hours on board QE2 with two more tests lined up for us. The following morning we three finalists were scheduled to cook the breakfast eggs for a thousand or so paying passengers, then later the same day prepare and cook a four-course dinner of our own creation for eight people at the Captain's table. The day after that, when the liner docked at Lisbon, we would disembark and fly home for a few days' rest prior to cooking our final three-course meal for the judges on the Saturday. We spent our first evening on board QE2 preparing for the breakfast service. Dean and Daksha prepped up for the omelette fillings whilst I was another deck below, trying my best to poach 250 eggs in a vat large enough to drown a horse. Poaching eggs can be tricky at the best of times, especially if the eggs are not absolutely new-laid and the water gets too hot. My little tricks for poaching eggs involve adding plenty of white vinegar to the water and waiting until the bubbles begin to rise from the bottom of the pan, when I pop the whole egg, shell and all, into the hot water for about 10-15 seconds to begin the process of setting the egg white. I then whisk the water to create a vortex, crack the egg, and let it fall into the centre of the spiral. The spinning water gently wraps the white around the yolk and after about three minutes (depending on the size of the egg) I take it out with a slotted spoon and drop it into iced water to stop it cooking any further. All well and good when you have the luxury of poaching your eggs one at a time. But I had to do 250! 250 times three minutes equals 750 minutes, that's twelve and a half hours. No, no, something horribly wrong with that: there had to be a better way.

I was standing, or rather swaying as by now the ship had set sail from Las Palmas in Gran Canaria, in front of a huge steaming brat pan about five feet by three feet by six inches deep. To my left were tray upon tray of eggs, and to my right a load of containers full of water and ice cubes. I genuinely felt that I could do with some words of advice from the resident head chef, but sadly he was nowhere to be seen and all the other chefs down there looked far too busy to be bothered with the likes of me. I could smell that the water had already been dosed with a liberal amount of vinegar, but instinctively felt that the water was too hot and looked about me for some sort of control to regulate the temperature of this vast cooking pan. I pulled the lid down; no, no dials or switches there, so quickly put it back up again as the water would get even hotter with the lid on. One young man working on the other side of the kitchen called over and pointed to a control panel on the wall that would not have looked out of place on the Starship Enterprise. This really worried me. If I got this wrong I might plunge the whole kitchen – or worse still the whole deck of the ship – into total darkness. I pushed a button and hoped. Sure enough, back at my brat pan I could see that the water had begun to go off the boil. Seizing my moment I thought I'd try my old technique and test just one egg. It didn't work very well as most of the white separated from the yolk before beginning to set. This didn't bode at all well for the other 249.

I retrieved my pitiful attempt from the water just in time for it to be seen by the chef who had returned at that very moment. 'Huh,' said he, 'You'll be here all night at that rate – and your water's too hot: it's stripped the white from the yolk.' 'Yes, I know Chef,' I pleaded rather pathetically. 'I was just testing one before wasting a whole load of eggs.' Chef didn't look too pleased. 'Here, use these,' he said, passing me one of those polythene-covered tubes of plastic cups you normally get at an office water fountain. 'You need to break about 20 eggs at a time into these plastic cups and then, when the water's the correct temperature, tip them all in at once. Don't break them, mind, and don't let them stick together.' I laid out a couple of dozen plastic cups and began to deftly break the eggs, one into each cup. 'Wait!' cried Chef, 'the water is getting too cold now – some idiot has turned the heater off!' I confessed to the misdemeanour and explained that I had no idea how to control the instrument on the wall. A very hurried and somewhat impatient lesson later and back at the brat pan I began tipping the eggs into the hot water. As I expected, the whites were separating from the yolks with boring and wasteful regularity. 'Chef, excuse me, but I usually put the unshelled eggs into the hot water for a few seconds before breaking them. That way…' 'Dreadful idea' said he, 'Don't you know what part of the bird eggs come from? Just get the temperature right and tip them in carefully – you'll be all right. And put these plastic gloves on, we maintain the highest standards of hygiene in this kitchen. I'll be back shortly to see how you're getting on.' With that he was gone again and I was feeling decidedly lacking in confidence. I had begun to feel decidedly off-colour as well – rather queasy and head-achy. Must be the heat down here in the kitchen, I thought, and the fact that I hadn't yet found my sea legs. Unperturbed, and determined not to be beaten by what in truth ought to have been a fairly simple task, I pressed on. The next twenty eggs were just as bad as the first, and if there is one thing I hate more than failure, its waste. I wondered if I dared use my old trick of dunking the unshelled eggs into the hot water – after all, what the eye doesn't see etc, and I'd always been sure that the hot water would kill off any problem bugs on the shells. So, with no-one looking, I used my own technique. It worked quite well and I soon had a hundred or so passably well poached eggs resting in the iced water. They weren't up to my usual standard, but I put this down to my belief that they were probably a week or more old. Meanwhile, the queasiness and headache were getting worse.

An hour or so later Chef returned and began to rummage through what must have been about 200 poached eggs. 'Some of these are quite passable. Come on, let's get them into the chiller and you can come upstairs and help the other two finish off.' Quite a relief, as it was very much cooler up there in the prep area.

Mis en place finished and surfaces cleaned down, we were free to shower and change ready for dinner in the ship's Mauritania Restaurant. Dean and I were sharing a reasonably comfortable cabin on One Deck, and little did I know as we changed out of chef's whites into something more appropriate for dining on the QE2 that this was to become both my hospital ward and my prison cell for the next three days and nights.

Upstairs in the restaurant, contestants, judges and production crew were tucking into a pretty good four-course meal whilst chatting about the early start and trials that lay before us the following morning. Food was the last thing on my mind. My stomach was getting worse by the minute, and the queasy rumblings were turning into severe pains. I realised I must have eaten something bad in Las Palmas the night before.

With such an early start ahead of us the 'party' did not linger, and I was thus able to retire to my cabin without appearing a wimp in front of the others. I just made it to the cabin bathroom before my body decided it was time to start rejecting whatever it was that was making me ill. The accompanying abdominal pains were excruciating, and my body became incapable of keeping anything within. Poor Dean had to put up with moans, groans and a wide range of other sound effects throughout the night. Come to think of it, the cabin couldn't have smelled that fresh either. By 5.30am it was time to get going as we were due in the kitchens by 6.00am, and even with no sleep and a night spent in or on the loo I was still determined to present myself for the tasks ahead. This was of course utterly ridiculous: I couldn't pass more than a few minutes without having to rush for relief, and even had I been able to the hygiene regulations on board QE2 would have prevented me from going anywhere near food preparation. Clutching my aching stomach I told Dean he'd have to go without me. He said he'd call the doctor for me and went off to work. I lay back on my bed in desperation, completely distraught. For months I had put so much of myself into this marathon competition, and up to this point maintained the belief that even at my advanced age I had a reasonable chance of winning it. By the time Dr Nikolas Hoffmann, Ship's Doctor RMS Queen Elizabeth 2, arrived at my cabin I had convinced myself that my attempt to win MasterChef 2006 was dead in the water.

The Doctor and his nurse gave me the kind of thorough medical examination that would cost a fortune in a private hospital ashore. They told me that, whilst they were fairly sure I was suffering from food poisoning, until proved otherwise they had to treat it as a possible case of *Norovirus gastroenteritis*, a highly contagious condition that can be easily spread by person to person contact. Worse still, if I had contracted this illness I would remain contagious for at least two days after my symptoms had subsided. They stuck needles into me, took samples of anything and everything, prodded and poked, tested heart, lungs, blood pressure and temperature, gave me massive doses of antibiotics and Loperamide Hydrochloride, told me to drink large quantities of water, then dealt the final blow. I would have to remain in quarantine for at least three days. For me the competition on board ship was over before it had even begun.

I hadn't realised, until the programme producer rang me later in the day, that poor old Dean had also been put in quarantine for twenty four hours because he'd slept in the same cabin as me. They had also been forced to postpone both the breakfast stint and the captain's table dinner. We wouldn't be disembarking at Lisbon next day, but staying on board for three more days and nights until docking back at Southampton. None of this made me feel any better. Instead of going home the next day I would be stuck alone in that cabin with nothing to look at through the porthole save for an ever-rising-and-falling horizon where grey sky meets even greyer sea. It was now Monday evening and the producer said that if I got the all-clear from the Doctor we could do the breakfast and dinner tests on Wednesday before arriving at Southampton on Thursday morning. My hopes were up, but by Tuesday morning I had to report to the Doctor that there was no marked improvement in my condition: if anything the diarrhoea had become even worse and the accompanying abdominal pains more intense than ever.

The programme producer rang me again to see how things were progressing. I wasn't allowed out and he wasn't allowed in. In fact no one was allowed in except for the Doctor and/or nurse and an 'Anti-bacterial Hit Squad' that descended on me three times a day. The latter, dressed in face masks and hoods, gloves, over-boots and baggy white overalls, looked like they belonged in a nuclear energy plant: it was their job to disinfect all surfaces in my cabin and spray everything, whether it moved or not, with anti-bacterial vapour. I wasn't enjoying any of this, and when the producer told me that the other two finalists were filling in time working in the ship's kitchens, under the guidance of Executive Chef Bernhard Stumpfel, my morale sunk to an all-time low.

Decisions had been made. I was definitely out of the picture, so the next morning Dean and Daksha would have to do the breakfast eggs without me – and they would have to do the Captain's table dinner without me too. This was a really tough call for them, but there was nothing whatsoever that I could do about it. The original plan for the dinner was that Dean would prepare and cook two starter courses of his own design, Daksha likewise with two main course options, and I was to do the soup course and the two desserts. All three of us had been given plenty of time to think about this important meal, and had been required to write down the ingredients for our dishes to be sure that everything needed was on board. Realising that Dean and Daksha now had to cook my three dishes as well as their own, it occurred to me that my lists of ingredients would be as good as useless if they didn't know what they were supposed to do with them. I suggested to the producer that the way out of this was for me to write down full recipes with detailed instructions for the methods. This I did in longhand, on some pages torn out of an exercise book and slipped under the cabin door for one of the crew to pass on to my two colleagues the night before their big challenge.

Late on Wednesday evening it was gratifying to learn not only that Dean and Daksha had done my recipes proud, but also that the dishes had been highly praised by the Captain and his guests. Not the same as having been there myself, but some compensation at least. Incidentally, when I saw this episode on television I couldn't help thinking that Daksha was being deliberately wound up. I wouldn't be at all surprised to learn that someone had 'inadvertently' moved her tray of fish from one oven to another without telling her, just to tighten the screw a little more.

Here are the dishes my fellow finalists cooked on my behalf on board QE2. The soup was made up on the spot, and of the two desserts one is a classic and the other is based on a classic with a bit of an idea of my own. I met the Captain before I was taken ill, so I knew from the soft lilt of his voice, similar to that of snooker player Dennis Taylor, that he was from Northern Ireland. It seemed likely that his guests would also be from some part of the British Isles, and I wanted to give them dishes that would be appropriate now that they were coming home after a round-the-world cruise. My recipes for these dishes are given below: if you try them for yourself, I hope you enjoy them.

Captain's Table QE2 Wednesday 14th December 2005: Second Course

Roasted pumpkin and garlic soup with Parmesan croûtons and parsley oil

8 to 10 servings

1 kg pumpkin
(butternut squash works just as well)

1 whole bulb of garlic

1 head of celery

2-3 shallots

A few sprigs fresh thyme

Olive oil

Butter

Salt and freshly ground black pepper

1 litre chicken stock (see right)

1 French loaf

100g lump of Parmesan cheese

1 bunch fresh parsley

Extra virgin olive oil

Lemon

For the stock

Chicken carcass

1 onion – including skin

2 carrots

1 stalk of celery
(taken from the whole head above)

Splash vegetable oil

A slug of white wine vinegar

Bottle of Muscadet
(or similar crisp, dry white wine)

2 bay leaves

Sprig of thyme

1 litre water

Cut open the pumpkin and discard the seeds and pith. Slice into segments about 2cm thick, leaving the skin on. Spread these out on baking trays, sprinkle with olive oil, salt, pepper and torn sprigs of thyme. Roast at 200°C for about 20 minutes. Test that the segments are cooked through – the edges should have taken on some colour that will add flavour to the finished dish. Remove from the oven and set aside.

Meanwhile break open the head of garlic, leave the skins on and add the cloves to a pan of boiling water. Boil for 7 minutes. Remove from the water; squeeze them out of their skins and fry gently in butter for 2 minutes. Set aside with the roasted pumpkin. Finely slice the shallots and celery and sweat in olive oil for 5 minutes, then set aside.

To make the stock, first roughly chop the chicken carcass, plus the onion and carrots (in their skins) and the stick of celery. Heat a splash of vegetable oil in a large saucepan until smoking hot then throw in the chopped chicken carcass. Cook over a high heat for a few minutes constantly shaking the pan, until the meaty bones have taken on plenty of colour. Add the chopped vegetables and again cook until they too are well coloured. Pour in a good slug of white wine vinegar and cook until completely evaporated. Then pour over a whole bottle of Muscadet, add the bay leaves and thyme and cook until reduced to about a third. Pour in a litre of boiling water and leave to cook uncovered at a rolling boil for 40 minutes.

Put the roasted pumpkin, cooked garlic, shallots and celery into a liquidizer and blitz thoroughly. You may need to do this in batches. Adding a little liquid from the stockpot will help achieve a smooth consistency. Strain the stock through a muslin-lined sieve into the purée, strain again, check for seasoning and adjust if necessary. Keep warm at the back of the stove but do not allow to boil again.

Slice the French loaf into small rounds about 10mm thick and toast on both sides. Blitz the parsley with a little salt and lemon juice and stir in enough extra virgin olive oil to make a thick pouring sauce. Ladle the soup into bowls; use a pastry brush to paint one side of each croûton with a little extra virgin olive oil. Float a croûton (oiled side down) into each bowl of soup. Sprinkle the croûtons with freshly grated Parmesan cheese and flash under a very hot grill. Just before serving, drizzle a little parsley oil into each bowl of soup.

Captain's Table QE2 Wednesday 14th December 2005 – Dessert Course 1

Rhubarb clafoutis

8 sticks good, fine, pink rhubarb

2 tablespoons caster sugar

Butter for greasing

Icing sugar for dusting

For the batter

300ml whipping cream

200ml milk

6 large eggs

50g plain flour

200g caster sugar

Pinch salt

1 level dessert spoon ground almonds

Splash Amaretto

400ml extra thick cream for serving.

Paint the inside of 8 individual ramekins with melted butter. Blitz all the batter ingredients in a blender and allow to rest while cooking the rhubarb.

Cut the rhubarb into lengths about 25mm and scatter over a baking sheet lined with baking parchment. Sprinkle with sugar and just a few drops of water. Place in a hot oven, 190°C, and cook for around 8 minutes for the rhubarb to just become tender. Carefully place into a colander over a basin to collect the juices while the rhubarb cools. Place a few pieces of rhubarb into each dish, pour over the batter mix and bake in the oven for about 40 minutes. Remove and allow to cool a little before serving.

Liquidize the remaining rhubarb with the collected juices. Place in a saucepan and warm through. If too sharp, stir in some icing sugar. This sauce can be stirred through the thick cream before serving with the clafoutis. Sprinkle with icing sugar before serving.

Captain's Table QE2 Wednesday 14th December 2005 – Dessert Course 2

Whisky syruped kumquats with snow eggs and bitter chocolate

For the kumquats

800g kumquats

The juice of 6 oranges

450g caster sugar

Blended Scotch whisky

For decoration

Good quality bitter chocolate

Finely pared rind of one lime

For the snow eggs

8 egg whites

Caster sugar measured to twice the weight of the egg whites

500ml milk

1.5 litres water

Icing sugar

Halve the kumquats and remove any pips. Bring the orange juice, sugar, and a cup of water to the boil in a saucepan, then reduce the temperature and allow to simmer for 5 minutes. Add the kumquats and cook gently for about 45 minutes, until the peel is cooked through and tender to the bite. Set aside to cool to room temperature. Before serving, stir in a generous measure of whisky.

Whisky syruped kumquats with snow eggs and bitter chocolate (cont)

To make the snow eggs, whisk the egg whites to soft peak stage and add half the sugar, whisking continuously. When fully incorporated, add the remaining sugar and continue to whisk until the mixture forms shiny firm peaks.

Heat the milk and water in a large, wide-topped pan to just below a simmer. Shape the meringue mixture between two tablespoons and poach a few at a time in the hot milk and water. Poach for about 3 minutes before carefully turning to poach the other side for a further 3 minutes. Remove with a slotted spoon and carefully place on greaseproof paper dusted with icing sugar.

Place a 100mm ring mould in the centre of a serving plate (black plates really set this dish off to its best). Spoon the whisky-syruped kumquats inside. Top with a snow egg (or two, depending on size) and lift off the ring mould. Spoon a little of the sweet orange sauce around the dish. Decorate the snow eggs with melted bitter chocolate and finally a touch of lime zest. Shavings of bitter chocolate may be arranged over the sweet orange sauce.

* * *

About midday on the Wednesday I began to feel a little better and it occurred to me that, apart from the doctor's medicines and copious amounts of water, I hadn't actually consumed anything since a few light sandwiches three days earlier. Audaciously I rang cabin service and ordered a three-course meal and a bottle of Muscadet – well it couldn't do me any harm, could it?

Sitting alone in that cabin for four nights and three days wasn't my idea of fun, but it had at least given me time to reflect on what a man almost sixty years old was doing entering a television challenge to find the country's most promising amateur chef. Why, when most people of my age are thinking about retirement or at least taking things a bit more easily, was I voluntarily competing in a championship that promised to change my life and open up the doors to a new and exciting career? I suppose, like most things that shape our destiny, it all began in early childhood.

CHAPTER TWO

EARLY DAYS

The fifteenth child of an austere Victorian working-class family, my mother was the hardest working person I have ever known. With precious little money at her disposal, the daily battle she fought against grime was the only way she knew to rise above being what she called 'common'. Her home – a rented, post-war, semi-basement flat – and her children were scrubbed daily from top to bottom. The latter was a ritual that involved being stood in the butler sink in the scullery where first my elder sister then I were lathered all over with green Palmolive soap and a flannel before being doused with warm water from a saucepan heated on the gas stove. After which, wrapped in winceyette pyjamas and dressing gowns, we would sit by the coal fire and eat. Sumptuous pies, fragrant soups, crusty bread and cheese, and on Saturdays the most delicious apple tarts.

How she managed it I will never know. On the meagre wage my father secured as a chauffeur, faced with shortages, queues and ration books, somehow my mother never failed to regale us with the most wonderful food.

This, of course, was how I came to love the kitchen and the endless possibilities that place holds for bringing pleasure to people. I don't know who said it before me, but it is certainly true that cooking is like making love: the pleasure received is through the pleasure given. Throughout the last - goodness, almost half a century - I have sought to provide something like the pleasure of my childhood feasts to everyone who has ever eaten the food I have prepared. And no matter how many uncertainties I have encountered in life, one constant remains: wherever I go, I find wonderful foods that only require care and a little passion to turn into a feast.

• • •

My arrival in post-war North London must have set a few tongues wagging. The gleaming black chauffeur-driven Phantom III Rolls Royce that conveyed me home from The Mildmay Road Nursing Home and pulled up outside 86 Finsbury Park Road was not exactly a common sight in that part of town. Neither was it usual for a new-born babe to be cradled in the arms of a black African nursemaid. Born in 1946, almost nine months to the day after my father's demobilisation from the RAF in the war, I was the second child of William and Maud, then living in the ground floor flat of a Victorian terraced house. William, 'Bill' as he was known to all, had returned to his pre-war job as a chauffeur to the wealthy industrialist Joseph

Swindon, hence the car and the driver. As for the 'nurse' the truth is that Dorothy was cook to the Swindon's London household and a close friend of my parents. There had never been any swank intended; it was just that my father had borrowed the car in order to transport my mother and his newborn son home after the delivery and compulsory 'lying-in' period. And, as it was Dorothy's day off, she had pleaded with him to come along to see my mother and the new arrival.

My father was a remarkable man, who from the very poorest of backgrounds somehow managed, through honesty and hard work, to create for himself and his family a home of which he could be justly proud. A home kept scrupulously clean by my mother, who took in machining children's clothes to augment dad's wages and to save for treats and our annual Summer holiday by the sea in a Cornish guest house.

Family legend had it that one of my father's uncles died by drowning in the Thames after leaping on a drunken bet from London Bridge. Folklore or not, it was certainly true that my paternal grandfather, Jack, would rather have had a jug of ale on the table than put food into his children's tummies. As a result my father hardly touched alcohol, save for the odd glass of wine or beer he allowed himself at Christmas. Food, however, was another matter. Maybe it was because as a child my father would often have to scavenge under street traders' stalls for a fallen apple for his supper. Perhaps it was because, as chauffeur to a grand household with cooks and maids, he daily saw masses of food go to waste: whatever the reason, my parents always prided themselves on laying 'a good table'.

In those days, when bombed-out buildings left gaps in the terraced rows of houses like rotted teeth in the mouth of an old crone, the streets were not an ideal place for children to play. It was better that I stayed indoors, and with coal as well as food on ration the kitchen was always the warmest and most welcoming place to be. I always loved food, and loved being allowed to help my mother in the kitchen. Stirring the puddings, making the pastry, peeling the vegetables – all seemed much more fun to me than kicking a ball or playing cowboys and indians out on the street.

My mother's unshakeable belief that it was her duty to provide food for her husband and children prevented my father from ever being permitted to cook. The one exception to this rule was the breakfast he prepared for himself at 5.30 every morning before leaving for work. Each and every day he indulged himself with a large bowl of cornflakes, sprinkled with All Bran and then doused with hot milk and brown sugar. Whenever he was asked if he cooked, my Father's well rehearsed, tongue-in-cheek response was always the same: *'no, but I do boil my own cornflakes'*.

I suppose that by today's standards my early childhood was very uncomplicated, and not particularly exciting either. Not that this thought ever occurred to me, because for most of the time I was blissfully happy, and food always seemed to be central to that happiness. Some of my earliest recollections of life before school age involve little excitements like being allowed to give a sugar cube to the milkman's pony, or running to open the front door when I heard the sound of the muffin man's hand bell. Once a week my mother would let me go out to the street to meet this man, who wore a floury white coat, long apron, and floppy white hat. He came from the baker's shop in Blackstock Road and carried fresh crumpets and muffins, teacakes and Chelsea buns in a wooden tray that he balanced precariously on top of his head. Just a couple of pennies guaranteed a scrumptious tea. 'Grandpa', my maternal grandfather, lived with us, and on these occasions he and I would sit in front of the coal fire where we toasted our bounty on long-handled brass forks. Mother would butter them while they were still hot so that the butter, or more often margarine, would soak right through and run down our fingers and chins as we ate.

Long before anyone ever dreamt of a supermarket, food shopping was almost a daily occurrence. I always accompanied my Mother on her shopping trips, and found wonder in the array of produce available in our local high street. When you are less than three feet high you see everything from a different perspective. I recall that the greengrocer always had muddy hands, that there was bloodstained sawdust on the floor of the butcher's shop. The ground was always wet around the open-fronted fish shop where men who wore heavy boots and leather helmets used huge metal hooks to drag great blocks of ice from a horse-drawn trailer onto their shoulders before depositing them on the fishmonger's marble slab.

Sainsbury's, a bit further up the road towards Nag's Head, was our local high street grocer and my mother held that 'emporium' in great esteem, demonstrating a high degree of brand loyalty long before anyone new what brand loyalty meant. For me it meant a very long walk there and back, but it was a real adventure to visit the place. I remember with nostalgia the wondrous Victorian tiled interior with black and white chequered stone floor, the marble-topped mahogany counters and gracious, immaculately dressed, assistants. The produce was real too and the whole place smelled of food, a kind of divine mix of cheese, coffee, bacon and dried fruit. There were great truckles of cheese and huge blocks of butter from which your slab would be carved and knocked into shape with wooden butter pats before being deftly wrapped in greaseproof paper. Sugar too was scooped from a sack then poured into beautiful blue paper bags to carry home. They even had wicker seated bentwood chairs for the elderly or expectant mothers to sit on while their orders were being made up. It was in Sainsbury's that I first saw a rabbit being skinned, and the whole sides of cured bacon hanging from metal rails on the wall behind the counter were obviously half of what had once been pigs. When my mother bought her 8 ounces of longback, the whole side would be lifted down onto the bacon slicer where it would be cut to exactly her preferred thickness. I remain convinced that it is right and proper for children to grow up with an understanding of where food comes from and how it arrives at our tables.

I am not sure that shopkeepers in those days studied retail psychology or product placement, but the sloping, glass-topped biscuit barrels along the front edge of the counter were at exactly the right height to delight the eyes of a four-year-old boy.

Sometimes, if I'd been a good boy and she could afford it, my mother would buy a little bag of broken biscuits for me to nibble at on the way home.

• • •

My father's job quite often kept him away from home. What with early starts, late nights, and frequent trips abroad, it always seemed rather special when we could all sit down together at the weekends to eat as a family. There was an underlying pattern or unwritten formula about the week's menu which, although varied in content, never failed to maintain its structure. Sunday lunch, or dinner as it was called in my family, was a very grand affair that always involved roasted meat of one kind or another. There would be roast and boiled vegetables and gravy, followed by a dessert – 'afters' – that usually comprised home made sweet pies or puddings served with Bird's custard or canned Carnation evaporated milk.

My mother seemed to spend the whole of Sunday morning in the kitchen: mixing, rubbing-in, stirring, beating, kneading, roasting, boiling and baking. The kitchen was filled with steam, and by the time 'dinner' was served at one o'clock sharp, mother was usually steaming too. All this work meant that there was no time for breakfast, and the rest of the family was sternly warned to keep out of the kitchen and not to get 'under her feet'. I took this threat literally, and carried with me a frightful image of ending up on the kitchen floor with my mother standing on top of me.

The immediate family of my mother and father, plus my sister Gloria, five years my senior, and Grandpa was often extended into a much larger group by the addition of one or more of my many aunts and uncles with accompanying cousins. On these occasions the supply of produce became a shared responsibility, as did the cooking of it, which necessitated (much to my mother's annoyance) two three or four of the women all getting steamed up in the kitchen together. Sometimes there could be twenty or more people at these impromptu gatherings, so the extending leaves on the dining table were pulled out to their full extent and all sorts of odd chairs and stools were collected from around the place to provide seating for everyone. Often the smallest person at the table, I frequently ended up sitting on some little stool with my chin slightly above table-height. Grandpa, who was always deferred to by dint of his seniority, would sharpen the bone-handled knife on the back step before performing his elected task of carving the meat. Grandpa couldn't bear to be fussed over, so would position his seat next to mine. He took it upon himself to ensure that I got the crunchy, gooey, well caramelised bits of meat from the outside edges of the joint, and a plentiful supply of gravy to go with them.

As soon as the 'afters' was done there was never any of that sitting on at the table like Mediterranean families do; instead everything was immediately cleared and scraped and washed-up and dried and put away. The tablecloth had its crumbs shaken off outside the back door before being replaced ready to lay up for the 'tea' that would be served no more than three hours later.

Tea, as it was served fifty years ago, has all but disappeared from our nation's culinary repertoire. Given that 'tea' requires everyone to sit down together in the afternoon, without watching television, sending text messages or grabbing a bite to eat whilst rushing off to do something else, it's hardly likely to make much of a comeback either. Yet I have the distinct impression that 'tea' was my parent's favourite meal of the day. There would always be a large bowl of salad comprising lettuce leaves, quartered tomatoes, sliced cucumber, and spring onions or radishes if they were in season, to which we helped ourselves using the special salad-server fork and spoon set provided for the job. Sliced beetroots in vinegar came in a separate dish. Onto the same plate we would add slices from a selection of cooked meats: jellied veal, ham, liver sausage, brawn, tongue, luncheon meat or corned beef. Occasionally the meats would be substituted by tinned fish: salmon, pilchards or sardines (we hadn't quite discovered tuna in the 1950s). It was customary to add a hefty slice of Cheddar, Edam or Gorgonzola to the plate before giving it a liberal dose of Heinz Salad Cream and possibly a spoonful of home made chutney for good measure. This dish would be followed by thinly sliced bread and butter spread with home made jam, and finally we would tuck into a wedge of home made fruitcake or Victoria sponge sandwich. The meal would be washed down with copious quantities of tea with milk and sugar before a repeat of the clearing away episode already seen earlier that same afternoon.

It didn't always fall to my mother to entertain, and we would often spend a Saturday or Sunday in the home of one of my many aunts. This must have provided my mother with a welcome break, but I always felt disappointed when I learnt that we were going to Auntie This or Auntie That for dinner. I had clearly developed a discerning palate even in early childhood, and soon discovered one of the reasons why Grandpa had elected to live with his youngest daughter when there were about twelve others he might have chosen from. Quite simply, my Mother was the best cook. None of my aunts could match the crisp yet softly crumbling texture of her pastry or the airy lightness of her sponge cakes. Her apple pies were legendary, and everyone who came to our home always hoped that she had just baked one. No one else cooked a roast dinner like my mother; their meat didn't taste right and their roast potatoes weren't golden on the outside and fluffy within. Their gravy was too thick or too thin, too strong or too insipid, and their Yorkshire puddings didn't rise two or three inches above the dish. And when it came to steak and kidney pies and puddings, boiled beef and carrots, Cornish pasties, Lancashire hotpot, rabbit stews and fresh whiting fried to a crispy skin finish in beef dripping, they just didn't have my mother's touch.

Monday's food depended entirely on what had been roasted the day before. If it was beef we could reckon on getting the leftovers minced and made into a cottage pie, while larger pieces of meat would find themselves mixed with vegetables under a suet crust or inside a casserole. However, the greatest joy of the day after roast beef was bread and dripping sprinkled with a little salt. If I got really lucky, some of the rich brown jelly from the bottom of the basin would find its way onto my slice of bread as well. Leftover lamb would become Monday's shepherd's pie or a kind of 'cheats' hotpot. Whilst chicken (a special treat in those days) would become a chicken and ham pie, pork never seemed to metamorphose into anything else. Instead it would be served as cold slices, either with pickles, salad and crusty bread, or with cooked vegetables and hot gravy to make a sort of second day roast.

By Tuesday the bones or carcass of the Sunday roast would become the basis of a hearty soup with potatoes and herby dumplings. Wednesday and Thursday were more of a challenge, because provisions would be running low and more imagination was called for. Wonderful things would be done with a pound of sausages: toad in the hole with onion gravy, giant sausage and onion rolls with a lattice pastry top, home made scotch eggs. A few rashers of smoked streaky bacon would be magically transformed into a bacon roly-poly pudding, and if the main course was going to be light there would always be something like baked jam roll, treacle tart, egg custard, or rice or tapioca pudding for afters. Friday was always fish day, not for any religious reason but simply because my mother believed we should have fish at least once a week. According to her the fishmongers offered fresher fish on Friday than on other days because it was on that day that the Catholic and Jewish communities ate fish. By Saturday family favourites came round in the form of steak and kidney pie, liver and bacon, or a marvellous rabbit stew made with potatoes, onions, and parsley. The liquor was white and creamy, and miraculously the potatoes didn't turn into wallpaper paste (over the years I have tried many times to recreate that dish, with varying degrees of success). Sunday of course was roast meat, and so the cycle repeated itself. And all the while, my love for and fascination with food grew ever stronger.

Steak and kidney pie

There have always been arguments about whether steak and kidney is best served as a pie or a pudding, but the great thing is that the ingredients are the same, it's just the method that differs. I prefer pie, so we'll kick off with that and do the pudding later. For 4 people:

500g lean braising steak	For the suet crust pastry
200g ox kidney (or lamb's kidney for a slightly lighter finish)	225g self-raising flour
1 medium onion, finely chopped	125g shredded beef suet
1 level teaspoon mustard powder	Pinch of salt
Seasoned flour for coating	Cold water to bind.
600ml brown stock	Beaten egg to glaze
25g butter	

Trim off and discard the fat and any sinew from the steak and cut it into cubes of about 40mm. Cut out and discard the nasty white core from the kidneys and cut them into pieces no smaller than 25mm (if you're using lambs' kidneys just quarter them).

Make up a bowl of seasoned flour by adding a good pinch of salt, at least 20 twists of freshly ground black pepper, and a teaspoon of mustard powder to about two tablespoons of plain flour. Give this a good mix and toss the meats in it to give all the pieces a good coating.

Melt the butter in a large saucepan and when sizzling add the chopped onion with a little salt and pepper and fry until transparent. Use a slotted spoon to remove the onion to a bowl.

In the same pan begin to sauté the pieces of steak and kidney, a few at a time. We want to get all the meat well browned on all sides, so don't try to cook too many at once or they'll begin to stew rather than fry and you'll get a horrible sticky mess in the pan. As each batch of meat is done, transfer to a bowl and continue in this way until all the meat is browned. If the pan starts to dry up add more butter as required.

At this point you'll find that there are lots of crispy brown bits stuck to the bottom of the pan; these will dissolve in the sauce and enhance the dish. Put all the meat and onions back into the pan and pour over the hot stock. You can cheat here by using a dissolved stock cube if you haven't any ready-made brown stock to hand. Bring the pan up to the boil, giving it all a good stir to scrape up those lovely brown bits from the bottom. Cover and simmer for about an hour. Check and stir every so often to make sure that it's not becoming too thick; if necessary, add a little boiling water to loosen the mixture. When cooked, transfer to a pie dish and set aside to cool completely.

Make up the suet crust pastry. Sift the flour into a mixing bowl, add the salt and suet and give it a good mix. Gradually add the water and mix to a firm dough. Turn out onto a floured work surface and knead briefly until smooth. Roll out to a thickness of about 5mm and use immediately. You'll need a piece quite a bit larger than the top of your pie dish.

Place a pie funnel (an upside down eggcup will do) into the centre of the meat, pushing it well down to the bottom. Moisten the rim of the dish with a little water and cut strips of pastry about 15mm wide from around the outer edge. Carefully line the rim of the pie dish with these strips, pushing down to make sure they stick. Moisten the strips with water and cover the dish with the pastry. Use kitchen scissors to trim off the excess pastry but leave 5-10mm extra over the edge of the dish. Use the palm of your hand to gently roll this lip of pastry down over the rim of the pie dish. Crimp the edges of the pastry all round using the back of a fork - if you feel adventurous you could do this by squeezing together between the backs of your thumbnails. Cut a small cross over the centre of the pie funnel, brush the whole top with beaten egg and place in the centre of a pre-heated oven at 200°C for about 30 minutes until the crust is crisp and golden brown. Serve with mashed potatoes and greens.

Steak and kidney pudding for 4 people

Everything is the same as for the pie up to when the meat is cooked. Instead of tipping the whole lot out into a bowl, use a slotted spoon to remove all the pieces of meat and kidney to a bowl, leaving the sauce behind in the pan. Let the meat cool, but keep a lid over the saucepan to prevent the sauce from skinning over as it cools.

Roll out the suet crust to a circle, but leave it a little thicker than for a pie, about 6-7mm thick this time. Cut from the centre to the outer edge once, then again to remove a piece just over a quarter of the whole, roll this into a ball. When you line your pudding basin with the main piece, the cut edges will come together and form a complete lining. The piece you've cut away will form the lid.

Grease a 150mm pudding basin and carefully work the suet crust down into it, making sure that the seam made by the cut edges coming together is sealed. Leave some excess hanging over the sides. Pile the cooled meat inside and add just a little of the sauce so the filling comes to just below the top. Make a lid by rolling the 'ball' left over into a circle larger than the top of the basin. Dampen the edges hanging over the basin with a little water and place the pastry 'lid' on top. Lift the basin into the palm of one hand and with a knife, blade pointing upwards, use a downward slicing motion against the rim of the basin to trim off the excess pastry and seal the top onto the pudding at the same time.

Steak and kidney pudding (cont)

Cover the top with a piece of lightly buttered greaseproof paper, then place an upside down saucer (as close to the size of the basin top as you can find) over the top of this. Cover the saucer with 3 layers of kitchen foil bent down the sides of the basin and tied tightly with string around the rim. Stand the basin in a saucepan with hot water that comes about halfway up the basin. Put the lid on the saucepan and bring to the boil. Once boiling, reduce the heat to a gentle simmer and cook for 2 hours. Check occasionally to see that the saucepan is not drying out; top up with hot water as necessary.

To serve, remove the basin from the hot water, cut the string and remove the foil, the saucer, and the greaseproof paper. Place a large serving plate over the top, invert the whole and lift the basin away. Carry it to the table like this and cut it open in front of everyone - it's a sight and an aroma not to be missed. Serve with whole onions that have been skinned and roasted with a drizzle of olive oil and a sprinkling of salt, together with some fresh greens. The sauce should be gently reheated and served separately for people to pour on as they wish, and don't forget some real English mustard as an accompaniment.

For the mustard, put 3 heaped teaspoons of mustard powder into a ramekin, add 1 dessert spoon of cold water and 1 dessertspoon of white wine vinegar and stir to a smooth paste. Don't use all vinegar as this can make the mustard very bitter.

Note: many traditionalists insist that the meat should be raw when it goes into the pudding prior to steaming. This makes for a pinkish-grey filling when cooked and slightly more bite to the meat. OK, if that is what you like, but I prefer the rich dark brown and melt-in-the-mouth steak and kidney in this recipe.

Poacher's (rabbit) stew for 3-4 people

1 rabbit, jointed
1 large onion, peeled and sliced
25g butter
1 tablespoon flour
100g white button mushrooms, finely sliced
150ml full cream milk

Salt and white pepper
A bouquet garni (a couple of sprigs each of parsley and thyme plus a small stick of celery, all tied up in the leaf of a leek - white part only)
4 potatoes cut into chunks about 25mm across
A little chopped parsley

Whiten the flesh of the rabbit joints by soaking them in salted water for about 8 hours or overnight. Place the joints in a colander and douse with boiling water. Put the rabbit into a large saucepan with the bouquet garni and add about 750ml water. Bring to the boil, skim off any scum that rises to the surface, then cover and simmer for an hour.

Melt the butter in a saucepan, add the onion, salt and pepper and cook until translucent, but not at all browned. Stir in the flour and cook for 2 minutes. Remove from the heat and stir in the milk. Return to the heat and cook, stirring continuously, until the sauce thickens. Add this sauce to the stewpan along with the potatoes and simmer for another 15 minutes until the potatoes are tender enough to take a knife blade without resistance. Add the sliced mushrooms, cover, and allow to stand off the heat for 5 minutes before serving. Remove and discard the bouquet garni and ladle the stew into pre-warmed soup bowls. Scatter with chopped parsley and serve with chunks of crusty bread.

Boiled beef and carrots

Boiled beef and carrots
Boiled beef and carrots
That's the stuff for your Derby Kell
Makes you fat and it keeps you well.

Don't eat like vegetarians
On food they give to parrots
From morn til night we'll eat just wight
On boiled beef and carrots.

Duddle diddle ar da
Duddle diddle ar da
Ows yer farver, awl wight!

Boiled beef, bully beef, and corned beef (not the pressed stuff that comes in tins), are all names for this classic old dish, allegedly originating in Ireland. They say it was the Irish Navvies (Navigators) that dug London's underground tunnels who brought this dish to the land of the Cockney. It's a nice story, but I rather fancy that Londoners have been boiling topside and brisket for a lot longer than that.

To feed a large family…

1 joint of topside of beef, about 2 kg
1 onion, peeled and stuck with a couple of cloves
2 bay leaves
A few whole black peppercorns
2 sticks of celery cut into big chunks
An 'andful or two of carrots peeled and cut into big chunks
A right ole daffy load of spuds peeled and cut into quarters

You need one of those great big enamelled iron casserole pots with a lid for this, and it couldn't be easier. Put the meat, which should have been tied up with string by your butcher, into the pot. Throw in the onion, bay leaves, peppercorns, celery and a few of the carrots together with a pinch of salt. Cover with water, put the lid on, and place on a direct heat on top of your stove to bring to the boil. Turn down the heat to a rolling simmer and skim off any scum that rises to the surface. Cover again and cook for 3-4 hours. Check occasionally, skimming off any further scum that rises to the surface and add more hot water if necessary.

About 20 minutes before the end (bearing in mind that the meat will benefit from a few minutes resting time) throw in the potatoes and the rest of the carrots. Carve the rested meat into nice thick slices and serve with the vegetables and a ladle full of the broth. Serve with chunks of crusty bread to mop up all the wonderful juice. Any leftovers of the meat will make great sandwiches with mustard and dill pickle. Or break it down with a fork, add it to grated potatoes and chopped onion, and fry up for a real corned beef hash.

Note: if you're feeding the 8th Army, you could always add some suet dumplings to the broth along with the potatoes. Naw that is a bit of awl wight!

Lancashire hotpot for 4 people

'ear all, see all, say nowt
Eat all, sup all, pay nowt
An if ever thou does owt fer nowt
Ollers do it fer theysen

1kg middle neck of lamb
(ask the butcher to cut it
into chop-sized pieces)

2 onions, sliced

2 carrots, sliced

800g peeled potatoes
cut into rounds about 10mm thick

500ml hot water

1 dessertspoon Worcestershire sauce

Beef dripping

2 tablespoons flour

A knob of butter

A good pinch of dried mixed herbs

Sea salt and at least 30 twists
of freshly ground black pepper

Place a large enamelled iron casserole directly over the heat and add a heaped tablespoon of beef dripping. When really hot put in the sliced onions with salt and pepper and stir-fry for a few minutes. Reduce the heat, cover with a lid, and cook for another 5 minutes. The onions should be just beginning to turn brown, but don't let them burn. Use a slotted spoon to remove them to a bowl. Toss the pieces of meat in flour and fry them a few at a time in the same pot. Cook until well browned all over, and transfer to the bowl with the onion. Add more dripping if necessary. When all the meat is browned, return the whole lot and the onions to the pot. Add the carrots and herbs and give everything a good mix. Pour over the hot water and Worcestershire sauce and bring up to a simmer. Remove from the heat and neatly arrange the potato slices on top of the meat, overlapping them like fish scales.

Lightly season the top of the potatoes and dot with butter. Cover with the casserole lid and place in the centre of a pre-heated oven, 160°C for 2 1/2 hours. Remove the lid from the casserole for the last 45 minutes of the cooking time to give the potatoes a rich brown crust.

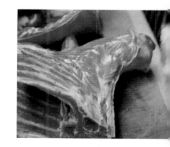

Roast beef and Yorkshire pudding

Roast beef and Yorkshire pudding is not only the best, but also the easiest Sunday lunch to cook. I am a great traditionalist when it comes to roast beef and I don't want 6 or 7 vegetables piled up on my plate. Just the beef, Yorkshire pudding, roast potatoes, cabbage and gravy. The only other thing needed is hot horseradish sauce.

For 4 people you'll need a joint of well hung beef of about 1.5kg. What I mean is a superb piece of rib on the bone, dark burgundy in colour with a good marbling of yellowy-cream fat running through it and a good coating of the same fat on the outside. None of that bright scarlet stuff covered in clingfilm and sitting in a polystyrene tray. I like my beef neither rare nor well done. I like it still pink in the middle, but not so rare that the dish resembles something out of an abattoir when you are carving the meat. That said, each to his own, so if you like it bloody cut back on the roasting time, and for well done leave it in the oven a bit longer.

A joint this size will take just 1 hour to be done to a turn, so cooking the whole dish does not mean spending all morning in the kitchen. Allow yourself about 90 minutes and all will be well. Put the oven on 240°C and while it's heating up put a large roasting pan (you need space for the roast potatoes to go around the meat) on top of the stove. Add a slug of cooking oil and a big knob of butter and heat it up until sizzling. Now sear the meat on all sides to begin the caramelisation. Give it a good few twists of freshly ground black pepper all over and a little sea salt on the outside fat only. Avoid salt directly on the meat as this will draw out the juices during cooking. Transfer the pan to the oven once it's heated and leave the temperature on high for 10 minutes, then turn it down to 200.

Now, peel and cut your potatoes to the preferred size and parboil them for 5-6 minutes. Drain off the water and, using a tea towel or oven gloves, put the lid on the saucepan and give it a good shake to rough up the outsides of the potatoes. These rough edges will form gorgeous crispy bits when roasted.

Chop up your cabbage and give it a wash in a colander under running cold water. Set aside to drain.

When the meat has been in for about 20 minutes take it out of the oven and turn the joint over. Put the potatoes round the meat and with two spoons roll each one over a couple of times to coat with the hot beef dripping. Sprinkle the potatoes with a little salt and a light dusting of flour and pop the whole lot back into the oven.

There's time now for a glass of wine before you do the next bit. What's that you say? What about the Yorkshire pudding? Well, contrary to popular belief, Yorkshire pudding batter doesn't need to stand for ages before use. Heresy? No, believe me, use this recipe and if you're not careful your pudding will rise so high that you'll have to scrape it off the oven roof.

About 15 minutes before the end of the joint's cooking time, break two eggs into a mixing bowl and add 300ml of full cream milk and a pinch of salt. Give it a good whisk, cover with a cloth and leave it like this for 10-15 minutes.

Right, the hour is up so take the joint out of the oven, wrap it in two layers of kitchen foil and set it aside to rest. Baste the potatoes in the pan and return them to the bottom of the oven. Now put a good slug of cooking oil into the Yorkshire pudding dish (yes, I prefer one whole one to those rather twee individual puddings) and put this into the centre of the oven to get really hot. Gradually sieve 4 tablespoons (about 100g) of plain flour into the egg and milk mixture, beating continuously with a balloon whisk to form a smooth batter. Take your dish out of the oven and pour the batter straight into the hot oil. Return the dish to the centre of the oven, close the door and don't be tempted to open it for at least 20 minutes.

Roast beef and Yorkshire pudding (cont)

Cook the cabbage in plenty of boiling water in an uncovered saucepan until just tender - 6 or 7 minutes should do it. As a rough rule of thumb, vegetables that grow above ground should be cooked uncovered and those that grow underground should be cooked covered. This way you will have green rather than brownish cabbage. Drain off the cabbage water and reserve for your gravy.

Gravy for the Sunday roast

Of course, if you happen to have a real brown stock ready prepared, nothing is better, but most of us will need a short cut and while I do like to do things 'properly' we can still have a delicious meal without spending two days in the kitchen first. All too often an otherwise splendid roast is spoiled by the gravy: too thin, too thick or lumpy, insipid, tasteless, greasy, something out of a packet or a jar that tastes of monosodium glutamate - ugh. So here's how to get it right in a jiffy.

Once you have removed your joint and potatoes from the roasting pan, amongst the brown gunk in the bottom of the pan you have the makings of wonderful gravy, so don't throw it away.

To make about 900 ml of gravy you'll need:

1 1/4 tablespoons plain flour	Pinch of sea salt and freshly ground black pepper
1 tablespoon butter	
1 meat stock cube (yes, I know it's cheating)	About a litre of the water you cooked the cabbage in
1 level teaspoon English mustard powder	Splash of dark soy sauce (optional)

Crumble the stock cube into a jug and use a fork to stir in the mustard powder. Add the cabbage water and give it a good whisk. Carefully pour off most of the fat from the roasting pan without losing all the meat residues and burnt bits. Now, place the roasting pan over a direct heat on top of the stove and add the butter. As soon as it starts to sizzle add the flour and stir with a wooden spoon until the butter has absorbed all the flour. Remove from the heat and let it cool just a little before pouring in all the stock. Give it a good stir and return the pan to the heat. Keep stirring and scraping up all the wonderful tasting gunky bits from the bottom of the pan. Cook gently whilst you start serving everything else. If the gravy thickens too much don't panic, just add a little more boiling water and keep stirring. If it's too thin you can use on old chef's trick to thicken it up. Beurre manié (kneaded butter) is quite simply a mixture of butter and flour - about twice as much butter as flour. Mix them together to form a paste and add in little bits about the size of a pea to any sauce you need to thicken. Keep going until you reach the desired consistency. This is best done off the heat, and as the butter melts the flour is absorbed into the sauce. Return to the heat for the last few moments, and if you like your gravy a bit darker add a splash of dark soy sauce. Taste, adjust the seasoning if necessary, and strain through butter muslin into a jug or gravy boat.

Unwrap the beef, put it on a large serving dish surrounded by roast potatoes, and carry it to the table for carving. Put the cabbage into a warmed serving dish, dot with butter and give it a few twists of the pepper mill, then take it to the table with the gravy. Now for the crowning glory - take your magnificent Yorkshire pudding out of the oven and carry it in. To everyone's amazement, it will have risen 4 or 5 inches and be as light as a feather. The whole thing only took 90 minutes, you're not hot and bothered, and you even had time for a glass of wine on the way.

Hot horseradish sauce

Freshly made horseradish sauce is very easy to make and so much better than the shop bought varieties. If you suffer tears when chopping onions the effect of grating horseradish can be even worse, but is still well worth the trouble. You can buy jars of pre-grated horseradish but they lack depth of flavour. It's worth buying a whole horseradish root and grating it all in one go. Seal up suitable quantities in polythene bags and freeze for later use.

2 dessertspoons grated horseradish

2 teaspoons white wine vinegar

A pinch each of salt and ground white pepper

1/2 teaspoon caster sugar

1/2 teaspoon mixed Dijon mustard

100ml double cream

Mix together the horseradish, vinegar, sugar and seasonings. Lightly whip the cream and fold into the other ingredients.

Bread and butter pudding for 8 people

We are told that bread and butter pudding was a favourite of the late Queen Elizabeth the Queen Mother and, no doubt, the chefs at Clarence House and the Castle of May had their own special ingredients designed to tickle her taste buds. This however is the recipe I learnt from my mother and frequently cooked in an earth oven for the other boys at scout camp. Whichever way, with all that lovely crunchy spicy topping and gooey inside, it's no wonder it's an all-time favourite of almost everyone.

12 slices of slightly stale bread, crusts left on

Butter

100g mixed fruit (currants, sultanas, raisins, candied orange and lemon peel)

4 eggs

800ml milk

3 tablespoons cream

3 tablespoons sugar

The finely grated rind of a lemon

Pinch of mixed spice

Grated nutmeg

Icing sugar

Apricot jam

Butter the bread as if for sandwiches and cut the slices in half diagonally. Arrange 8 of these triangles, overlapping like fish scales and butter side up, in the bottom of a baking dish. Scatter half the fruit over the bread and then arrange the next 8 half slices in the opposite direction. Add the other half of the fruit followed by the final layer of bread - again reversing the direction.

In a bowl or jug, whisk up the eggs with the milk, cream, sugar, mixed spice and grated lemon rind and pour the whole lot over the bread and fruit. Finish off with a little freshly grated nutmeg and bake in a pre-heated oven at 180°C for about 45 minutes. Remove from the oven and dust the top with icing sugar. Place under a hot grill to caramelise the sugar. Finally, warm a little apricot jam in a saucepan and, when runny, paint it on to the crusty topping of the pudding to glaze just before serving.

• • •

Doing things 'properly' and maintaining 'standards' were very important in our family. I suppose because my father worked 'in service', my parents made sure that my sister and I 'knew how to behave' in polite company and 'would never let them or ourselves down'. Knowing which knife and fork to use, how to hold them, how to use them, what to do with them when I'd finished eating – such things were as important as cleaning my shoes, combing my hair and checking that my tie was straight before going outdoors. I was taught to stand up when adults entered the room, to offer my seat to a lady or elderly person if there were no others vacant. I was taught to hold back the door to allow others to pass and, if I was wearing one, to raise my hat when spoken to in public. All this 'correct behaviour' was about not being 'common' a condition which, to my mother, was about as despicable as it is possible to be.

My first school was Blackstock Road Primary, about a 10-minute walk from home. In the beginning my mother would walk me there and meet me after school to walk me back home again. This journey took us past a shop that was to take on a fascination for me out of all proportion to its value.

Bellowes – newsagent, tobacconist and confectioner – had been declared 'COMMON'. The peeling grass-green painted shop front had one large window and one smaller window with the door off-centre. Inside the dingy looking windows were row upon row of screw-topped glass bottles filled with brightly coloured sweets of every conceivable kind. On the pavement outside was a cream and blue vitreous enamel sign advertising Wall's Ice Cream. Another in yellow, brown and blue espoused Ogden's Ready Rubbed tobacco, and several wire-fronted billboards had the day's newspaper headlines scrawled across them. Whenever we passed Bellowes there was always a knot of children hanging around the door; licking ice-lollies, sucking at sherbet dabs or chewing on black liquorice shoelaces. I longed to step over the threshold and plunder the delights within, but I was always ushered quickly past with a sharp intake of breath, a tut tut and a shake of the head from my mother. Naturally, the more she condemned Bellowes and told me never to go inside, the more I longed to do just that.

It seems strange now, almost outrageous, to say that it wasn't long before I was allowed to go to school by myself – that is to say without being accompanied by my mother. All the children in the area attended the same school and the older ones, who would look out for us juniors, either went to Blackstock Road Secondary or, if they'd passed the eleven plus, Highbury Hill High School, a trolley bus ride away in the other direction. I don't believe anyone thought it dangerous for children to go to school unaccompanied by adults, so that's what we did, even in the winter when the smog swirled thickly around the yellow glow of the gas lamps along the street. Anyway, you've guessed haven't you? Just as soon as the opportunity presented itself to me and I'd managed to smuggle out a few pence from my moneybox at home, I ventured inside Bellowes for the first time.

It was a revelation. I'd never seen so many sweets in my life, and wanted to try all of them. The shop was very dark and dingy, with one whole wall taken up with newspaper and magazine racks. High up on the racks my eye stopped at a black and white picture on the front of a paper called 'Health & Beauty'. It was a picture of a man and a woman standing on a beach somewhere. The woman was in the process of throwing a large beach ball to the man and he was preparing to catch it, but what made it fascinating was that neither of them was wearing any clothes. So that's what tits look like, I thought, but I had no idea what the dark patch between her legs was all about. I will never be quite sure why, but my face flushed up. At the age of seven I felt guilty, I'd seen something I wasn't supposed to see; that's why my mother had forbidden me to go in there, this was obviously what being 'common' was all about, and that must mean that I was now common too.

Bellowes just stood there behind the counter peering at me over the top of his heavy-rimmed spectacles. He gave a look as much as to say; 'Was there something…?' I took in the image of him in that moment; grey tousled hair, a grimy shirt and greasy necktie inside his shopkeeper's brown overall. He retrieved an indelible pencil from behind an ear, wetted the lead on the tip of his tongue, leaving a purple smudge on his lips, and, with a sort of half shrug, returned his glance to the open book on his counter top.

Outside I ran into a couple of school friends who were on their way in. I stopped them and mentioned the picture. 'Oh that's nothing,' said one of them, 'Old Bellowes has got the real stuff behind the counter, but he won't sell it to you 'til you're fourteen. Coming in for a lolly?' Inside, my chums headed straight for the fridge opposite the wall of magazines without so much as a glance back. My eyes however were drawn back to the front of the paper on the top shelf like iron filings to a magnet.

Bellowes made his own ice-lollies, they were cone-shaped and made with coloured, sugared water with a stick stuck through them. No wrappers, no names, and the sticks all skew-whiff because he put them into the liquids in the mould before they were frozen. I bought a bright red one for a penny and my friends bought the dark purple ones. 'Blackcurrant's best', said my friend, 'but they make your tongue black for days.' I hadn't thought about the dye in the lolly; my tongue would be bright red, and my mother was sure to find me out. When inevitably she did, my tongue wasn't the only part of my anatomy to remain red for several days thereafter.

CHAPTER THREE

I DO LIKE TO BE
BESIDE THE SEASIDE

5.30am, and Grandpa is sitting on his upturned suitcase by the open front door, his best brown shoes newly polished, his summer white cheese-cutter cap on his head and his raincoat neatly folded over his arm. Although the sleeves of his striped shirt are rolled up above the elbow, he still wears a stiff white collar and a tightly tied necktie tucked into a sleeveless v-neck jumper knitted for him by my mother. It would have been unthinkable for Grandpa to venture outside the house for any purpose without wearing a tie.

'We're not going for half an hour yet Grandpa!' my mother called from the kitchen. 'All right Maudie – I don't want to hold you up, and I'm out of everyone's way here' Outside, father had his head inside the engine compartment of the black Austin 10 he'd hired the previous day for our fortnight's holiday, checking the oil and water levels. Gloria and I were almost sick with excitement. We ran up and down the hallway with our buckets and spades and water wings, having no regard whatever for Mr and Mrs Plummer who lived on the first floor with their rather odd daughter called Sukie, or for old Mrs. Silence who lived alone in the attic. My father was now strapping our luggage to the car's roof rack and rear luggage carrier, whilst my mother was in the kitchen packing sandwiches, cakes, tea, milk and sugar into the wicker hamper in preparation for our journey to Cornwall. One last check that the back door was locked and the Ascot water heater and gas-stove taps were off, and one last vitally important piece of equipment to stow on board before we could head off. According to my mother Thermos flasks made tea 'taste funny', so whenever we went away, even for one day, we had to take tea-making equipment with us. This meant taking a water carrier and a camping kettle, Primus stove, paraffin and methylated spirit, prickers to clear the fuel jet and a special box of matches. All this was packed into a large tin box that then had to be separately strapped to the rear luggage carrier. Mother used to say that that was 'in case it catches fire', leaving me to worry that by some trick of spontaneous combustion the box would burst into flame and our little Austin would leave a trail of fire behind it all the way to Cornwall. In the days before motorways, and with the average car capable of speeds not much more than fifty miles per hour, the journey from Finsbury Park to Newquay with three adults and two children was always going to be a very long day.

We used to stay at a guesthouse in St Columb Minor, a little place just outside the resort of Newquay. It was run by the lovely Mrs Nichols, a widow lady with whom my mother stayed for over a year during the war while my father was stationed at RAF St Evel. Despite the war I think my parents had quite a good time there, and my sister Gloria was both conceived and born during their time in Cornwall. Mrs Nichols was a naturally very fine cook, with the added benefits of a garden full of fruit and vegetables and an obliging neighbour who farmed Jersey cattle and produced the finest milk and butter and clotted cream. Thanks to Mrs Nichols I tasted my first junket made with cream and rennet and my first 'real' Cornish pasty.

• • •

Cornish pasties

The mysteries and folklore surrounding the 'correct' way to make a Cornish pasty are almost as deep, and nearly as fraught with danger for the unsuspecting, as those in the various parts of the western Languedoc over what constitutes the finest cassoulet. The arguments and bitter rivalry on both sides of the Channel go back a very long way, and will probably never be satisfactorily resolved. One thing I can confirm though is that carrots have no place in a genuine Cornish pasty.

It is generally believed that the origin of the pasty lies in the meals prepared by Cornish tin-miners' wives so that their husbands could eat a decent meal at the bottom of the shaft. Some have even suggested that meat and potatoes went in one end of the pasty, with fruit and custard in the other end - who knows for sure? But one piece of folklore I can believe is that pasties were designed with an extra large twist of crust round the outside so that the tin miner could hold it by this whilst eating his meal. He would then chuck this crust away so that he did not eat the part contaminated by the toxic minerals on his hands. Makes sense, and good enough reason not to be too hard on those who leave this extra crust on their plates.

Whatever the truth, that lovely rolled plait of pastry is what identifies it as a true Cornish pasty. So what of the ingredients? Easy. According to the instructions given to my sister by Mrs Nichols: 'Taters, turnip, onion, meat, sage, salt and pepper. Yoom doan need nothin more me ansome'.

I have been making pasties like this for years and I must say that even after repeated visits to Cornwall I have yet to find a better recipe.

To make 4 pasties

450g short crust pastry
150g lean beef steak
2 medium potatoes
1 medium turnip
1 small onion
A good pinch of dried sage
Salt & pepper
Beaten egg to glaze

The pastry

I give here the recipe from Mrs Nichols. Sometimes it works for me and sometimes it doesn't - do give it a try though, and if it doesn't work out, reach for the packet of ready-made.

300g plain flour
75g lard
75g block margarine (not the soft stuff used for spreading)
A pinch of salt
A little iced water

Put some ice cubes in a jug and cover them with cold water. Sift the flour and salt into a mixing bowl from a great height. Mrs Nichols used to put the bowl on the floor and gently sift the flour into it from about bust height. 'Yoom gotta get plenny of air en it.' Now add the lumps of lard and margarine, straight from the fridge - it's OK, you can put the bowl back on the work surface now. Use an old round-ended table knife and 'cut' the fat into the flour until you end up with bits of fat about the size of a pea, or smaller. Chill your fingertips by holding them against the jug of iced water. Dry them and then begin to rub the fat into the flour using only the tips of your fingers. Lift the mixture up into the air as you do this and let the crumbles fall back into the bowl to add more air to the pastry. Once the fat is all incorporated into the flour and it looks like coarse breadcrumbs, you can begin to add the iced water a few drops at a time. Sprinkle the water from a spoon and go back to cutting the pastry with the knife. As soon as it starts to form a homogenous lump stop adding water and pull the piece of dough together with the flat of the blade. Wrap it tightly in clingfilm and refrigerate for an hour before rolling out.

Cut the steak into tiny dice. Place in a bowl and add the sage, salt and pepper. Give it a good mix and set aside. Peel the potatoes and cut in half lengthways and then across in very thin slices to give you half-rounds about 2mm thick. Treat the turnip in the same way. Peel the onion, cut it in half from top to bottom, then slice lengthways to give fine slivers. Mix the vegetables together with the meat so that all the ingredients are evenly dispersed.

Divide the pastry into 4 and roll each quarter into a ball. On a floured surface roll each ball out to a circle, only about 2mm in thickness. Place a quarter of the meat and vegetable mixture to one side of an imaginary line that bisects each of the pastry circles, leaving 50-60mm of pastry beyond the filling. Lightly dampen this edge of the pastry with water and bring the other side of the pastry over the filling to form a semicircle. With your fingers, lightly press down around the filling to bring the spare 50mm+ of unfilled pastry together. Starting at one end, roll and twist this flap up to meet the filled section. Keep going like this about every 10mm or so until the whole pasty is sealed. Place the completed pasties on a floured tray, cover with clingfilm, and chill in the fridge for about an hour.

Pre-heat the oven to 180°C. Place the pasties on a baking sheet covered with non-stick baking paper. Give them a few pricks with a fork and paint with the beaten egg. Pop them in the oven for 40-45 minutes or until the pastry is cooked through and golden on top.

Those early holidays in Cornwall were responsible for introducing me to foods that have remained favourites throughout my life. I learned that it is good to eat kippers, smoked haddock or smoked mackerel for breakfast, and that it isn't remotely common to hook freshly boiled winkles out of their shells with the aid of a pin. And I discovered that fried fish and chips always taste best when eaten out of newspaper in the open air.

The best fish and chips

Much maligned and often scorned, really good fish and chips are for me one of the finest dishes in the world. As a child, fish and chips were a rare treat and being allowed to eat them, straight out of the paper while sitting in a promenade shelter on the seafront in Cornwall, was always one of the highlights of our summer holidays.

The fish has to be white and very fresh, the batter crisp and golden, and the chips hand cut and fried immediately before eating with lots of salt and a good splash of malt vinegar (I'm enjoying this so much that I may just have to cook fish and chips tonight). Cod or haddock make the best fish and chips, although hake, huss, pollack and even skate wing also work well. There are lots of different ways to make good, crispy batter. I used to make a really complicated batter with beer and egg yolk, then stiffly beaten egg whites folded in at the end, but I now find the simplest is the best: just self-raising flour, ice-cold water and a teaspoon of bicarbonate of soda. Whisk it up to a smooth coating batter, and that's it.

If you want the true taste of 'real' British fish and chips there is only one thing to fry them in. Forget about your waistline and forget about poly-unsaturated fats – beef dripping gives an incomparable flavour to both the fish and the chips. You'll then have all that is best in the best of British food. Fresh white fish from our own shores, good quality potatoes like King Edwards or Maris Piper, and the rendered fat of British beef that gives the chips the flavour of roast potatoes and somehow manages to enhance the flavour of the fish in a way that no oil can ever do.

With the exception of huss, which like an eel has only one big bone down the middle, the fish must be filleted. Before cooking, always run your fingers lightly up and down the fillet to identify any bones that have escaped the fishmongers knife. Pull out any stray bones with tweezers, or pliers if they're obstinate, because the whole eating experience can be ruined by a fishbone in the mouth. It's also a good idea to ask your fishmonger to skin the fillets for you, as this is a tricky skill that requires a bit of practice to get right. Cut your fillets into nice serving sized pieces (about 150g each) and set aside while you make the batter.

The batter for 4 servings

150g of self-raising flour

150ml water

1 teaspoon bicarbonate of soda

If you use soda water you don't need to add the bicarb. Sieve the flour and bicarbonate of soda into a bowl, add half the water, and whisk to a thick paste with a balloon whisk. Now gradually add the remaining water, whisking continuously until smooth and free from lumps. Different flours have different absorption rates so you may need a little more or less water to achieve the consistency of good quality double cream.

Peel and cut the potatoes into nice chunky sized chips. Rinse in a colander under running water. Set aside to drain. Heat the dripping in a deep pan. To test that the temperature is right, drop a little of your batter mixture into the hot fat. If the batter floats with little bubbles round the edge, you are ready to start.

Fry the chips in batches so they have plenty of room to move around. If you try to cook too many at once they'll stick together and become soggy. Cover the pan with a lid to prevent splashing and to help maintain the temperature of the fat. Check every couple of minutes and

The best fish and chips (cont)

give them a stir with a long-handled slotted spoon. As soon as they take on a little colour remove with a slotted spoon and spread out onto baking trays that have been lined with a few sheets of paper kitchen towel. Continue like this until all the chips are done. They may now be left to cool completely until you are ready to give them their second frying. At this first stage the chips may be covered, refrigerated, and kept overnight.

Check that the fat is back up to temperature before frying your chips for the second time. Again do them in batches and transfer each batch to trays as before. Sprinkle with sea salt and keep warm in the oven. When all the chips are ready place one piece of fish into the batter and make sure it has a good, even coating. Lift the fish by a corner between two fingers and gently lower it away from yourself into the hot fat. The batter will set and form a barrier around the fish as soon as it hits the hot fat - and this is the secret. Crisp, crunchy batter on the outside, and pure white fish on the inside that has been 'steamed' inside its coating. The fat should not actually touch the fish at all.

Depending on the size of your pan you may be able to cook more than one piece at a time, but be careful not to let them stick together. When the batter gains a deep golden brown the fish is ready: this usually takes about 6 minutes. Transfer to a wire rack over a baking tray to allow the excess fat to drip off. Keep warm in the oven and cook the other pieces of fish in the same way.

Serve your fish and chips on warmed plates with a wedge of lemon, garnish with a sprig of parsley, and hand around the bread and butter so everyone can make themselves a 'chip buttie'. Apart from sea salt and malt vinegar, nothing else is needed.

• • •

Paradoxically, my father's humble occupation was also the reason why my infant palate became educated to enjoy many of the finer foods in life. Among the perks associated with my father's job as a chauffeur were the gifts we used to receive from his employers. Mostly these were in the form of foods that were surplus to requirements up at the house. Occasionally a whole case of Arbroath Smokies would arrive directly from Scotland. A breaded ham would suddenly appear, as would the odd side of smoked salmon or a great tranche of pâté de foie gras. Foremost among these gifts were the ones we would receive at Christmas. My earliest recollections of Christmas 'Up at the House', as my father referred to his employers' home, were not at a house at all. Rather they were at an apartment in the Albert Hall Mansions, right beside the Royal Albert Hall in Kensington.

On a convenient evening just before Christmas there would be a grand dinner party for all the staff and their families. The table was laid in the kitchen, not in the formal dining room, but that didn't seem to mar the experience. Joseph Swindon's wife Phyllis, having graciously given her staff the day off, would even make a show of helping 'Cook' prepare the food for our party. The food was of course wonderful, and I seem to remember that we were even permitted a glass or two of wine. Sharp at 8.30pm the Master and Mistress would appear at the kitchen door and lead us all through the hall to where a giant Christmas tree bore the gifts we were to receive. Lovely days, and I didn't feel at all patronised by them.

To complete their acts of largesse, the day after the party the Swindons sent my father to Coopers of Piccadilly to collect the goose and turkey that were to be our Christmas lunch at home. My mother always got in a flap – why couldn't they give us just a turkey, rather than both. And anyway she didn't much like goose, proclaiming it too greasy and not enough meat on it. The upshot of all this was that we ate both goose and turkey on Christmas day and pretty well every day thereafter for a week to ten days.

Roast goose with sage and onion stuffing

There is a lot of fat on a goose. A great thick layer of it, between skin and flesh, but well roasted and allowed to rest for 30 minutes before carving goose can be truly sublime. There are, of course, plenty of different ways to 'cook your goose' but the recipe below is a favourite of mine.

1 young goose, 4.5-5.5kg

50g butter, slightly softened

2 teaspoons made English mustard

A good pinch each of salt and cayenne pepper

1 glass of port (or two if you'd like one to drink while you're cooking)

For the stuffing

2 large onions, peeled and finely chopped

450g freshly made white breadcrumbs. Use a two-day old loaf, cut into thick slices, and break the bread into little bits. Give them a whiz in a food processor.

2 tablespoons dried sage

Salt and freshly ground black pepper

Freshly grated nutmeg

350ml chicken stock

Begin by making the stuffing. Boil the chopped onion in slightly salted water for ten minutes and then drain through a sieve. Put the breadcrumbs in a mixing bowl and add the sage, salt, pepper and nutmeg. Mix together with the onions. Gradually add the stock and mix until the stuffing just begins to cling together.

Wipe the goose inside and out with a clean damp cloth and fill the body with the stuffing. Tie the bird up tightly at both ends with kitchen string. Take a sharp skewer and make a few stabs through the skin of the goose, around the back, and through where the thighs meet the body. This will help the fat to run away during roasting. Mix together the butter, mustard, salt and cayenne and smear this all over the breast and legs of the goose. Set the bird on a rack over a pan to catch all the dripping fat, and roast in the centre of the oven at 180°C for 2 1/2 to 3 hours. At the end of this time, remove the pan from under the bird and decant the hot fat into a bowl. Keep this, it's precious. Goose fat makes the finest roast potatoes, and stored in a sealed container it will keep for months in the fridge. The goose will generate about a litre of fat during cooking, so you'll need to do this at least a couple of times.

Put the pan back under the bird. Douse the skin of the goose with the port and turn the heat up to 220° for about 15 minutes. When the skin is crisp the bird is ready. Place it on a carving dish and allow to rest for half an hour. Serve with potatoes and parsnips roasted in goose fat, with mountains of dark winter greens or Brussels tops and apple sauce and gravy.

• • •

After 1954, when the Swindons moved home to a mansion on the exclusive seaside estate of Kingston Gorse in West Sussex, the staff Christmas dinners seemed to lose just a little of their magic, but maybe it was just me growing up. At any rate my London days were over for the time being as we also were plucked from our flat in Finsbury Park and went to live in a little terraced cottage in the village of Angmering.

We moved from North London to West Sussex on 10th June 1954. Grandpa came with us, but this proved to be the last move he would make as he fell ill soon after we arrived and died before having a chance to enjoy life in the countryside. It, life in the country that is, had been sold to my sister and me as a great adventure. We would be leaving behind us forever the bombsites, the backstreets, the hustle and bustle – all the stuff that had, of course, made us precisely what we were. Instead we would live in a country village with village green, village hall, farms, fields, cows, sheep and even a blacksmith at the bottom of the lane. For many people, the rural idyll can be no more than a dream in the minds of those who have never been there – for me though, at the tender age of eight, it became reality.

I was enrolled at the village C of E primary school called Older's Charity, so named after its Victorian benefactor, one William Older, late of the Parish. The building itself owes much of its style to Victorian Gothic revivalism and the combination of red brick with Sussex flint infill makes it an attractive partner to the original Gothic church of St. Margaret that stands opposite. There were only three classrooms in the school, one of which accommodated children aged five to seven under the tutelage of a kindly lady named Miss Peters. The seniors, ten and eleven year olds, were in class three under the Headmaster Leslie Baker, who lived in the beautiful school house next door with his wife and equally beautiful daughter Penny, whom I long admired from afar. I went straight into class two for the eights and nines, where my teacher was the stern and somewhat frightening Mrs Springett. Mrs Springett united a long, sharp nose with full but tight lips that were always painted a deep red to match the varnish on her fingernails. Her dark hair was scraped back off her face and tied into a bun at the nape of her neck, while her dresses had starched collars pressed back like lapels outside her buttoned up cardigan. Around her neck she wore a black band with a large cameo brooch fixed to it at the front.

Mrs. Springett was a stickler for discipline, which she imposed unbendingly with a rod of iron, in point of fact a twelve inch wooden rule that she would deliver with alarming accuracy to the palm of one's outstretched hand. Miscreants would not be allowed out at playtime or would be forced to stand in the corner, or worse still have to stand on their seat with their hands on their head, looking and feeling very foolish. Anything that we weren't supposed to have about us in class, like sweets, an apple or a toy of some description, would be confiscated and locked inside Mrs Springett's cupboard for retrieval at some later date when she felt due penance had been done. The final sanction for the most serious offences or lapses in discipline was to be sent to Mr Baker. Often just the sending was more than enough punishment, reducing even the most hardened recidivist to floods of tears. Sometimes though, the plimsoll was applied with force to the rear of the naughtiest pupils. My father gave me a fearsome warning about corporal punishment: as far as he was concerned, if I had been subjected to such a punishment at school then by definition I must have deserved it. Furthermore it would mean that I had let my family and myself down badly and must therefore receive a similar punishment from him. Although I struggled mentally to find the justice in this, it was a highly effective deterrent and did make me err on the side of caution in my behaviour at school.

I had not realised until Mrs. Springett pointed it out to me that I spoke with a slightly Cockney accent. Apparently I dropped my 'aitches', neglected to give due importance to my double 'tees', as in 'bottle' or 'kettle', was inclined to make 'no' sound like 'nah' or 'down' sound like 'dahn'. Worst of all I occasionally made 'th' into an 'f' or 'v' as in: 'I fought I 'ad one wiv me Mrs Springett.' Elocution lessons were called for, and out of the kindness of her heart Mrs Springett took it upon herself to teach this poor unfortunate boy how to speak 'properly'. Thus it was that 'RP' was drummed into me at an early age, and has stayed with me ever since.

One day in the late Summer of 1955 my father came home from work and presented me with a gift from Mrs Swindon. It was a book, a huge and beautiful book with a cream leather binding: *Bouquet de France, an Epicurean Tour of the French Provinces* by Samuel Chamberlain. This sensational volume recounted the travels through provincial France of an American food writer, and contained literally hundreds of recipes collected from French chefs and home cooks alike. Instantly this book became my most treasured possession, and its influence on me was so profound that fifty years later I still seek to perfect the classic French cooking skills. Apparently Mr and Mrs Swindon had been on a trip to America, and when my father was driving them to the airport on their outward journey Mrs, Swindon had asked what interests his young son was showing. Of course he replied that I was fascinated with food and cooking. I still find it touching that such a grand lady of the '50s should have bothered to go to a bookshop in New York and buy that book specially for her chauffeur's son. Sadly, Mrs Swindon died in tragic circumstances only a couple of years after this incident, and I was never able to properly demonstrate to her how influential her present to me had been.

• • •

I failed the 'eleven plus'. Possibly because I was spending too much time observing the ripening seeds around me in the forms of Penny Baker and Margaret Ansell, another very pretty girl from the village who wore her long blonde hair in a pony tail tied with ribbons. Or perhaps I failed because the exam papers didn't feature any questions about food. Anyway, unlike my sister who was now in lower VI form at Worthing Grammar School, I was sent to Littlehampton Secondary Modern.

Many people thought then that failing the eleven plus was the equivalent of not gaining a degree now – in other words, one would be on the scrap heap, with little or no chance of redemption. It wasn't true then and it isn't true now: talent, persistence and a liberal dose of good luck are worth more than any old eleven plus or degree. In the event, failing that exam was probably one of the best things that could have happened to me. Instead of struggling to achieve academic success at a Grammar school, or battling with science and mechanics at a Technical High, I attended a school where any and every talent or useful inclination was identified, encouraged and nurtured. Andrew Cairns Secondary School for Boys was one of the brand new model schools in an age of educational enlightenment. Built to replace the ghastly old Victorian Secondary school where half the classes had to be held in pre-fabs, Andrew Cains was light, bright and modern. Set among playing fields and surrounded by semi-formal gardens, the school, large enough for eight hundred pupils, boasted two fully equipped science labs and an arts and crafts wing for painting, sculpture, print-making, pottery and calligraphy. There were workshops for metalwork with a forge, lathes, power machinery and facilities for building a whole car from scratch. The woodwork classes taught boys how to make everything from furniture to doors and window frames. Even gardening was on the curriculum, and pupils could learn about propagating plants in the extensive gardens and greenhouses. The sporting facilities included a large gymnasium and facilities for football, rugby, hockey, cricket, tennis and field athletics all within the school grounds. There was music, drama, debating and even dancing classes organised in conjunction with the Maud Allen School for Girls on the other side of the playing fields. All this was alongside formal academic studies that gave intellectually late developers a second chance of gaining exam passes and making it on to college or university. I've yet to be convinced of the efficacy of the radical educational reformers who did away with the three tier system and replaced it with co-educational comprehensives.

For my money the most enlightened investment at Andrew Cains School was their fully equipped catering department run by a French chef, Monsieur Bournet. The department had professional kitchens and a classroom that doubled as a restaurant. They taught cooking and catering skills alongside front of house and hotel management, and young lads from the age of thirteen from all over the county and beyond applied for a place there. Throughout my first and second years at the school I had many conversations with Monsieur Bournet, who was impressed that one so young had acquired so much knowledge of French cuisine. Naturally M Bournet encouraged me to apply for entrance to study under him from the third year onwards.

• • •

I joined the village Wolf Cub pack pretty well as soon as we moved into the village and, surviving the rigours of 'Akela', DYB DYB DYB and we'll DOB DOB DOB, by the age of eleven had moved on to the Boy Scouts. I never really saw any of this as being trained to be a baby soldier, but rather as a means of coming to terms with self-reliance and gaining an understanding of what may be achieved if one tries hard enough. What with my cooking, painting, scouting and being a member of the church choir, my hours out of school were kept pretty full. Nothing, however could have trained me to cope with the terrors I suffered going to choir practice during the winter months.

We lived about 15 minutes' walk from the church. I doubt if even now a village like Angmering has any streetlights, and certainly in those days, on a starless night, it could be pitch black on the lane to the village green then on up the hill to the church. I'd been given a pocket torch but I didn't like to use it because when it was on it only served to illuminate a small circle of the ground that made everything beyond blacker than ever. Without the torch one's eyes gradually became accustomed to the ambient light, making progress just that little bit easier. Once into the church car park and under the lytch gate, the terrors took hold of me. The path to the vestry door took me through the churchyard, under yew trees that creaked and groaned and always seemed to be reaching towards me in some malevolent fashion. The ancient tombstones appeared to rise up out of the ground and confront me menacingly as I ran to the safety of the single light that shone over the vestry door. Back home from choir practice there was always something warm and comforting to eat and, safe by the fireside, I never once let on to anyone how scared I had been.

I went to my first Boy Scout Summer camp in the summer of 1957 and it was there that I discovered not only that I was the only boy who could cook, but that what I cooked brought pleasure to others around me. I was immediately proclaimed Camp Cook. I found to my delight that being so elevated brought considerable advantages. No latrines to dig, no firewood to chop, no water to fetch and carry, and no pitching or striking of tents. No, all they wanted me to do was to carry on cooking. By the age of thirteen, at my third Summer Camp, I was now happily catering for three meals a day for 50 odd people on no more than a campfire and an improvised earth oven.

Once the technique for baked jam roll was learned from my mother I quickly adopted it, and became a bit of a hero at Scout Camp where I managed to bake jam rolls in an earth oven. The oven itself is worth a mention, because I was very proud of the one I built in The New Forest in the summer of '59. Several weeks before I had sat down and designed my oven, then drove the neighbours crazy by scavenging all the various bits and pieces required to make it work.

41

Here's my list:

A six-foot length of metal drainpipe with a broken end,
the importance of which will be revealed later

4 square biscuit tins (you don't see these any more but they were each about a foot
square and a foot deep with overlapping lids that were hinged on one edge)

Assorted nuts and bolts

A few lengths of stout wire

A lump of corrugated iron roofing sheet cut to size with loads of holes drilled
through it and a chunk cut out of the side about the diameter of the drainpipe

3 iron rods of similar length

4 roasting trays of a suitable size to fit inside the biscuit tins

A shovel with a blade less than a foot wide

You can imagine what the Scout Master said when I arrived to go to camp with not only my kit bag but also with an old pram in which I was pushing all my prized bits of scrap metal. After a protracted conversation during which I convinced him that this year we were going to roast and bake food as well as stew and fry it, he reluctantly agreed to let me load my kit-form oven onto the wagon.

I'd worked everything out so carefully that once we arrived at our destination in the forest it only took about an hour to build an oven capable of matching anything that Mr Aga could have achieved. First I had to ascertain the direction of the prevailing wind, as the front of the oven must face into the wind. Now the shovel was employed in the first of its two vital roles. Here goes (and in honour of its vintage, all dimensions are given in Imperial measurements).

Dig a hole in the ground, 2 feet wide and 6 feet long with a base that tapers from ground level at the front to 2 feet deep at the rear. Secure the metal rods across the deep end of the trench about 6 inches down from the surface. Jam the corrugated iron sheet on top of the rods. Shove the drainpipe through the hole previously made in the corrugated iron and push through to the bottom of the pit. This is the really ingenious bit: the broken end faces up the pit, allowing the air and the smoke from the fire that's going to be down below to escape up the chimney. Brilliant, eh?

Now for the biscuit tins. Having already fixed bolts through the tin lids to make oven door handles, all that's left to do is to pile the tins on top of the corrugated iron sheet, two across and two high, and fix them all together with nuts and bolts and wire. Pile all the earth that came out of the hole over the tins, and finish off with the carefully cut turf, green side up. Light a fire in the bottom of the pit under the iron sheet and stand back. Amazingly, it works. The chimney causes the fire to draw beautifully, and all the smoke blows away from the direction of the cook. In a matter of a few minutes the bottom two ovens are hot and the top two are moderate.

I cooked in that oven with varying degrees of success over the two-week period of our Scout camp, and was very sad when at the end it all had to come down and be dumped at a municipal tip on the way home. By the way, the second vital function of the shovel was to insert and retrieve the baking trays from the hot ovens.

I don't suppose a thirteen-year-old would be allowed to recreate my oven these days. I am sure our Nanny State would consider it far too dangerous for a child to be permitted to play with fire.

Anyway, here at last is the recipe for Baked jam roll and custard.

Baked jam roll and custard

Makes 4-6 servings

200g plain flour
100g shredded suet
A pinch of salt
A little cold water
1 jar of mixed fruit jam
Milk

Sift the flour and salt into a mixing bowl from a great height to get plenty of air incorporated. Don't trust the information on the bag that says it's ready sifted. Add the suet and mix well into the flour. Lift the mixture up into the air as you do this and let the crumbles fall back into the bowl to add more air to the pastry. Begin to add the cold water a few drops at a time. Sprinkle the water from a spoon and use a round-ended table knife to cut the liquid into the dough. As soon as it starts to come together stop adding water and pull the piece of dough together with the flat of the blade. Wrap it tightly in clingfilm and refrigerate for an hour before rolling out. Of course, at Scout camp we didn't have a fridge and clingfilm wasn't invented, so I used to put the dough in a basin covered with a tea towel and stand it in a bucket of cold water.

Roll out the dough on a floured surface into a big oval shape. Spread the jam all over to within 50mm of the edges. Dampen the edges with water and roll up. Finish with the seam on top and tightly fold in the two ends. Brush the top with milk and bake at 200°C for half an hour. Allow to cool a little before cutting into slices as the jam will be scalding hot. Serve with lashings of custard.

• • •

I always had a natural ability to draw, and when I was five Mrs Sillence, who lived alone on the top floor of 86 Finsbury Park Road, gave me an oil painting box that had belonged to her late brother. The lovely wooden box opened to reveal a palette, palette knife and long-handled brushes – rounds, flats and filberts – tubes of oil paints and bottles of linseed oil and turpentine. My father used to coat sheets of paper with size so that the oil paints didn't soak through when I painted my pictures of birds and trees. Bernard Hickey, a very fine and inspirational artist and calligrapher, was head of my school's art department. It was Mr Hickey who, having identified a pupil with a natural talent, encouraged me to take the subject seriously. I went to extra lessons after school and learnt lithography and silk screen-printing. I helped him paint the sets for the school plays and, further encouraged by the Headmaster Kenneth Hodges, a Sunday painter himself, I invariably had my paintings and drawings framed and hung on display in the school hall or foyer. Secondary Modern Schools encouraged their pupils to pursue the subjects they were good at, and both Mr Hodges and Mr Hickey told me I was good enough to go to Art College. I remember mentioning how much I enjoyed cooking, and that I was thinking of applying to join Monsieur Bournet. They said that cooking was all right if you wanted to work sixteen hours a day for a pittance. However, if I went to Art College and achieved a National Diploma of Design, it was equivalent to a degree and would open doors to all sorts of fine careers. At the age of thirteen I had reached the first 'Y' junction of my life, and I had to make the decision as to which branch I should take.

At that age I had a voracious appetite for reading, and alongside the books on the school's recommended reading list I was devouring not only Auguste Escoffier's *Ma Cuisine* but also every biography of nineteenth century French painters I could lay my hands on. Being a bit of a romantic, I found myself drawn to these stories, and when I read Picasso's edict that great art emanates only from poverty it somehow struck a chord with me. Monsieur Bournet said that chefs and painters were both artists, but that the difference lay in that painters starved for their art whilst chefs got to eat the fruits of their labours. All good stuff, but I decided on a course that led to Art College and turned my back on the notion of making my living as a chef. There is no point in wondering what if: people are divided into two groups; those who do and those who merely talk about it. Maybe I could have cooked for a living, but I was always afraid that I might have stopped enjoying it if I had.

CHAPTER FOUR

THE FLAVOURS OF FRANCE

Having been married on 4th August 1935, my parents were determined to do something really special to commemorate their Silver Wedding Anniversary in 1960. My father, as a chauffeur, had travelled extensively throughout Europe, always dressed in his smart black uniform, with the shiny-peaked hat emblazoned with the red and silver RR badge that signified his status as a registered driver/mechanic of the gleaming Rolls Royce he drove. Mother alas, had never been further away from home than Cornwall. Thus it was that, after something approaching two and a half years of saving every penny they could, we went as a family for a holiday to the Côte d'Azur.

My father drove us there in his little powder blue Ford Anglia. It took two whole days, but what a magical experience. Travelling down the length of the old Route Nationale, mile upon mile of tree-lined roads with acres of vineyards stretching out to the horizon, was an experience I would never forget.

Dieppe, Rouen, Versailles, Fontainebleau, Auxerre, Chalon, Mâcon, Lyon, Valence. A stop off in Montélimar to buy me a giraffe and my sister a donkey made of the sweet and fragrant nougat for which the town is most famous. Avignon, Aix, Fréjus, Cannes, Antibes, Nice, then on up the Moyenne Corniche to Eze Village. What a miracle for a boy who had never before been away from his home shores. The sights, the smells, the temperature perceptibly getting warmer the further south we drove. Wherever else I have travelled in the ensuing years, nothing has ever quite matched that first experience of France, creating a love in my heart and a notch on my soul that have remained with me ever since. And all around me I saw people eating the dishes that previously I had only read about in books.

We stayed for our fortnight in Eze at a tiny pension called l'Arc en ciel, a place where my father had stayed many times before whilst his employers were at l'Hôtel Négressco in Nice or l'Hermitage in Monte Carlo. l'Arc en ciel was a café-bar with a souvenir shop downstairs and a few scant, but scrupulously clean, rooms above. Monsieur et Madame Dannin ran the place with their daughter and son-in-law, Monsieur et Madame Dreyfus. It seemed to my child's mind that, with the notable exception of Monsieur Dreyfus, who spent most of the day smoking Gitanes whilst languishing behind the bar, the rest of the family never stopped working.

Madame Dreyfus was the cook, and I was completely enraptured by watching her perform in the kitchen. It was through my mother that I was first attracted to the kitchen, but it was Madame Dreyfus who opened my adolescent eyes to the wonders of Provincial French food. She cooked with olive oil, garlic and mountain herbs. She used aubergines, courgettes, black olives and the deepest red tomatoes I had ever seen. She cooked with pasta and made daubes in which the meat was made meltingly tender and succulent by long, slow cooking in wine. It was Madam Dreyfus who introduced me to her Provençal version of an Italian dish that instantly became one of my all-time favourite meals.

Pappardelle con coniglio -
Pappardelle with rabbit in a rich tomato and wine sauce

This is not a dish for the faint of heart. I say that not because of eating a little bunny, but because it's incredibly filling and leaves you with little room for anything else.

For two hungry people

150g freshly made pappardelle *

1 wild rabbit,
jointed and including the liver and kidneys

4 large ripe tomatoes,
skinned, de-seeded and chopped

1 large onion, peeled and finely chopped

2 cloves of garlic, skinned and finely chopped

1 thick rasher of smoked streaky bacon
cut into lardons

375ml red wine

1 tablespoon brandy

300ml rabbit stock

A few mushroom, sliced

A little flour

Salt and freshly ground black pepper

A good pinch of dried oregano

2 bay leaves

1 stick of celery

1 carrot

Olive oil and butter

* see page 140 for the pasta recipe

Ask your butcher to joint the rabbit for you so you get two haunches (hind legs and thighs) and two nice pieces of saddle. The forelegs and ribcage are going to be used for making the stock. Remember to keep the liver and kidneys.

To make the stock, roughly chop the unpeeled carrot and the celery and put these in a roasting tray along with the outer peelings of the onion and garlic. Add to this the forelegs and ribcage of the rabbit chopped up into little bits. Sprinkle with a little olive oil, salt and pepper, and roast in a 200°C oven for 30 minutes. Bring the pan up onto the top of the stove and over a moderately high heat pour in 600ml of boiling water and add one bay leaf. Bring to the boil, stirring and scraping up all the residues from the bottom of the pan. Reduce the heat and simmer for 30 minutes. Strain through a fine sieve and reserve. All the bits from the pan can be thrown away now.

Put a good slug of olive oil and a knob of butter into a sauté pan over the heat and, when sizzling, add the onions and lardons. Cook until just beginning to brown at the edges, then remove with a slotted spoon and set aside.

Rub the rabbit joints all over with salt and pepper and then roll them in flour until well coated. Fry the rabbit in the same pan you cooked your onions until well-browned all over - about 10 minutes. Take the pan off the heat and pour over the brandy. Flambé to burn off the alcohol. Return the onions and lardons to the rabbit and add the tomatoes, garlic, bay leaf and oregano. Pour over

Pappardelle con coniglio (cont)

the wine and the stock and bring to the boil. Reduce the heat, cover the pan and simmer for 2 1/2 hours. Check every so often to see that the sauce is not drying out; if necessary, add a little hot water.

About 10 minutes before the end of the cooking time chop the rabbit liver and add this to the pan together with the whole kidneys and sliced mushrooms.

Cook the pappardelle in the usual way and drain. Have ready two pre-warmed glazed terracotta pots and divide the pasta between them. Place the rabbit joints on top of the pasta and spoon over the sauce, which should be rich and thick. If the sauce is thin, you will have to cook it a little longer without the lid on to reduce it down. Try to be fair about how you apportion the servings and make sure each person gets one kidney. If you catch it in time, chuck out the bay leaf.

• • •

Single-handedly producing all the café meals, Madame Dreyfus was renowned for the quality of her Tartes aux citron. Every other day she made two enormous ones, enough for 20 or more portions each. And they were delicious. Madame Dreyfus told me that chefs from many of the finest hotels between Cannes and Menton had quizzed her over her recipe, but that she had always kept it a secret. She would, however, permit me to watch while she prepared one, on the understanding that I never spoke of what I saw to anyone else. Considering that this was more than 45 years ago, I trust that Madame Drefus - wherever she is now - will forgive me for recounting here what I can remember of it.

Pâte brisée sucrée (sweet shortcrust pastry)

Enough to line a 20-25cm flan case, ie 6 portions

150g plain flour
100g unsalted butter, softened
2 egg yolks
50g icing sugar
A good pinch of salt
The finely grated rind of half a lemon
1 tablespoon brandy

In a bowl, cream together the butter, egg yolks and icing sugar (I use a small balloon whisk for this). Then add the lemon rind and salt and sift over the flour. Work this all together with a knife using a cutting action. When well mixed and crumbly, sprinkle over the brandy and keep working with your knife, then start to pull it together into a ball using the flat of the blade. If it will not hold together, add a few drops of iced water, but be very careful not to make the dough too wet. Now take a spatula and dig out about a tablespoon of the mixture. Place this on your work surface and smear it out by using the heel of the palm of your hand. Scrape this up with the spatula and plonk it onto the centre of a large piece of clingfilm. Keep going like this until all the mixture is used up. Pile each piece of smeared dough on top of the last and pull it all together by wrapping the film tightly around it. Refrigerate for at least 2 hours before using, as in the following recipe.

Tarte aux citron

Lemon filling

3 tablespoons of cornflour

2 egg yolks

60g caster sugar

50g unsalted butter

Finely grated rind of 2 lemons
plus the juice of 3 lemons

250ml cold water

1 tablespoon of Limoncello (lemon liqueur)

Meringue topping

4 egg whites

200g caster sugar

You will have noticed that, conveniently, all the eggs and lemons get used up in this recipe. Do try to buy the best lemons you can find, they won't be as good as those wonderfully fragrant, rough-skinned ones they grow in the south of France and Italy, but do make sure that they are un-waxed. This dish is best served cold or only slightly warm, and needs no accompaniment other than a small glass of freezing cold Limoncello. The meringue should be slightly crunchy on top and lovely and gooey inside.

Limoncello is a delicious Sicilian lemon liqueur that may be obtained from high-class wine and spirit merchants. Although more usually served almost frozen in tiny glasses at the end of a meal, Limoncello is undoubtedly Madame Dreyfus's 'secret' ingredient.

Start by making the sweet shortcrust pastry and chill in the fridge for at least 2 hours before using. Brush the inside of a deep-sided 25cm flan dish with melted butter and sprinkle with flour. Shake out any excess flour. Roll out the pastry to a circle quite a bit larger than the dish. Now line the dish with the pastry, making sure to work it well down into the base and up the sides. This can be a little tricky, but don't panic if the pastry tears as you can easily repair any breaks by gently pushing back together with your fingers. Trim off the excess pastry by placing a rolling pin across the centre of the top and rolling once outwards. Go back to the middle and roll back the other way to give a really clean finish to the top of your pastry. Prick the base with a fork and chill in the fridge for 30 minutes.

Pre-heat the oven to 160°C. Paint the base of the 'pie' with a little unbeaten egg white and place in the oven towards the top. Bake for 20-25 minutes until quite well done. When cooked, remove to cool and turn the oven down to about 140 degrees.

To make the lemon filling, mix the sugar and cornflour together in a bowl and add a little of the water to form a smooth creamy consistency. In a saucepan, boil the lemon rind in the rest of the water and gradually pour this into the sugar and cornflour, stirring continuously until smooth. Put it all back into the saucepan and bring back to the boil again, stirring continuously. Simmer for a minute or two. Remove from the heat and beat in the egg yolks, lemon juice and Limoncello. Finally beat in the butter until completely dissolved. Pour into your pre-cooked pie case.

To make the meringue, simply whisk the egg whites until firm. You know the old test: tip the bowl upside down over your head and if it all falls on top of you, it wasn't firm enough! Now whisk in one dessertspoon of the caster sugar and gently fold in the remainder of the sugar with a metal spoon. Use a palette knife to spread this all over the top of the lemon filling. Don't worry if it looks a bit rough, but do spread well out to the edges. Bake in the centre of the oven for about 40 minutes. The meringue should be lightly browned on top with a few tips of the peaks just beginning to catch and turn darker.

Here are my versions of some of my all-time favourite French dishes, dishes that I continue to revisit over and over again.

Noisette de porc aux pruneaux (pork chop with prunes)

All over the world we find dishes that mix pork with fruits. It's a marriage made in heaven, but this one with prunes is one of my favourites.

For 4 people

4 large pork chops
50g butter plus a little slug of vegetable oil
Salt and freshly ground black pepper
Finely chopped parsley
200-250g dried prunes

sauce

1 stick of celery, finely chopped
2 shallots, finely sliced
1 carrot, chopped into very small dice
Butter for the sauté
1 bouquet garni (a few mixed herbs plus 1 whole clove tied up in the outer leaf of a leek)
A glass and a half of red wine
plus a splash of red wine vinegar
Salt and freshly ground black pepper
About 20g kneaded butter (beurre manié)

Some prunes need to be soaked in water for a couple of hours before cooking, others don't. So do check the packaging and follow the recommendations before proceeding with this dish.

Sauté the vegetables and bouquet in a generous amount of butter (20g), adding salt and pepper as you cook. As soon as they are slightly browned all over, pour in the red wine and vinegar. Simmer for about 20 minutes. While you are doing this, stew the prunes in plain water for about 20 minutes (again check the packers' recommendations because we want them to stay whole, not turn into a mushy mess). Drain and keep warm.

Add the butter and oil to a pan large enough for all 4 chops and, when sizzling, sauté the chops well on both sides. Remove and keep warm.

Strain the sauce into the pan in which you've cooked the chops. Bubble up and stir to deglaze the pan. Strain once more into a saucepan over a low heat and begin to add the kneaded butter a little at a time. When the sauce is smooth and thickened, add the drained prunes.

This dish must be plate served. Place one chop on each of 4 pre-heated plates and surround with prunes. Pour the sauce over and finish with a little chopped parsley. Offer a bowl of creamy mashed potatoes as the perfect accompaniment.

Tarte au citron

Confit de canard (preserved duck)

Long before the arrival of the refrigerator and deep-freeze, inventive cooks had developed all sorts of marvellous methods of preserving their foods. Pickles and jams, salting and smoking, drying and bottling in oil. But few preserving methods can be as simple or as inventive as a confit. It consists of pieces of goose (confit d'oie) or duck (confit de canard) which have been marinated in aromatics, slow-cooked, and then preserved in their own, rendered fat. The method is also used to preserve chicken which, for some reason best known only to the French, is called poulet en confit: on rare occasions, other meats and even fish may be found preserved en confit.

Confit de canard usually consists only of the legs and thighs preserved whole. The magnificent breasts having been eaten pan-fried and pink-centred, and the carcass and wings used for making soups and stocks, a confit is the perfect way to make the best of the remaining legs and thighs.

The confit may be eaten hot straight from the oven with shredded cabbage and l'aligot, that wonderfully smooth, creamy, garlicky, cheesy mashed potato, or it may be preserved in airtight jars. Like this, it will keep for anything up to a year, but it does take on a decidedly gamey flavour as the weeks pass into months. After this, the confit may be eaten cold, or re-heated and served as an assiette de canard alongside slices of quickly seared duck breast and duck sausage. But for me, its finest use is an integral ingredient of cassoulet.

These days supermarkets sell trays of duck legs very cheaply, and this is a great way to buy the duck for a confit. After all, you want to prepare at least 8 legs, and how often do you go out and buy 4 whole ducks?

8 whole legs (and thighs) of duck	A handful of coarse sea salt (Maldon is brilliant)
A few juniper berries	A couple of spoons of whole black peppercorns
3 or 4 cloves of garlic	250g duck fat
A few sprigs of fresh thyme	
A few dried bay leaves	

Use a pestle and mortar to crush the peeled and sliced garlic into a pulp with a little sea salt. Rub this all over the duck legs. Gently crush the juniper berries and set aside in a bowl. Now crush the peppercorns and add to the juniper berries with the remaining sea salt, thyme and broken bay leaves. Mix this all together and then coat the duck legs, pressing the herbs and aromatics into the skin and flesh with your hands. Pile the duck legs tightly together in a large dish, cover with clingfilm (to prevent your fridge from stinking of the mixture for months afterwards), and refrigerate for 12-24 hours. The salt will draw moisture out of the meat.

Before cooking, wash off all the salt and aromatics under running cold water and dry the legs with paper kitchen towels. Pack the duck legs into a large ovenproof dish, cover completely with melted duck fat, and roast at 140°C for 2 to 2 1/2 hours. During this time, all the molecules of water within the meat will be replaced with duck fat, and it is this that acts as the preservative.

Note: The fat will not set at room temperature, so when cool pack the legs into sterilised and completely dry preserving jars and cover with the liquid duck fat. Seal the jars and store in a cool dark place.

Cassoulet

Over the years, I must have read more on the subject of cassoulet than almost any other dish, and still I can't find the definitive recipe. To be perfectly honest, I don't believe there is one, although in Southwest France, where the dish is indigenous, arguments abound about its origins, ingredients and method of cooking. In its simplest form, cassoulet is a dish of various meats cooked slowly with haricot beans, garlic and tomatoes. But in Castelnaudary, Toulouse and Carcassonne, the three main centres of cassoulet cooking, they argue endlessly about the ingredients. Some use pork and sausages, whilst others add lamb and even game birds when they are in season. One thing they all seem to agree on though is that a true cassoulet must include confit d'oie or confit de canard.

The history of cassoulet is equally fraught with problems. It is said by some that the dish originated in the seventh century, when the Arabs brought a dish of white beans and mutton to that part of France. Others ascribe it to Castelnaudary, to an occasion in the fourteenth century when that town was besieged by the English under the Black Prince and meat and beans were all that remained in their stores. Yet another twist to the story is that the white kidney bean, so essential to the dish, didn't even arrive in France from The New World (South America) until much later in the sixteenth century. Whatever the truth, the good people of this region take cassoulet very seriously indeed and even have a Grand Brotherhood of the Cassoulet (Grande Confrérie du Cassoulet), a kind of quasi-Freemasonry of the cassoulet. Hey ho, we'll never get to the bottom of it, but no matter. If you find yourself in that part of France, you absolutely must try a dish of cassoulet, but don't plan on doing too much afterwards - it's very filling, and all you'll probably want to do is lie down in a darkened room with a cold flannel on your forehead. Oh, and one more thing, I honestly don't think it's worth all the work over two whole days to try to make an 'authentic' cassoulet - leave that to the people of the Languedoc who really know what they're doing.

Loosely based on the idea of cassoulet I have developed a recipe which is easily prepared at home and a great favourite of family and friends - just don't tell the Grand Master of the Confrérie.

Cheats' Cassoulet for 4 very hungry people

450g good quality pork sausages
(Toulouse sausages if you can get them)

2 whole duck legs (confit de canard)

250g belly of pork

100g unsmoked streaky bacon,
cut across into strips 3-4mm wide

2 x 300g tins of white cannellini beans

1 onion, finely sliced

3 or 4 cloves of garlic, peeled and finely sliced

1 carrot, peeled and chopped

1 stick of celery, finely sliced

2 tomatoes,
skinned, de-seeded and roughly chopped

2 bay leaves

A few sprigs of thyme

Good pinch of sea salt

About 30 twists of freshly ground black pepper

1 large cupful of fresh white breadcrumbs

1 glass dry white wine

600ml chicken stock
(you can use a chicken stock cube, but if you
do remember to cut down on the salt because
even the best stock cubes are already very salty)

Ideally, you want a large, glazed terracotta bowl (a cassole - that's where the name of the dish comes from) in which to cook your cassoulet, but any wide-topped open casserole dish will do if you haven't got the real thing.

Cheats' Cassoulet (cont)

Begin by cutting up the belly pork into bite-sized pieces and fry these off in a little duck fat from the confit. When nicely browned all over transfer to the cassole. At the same time, fry the sausages in another pan with a little more duck fat. Cut the sausages in half and add to the pork along with the duck legs, which should also be cut in half so that there's a piece for everyone in the final dish.

Put some more duck fat into a large saucepan over the heat, and when sizzling add the onion, bacon, salt and pepper. Cook for about 5 minutes without browning, then add the garlic and tomatoes and cook a little longer. Add the carrot and celery, along with the bay leaves and thyme (leaves stripped from the stalks). Give it all a stir and then pour in the stock and the wine. Cover and simmer for 15 minutes.

Empty the beans from their cans into a sieve and rinse thoroughly under cold running water to get rid of all the sugared salt water they've been stored in.

Strain the stock through a sieve and add the contents of the sieve to the meats in the cassole, mixing well together. Cover with the beans and then pour the stock over everything. Finally sprinkle the breadcrumbs over the top and cook in a moderately hot oven, 180°C, for about an hour. Every 10 minutes or so push the crumb topping down into the liquid using the back of a spoon. The final dish should have a crisp, golden topping.

Amusingly, there is even a mythology about this 'crust' on top of the cassoulet: should it be the breadcrumbs, or should it be the beans? Are you supposed to push the topping down once, five times, seven times or not at all? No, there will never be a definitive recipe for cassoulet.

Gigot d'agneau (leg of lamb with beans)

While I think that lamb is an unnecessary addition to cassoulet, here is a dish of lamb and beans which is an all-time favourite. The original dish from Brittany calls for white haricot beans, but I favour those lovely little green flageolet beans for a slightly sweeter flavour and the perfect accompaniment to lamb.

For 4-6 people

1 leg of lamb, 2-2.5 kg	**For the beans**
Some softened butter	3 x 300g tins of flageolet beans, drained and washed
2 cloves of garlic, cut into fine slivers	
6-8 shallots, sliced	50g butter
3 carrots, sliced	3 finely chopped shallots
A few sprigs of thyme	1 carrot, very finely diced
Pinch of sea salt	Pinch of sea salt
A few good twists of freshly ground black pepper	A few good twists of freshly ground black pepper
1 glass dry white wine	A large bouquet garni
250ml brown stock	(a couple of sticks each of carrot and celery, 2 bay leaves, and a few sprigs each of thyme and parsley all tied up in the outer leaf of a leek)
	Finely chopped parsley

Ask your butcher to bone out the leg of lamb, leaving the shank intact, and to tie it into a neat roll with string. Use a sharp-pointed knife to make little cuts into the meat and push in the slivers of garlic. Season well with salt and pepper then smear softened butter all over it.

Heat the oven to very hot, 240°C. Melt some more butter in a roasting pan not much bigger than the leg of lamb and cover the base with the chopped shallots and carrots. Sprinkle with thyme and place the lamb on top of the vegetables. Roast for 10 minutes at full heat and then reduce the temperature to 200 degrees. A leg of 2kg prepared weight will take 55 minutes for rare, 75 minutes for medium and 2 hours for well done. Remove the meat from the oven and leave to rest for 10-15 minutes before carving.

To prepare the beans put half the butter in a saucepan over the heat and, when sizzling, add the chopped shallots with the salt and pepper. Cover and cook over a low heat for 10 minutes until soft but not browned. Add the carrot and bouquet garni and pour in about 400ml of hot water. Cover and simmer for 20 minutes before adding the washed and drained beans to just heat through.

Put 2 dessert spoons of beans together with 4 dessert spoons of the cooking liquid into a liquidizer and pulse to a smooth creamy purée. Drain the rest of the beans and discard the bouquet. Stir in the purée, together with the parsley and another knob of butter. Re-heat, check for seasoning, and keep warm before serving.

To make the sauce for this dish, simply remove and discard the roasted vegetables and most of the fat from the roasting pan. Place the pan over a direct heat and 'deglaze' by pouring in the wine and stock and stirring to loosen up all the juices from the roasted meat and vegetables. Strain into a small saucepan and simmer for about 15 minutes while the meat is resting.

Serve on well-heated plates by spooning on the beans and partially covering them with slices of carved lamb. Pour the sauce over the meat.

Coq au vin (chicken in wine)

There must be over a hundred variations of this classic dish, but here is a really easy one that I used to make as an art student and continue to enjoy to this day. Serve with stacked roast potatoes and some steamed curly kale or broccoli. Serves 4 people.

Chicken, about 1.5 kg

100g unsmoked streaky bacon, cut into thin strips (lardons)

4 shallots, finely chopped

375ml dry white wine (preferably Burgundy)

300ml chicken stock

Seasoned flour

A handful of button mushrooms

A few tiny onions (the ones used for pickling)

Pinch of sea salt

A few good twists of freshly ground black pepper

A large bouquet garni
(a couple of sticks each of carrot and celery, 2 bay leaves, and a few sprigs each of thyme and parsley all tied up in the outer leaf of a leek)

2 tablespoons of brandy.

12 slices of French bread, cut diagonally about 12mm thick

Butter for cooking

Joint and skin the chicken. This is much easier than you might think: all you need is a sharp knife and a little nerve. Start by pulling one of the legs and thighs away from the bird. Cut through the skin between thigh and breast and pull away to expose the ball joint. Cut through the flesh behind the joint. Repeat on the other side. Cut off the wings (two joints each) and cut away and discard the pinions - those little pointed bits at the end of the wings. Now take your knife and cut boldly down the centre of the breastbone. Beneath the breast meat there is a diagonal line of fat to follow so you can cut away each breast in one piece. Go either side of the backbone and cut right through. Discard the backbone. Cut each breast in two and separate the legs from the thighs - again there is a line of fat to follow, showing you where to cut. So, now you have 4 pieces of breast, two legs, two thighs, two wings and two pieces of back without the backbone; cut these last in half. Remove and discard all the skin by pulling it away from the flesh, holding it with kitchen paper to stop the skin slipping through your fingers.

In a heavy casserole, sauté the shallots and bacon lardons with a little salt and lots of pepper. Remove to a dish. Roll the pieces of skinned chicken in seasoned flour and sauté a few at a time in the hot butter. When the chicken pieces are well browned, return them all to the casserole. Pour over the brandy and flambé (just set light to the hot brandy with a match and step back so you don't singe your eyebrows). Put the shallots and bacon back in and add the wine, stock, bouquet garni and small onions. Cover and transfer to a pre-heated oven at 180°C. Cook for one hour. After this time add the button mushrooms, stirring them in, and return to the oven for another 15-20 minutes.

Meanwhile, peel and thinly slice up 4 large potatoes. Put them in a bowl and toss in a good slug of olive oil, salt and pepper. In a roasting pan, stack the potatoes up to form 8 reconstituted halves. Roast these in the oven for 45 minutes. Towards the end of the cooking time strip the curly kale from its stalks (or break the broccoli into florets). Give them a good wash through a colander under running cold water, then steam in a (metal) colander for 6-7 minutes over a pan of boiling water with a saucepan lid to cover.

Fry the bread slices in butter until crisp and golden.

To build the dish spoon three pieces of chicken onto each of the four warmed plates with lots of sauce to cover. Surround with the croûtons and finish the plates with two halves of stacked, roasted potatoes and a little curly kale or broccoli.

Coquilles Saint-Jacques au gratin

Scallops in their shells with white wine sauce and a crunchy cheese topping: for 4 people

12 scallops

25g butter

1 large glass dry white wine

300ml water

75g button mushrooms, sliced thinly

A light roux made with 15g butter and 20g flour

A pinch each of salt and ground white pepper

1 small cup fresh white breadcrumbs

25g grated Parmesan cheese

Get the fishmonger to clean the scallops for you and ask for 4 of the deep shells. Poach the scallops and mushrooms in the wine and water plus the seasoning for 5 minutes. Remove from the liquor and slice up the white parts but leave the orange corals whole. Transfer the mushrooms to a plate using a slotted spoon.

Make the light roux and, off the heat, stir in the poaching liquid. Return to the heat and simmer until thickened.

Scrub the shells and scald with boiling water. Put a little of the sauce into the bottom of each shell and divide the scallops and mushrooms between them. Cover with the remaining sauce. Mix together the breadcrumbs and Parmesan and scatter this over the filled shells. Melt the butter in a pan and drizzle over the crumbs. Place under a hot grill until golden brown and crunchy on top.

Brochettes de foie de veau (calf's liver kebabs)

For 4 people

350g calf's liver

6 rashers unsmoked back bacon

24 closed cap mushrooms

50g butter

Half a cup of dry breadcrumbs

Salt and freshly ground black pepper

Cut the liver and bacon into squares roughly 25 x 25mm. Season the liver with salt and pepper and quickly fry in hot butter until just browned. Toss the mushrooms and bacon in the hot butter for a few seconds. Thread the liver, bacon and mushrooms alternately onto skewers. Roll in breadcrumbs and drizzle with the pan juices before transferring the brochettes to a hot grill. Turn frequently until golden and crunchy.

Serve on a bed of rice with a piquant sauce made with a dark brown roux, meat stock with a splash of vinegar and a generous spoonful of Worcestershire sauce.

Note: You can give this sauce a real kick by adding some finely diced chilli peppers – jalapeño or Scotch bonnet if you're a real masochist.

Daube de boeuf (beef slow-cooked in red wine) for 6 people

This is a truly magnificent Provençal version of the world-famous Boeuf Bourguignon, but using cheaper cuts of beef like ox cheek - and yet another recipe I have 'borrowed' from Madame Dreyfus.

1.5 kg stewing beef, cut into cubes of 4-5 cm (ox cheek is best)

4 shallots, finely chopped

200g unsmoked streaky bacon, cut into thin strips (lardons)

A couple of good slugs of olive oil

Sea salt and freshly ground black pepper

A handful of pitted black olives

Marinade

1 litre red wine

1 glass red wine vinegar (approx. 150ml)

3 cloves of garlic, crushed to a paste with a little sea salt

2 large onions, peeled and sliced

3 or 4 carrots, peeled and sliced

A large bouquet garni (a couple of sticks of celery, 2 bay leaves, a few sprigs each of thyme, parsley, oregano etc. and a couple of strips of orange peel all tied up in outer leaves of a leek)

1 teaspoon of dried, mixed herbes de Provence

The day before, put all the marinade ingredients into a large china or glass bowl. Add the cubed meat and give everything a good stir. Cover with clingfilm and refrigerate for at least 12 hours.

The secret to this dish is long slow cooking, so about 6 hours before you want to eat remove the meat from the marinade and dry the pieces well with paper kitchen towels.

Heat the olive oil in a large enamelled iron casserole and sauté the shallots and bacon lardons with a little salt and a lot of freshly ground black pepper (about 40 twists). When nicely cooked and beginning to take on a little colour, use a slotted spoon to remove to a large dish. Now sauté the pieces of meat, a few at a time, in the same casserole. Cook them until well browned all over and transfer to the dish with the shallots and bacon as you go.

Strain the marinade and add all the vegetables (but not the bouquet) to the casserole and cook for a few minutes until the onions start to brown. You may need to add a little more olive oil at this point. Now return the meat, shallots and bacon to the casserole and give everything a good stir around. Bury the bouquet deep inside and pour the marinade liquid over to cover everything - if necessary, add some more wine. Cover the casserole with two or three thicknesses of kitchen foil and press the casserole lid down hard to form as tight a seal as possible. Bring to the boil, and when you hear the liquid bubbling turn the heat down and simmer gently for 4 hours. If preferred, you may cook the casserole in a low oven, 125°C. Stir in the olives and discard the bouquet before serving.

Madame Dreyfus always served this with a delicious pasta dish, which she called 'macaronade'. I have never found a recipe for this dish, but I remember it as going something like this. Certainly this version tastes just great.

Boil the macaroni in lots of water until just tender, but still retaining a bite (al dente). Drain the macaroni and toss in a little olive oil. Put a layer of the macaroni into the bottom of a glass or terracotta oven dish and sprinkle with a mixture of grated cheese. Gruyère and Parmesan are a good combination, but you may use almost any strong flavoured hard cheeses. Keep building up layers like this and finish with a sprinkling of cheese. Pour over a ladle or two of the liquid from the casserole and put into a hot oven, 220°C, for about ten minutes until the top is nicely browned and glistening.

Gratineé Lyonnaise (French onion soup)

It is always a mistake to serve French onion soup as a first course. It is so robust and filling that once you've downed the last spoonful and munched on the final piece of cheesy croûton, it's doubtful you'll need anything else for a good few hours.

To make enough for 6 people

1kg onions peeled and finely sliced

3 cloves of garlic, two peeled and crushed to a paste with a little sea salt, the third just cut in half

1 bottle of dry white wine

2 tablespoons brandy

1.5 litres meat stock (beef for a robust flavour, chicken for a lighter finish)

2 rashers of smoked streaky bacon cut into very fine lardons

2 tablespoons vegetable oil

50g unsalted butter

2 tablespoons of plain flour

1 whole French loaf cut into about 24 slices

A little olive oil

60g grated Parmesan and Gruyère or Emmental

Salt and freshly ground black pepper

Heat the butter and vegetable oil in a large, heavy-bottomed saucepan and when sizzling add the onion, bacon, salt and pepper. Cook gently for 30-40 minutes, stirring occasionally, until soft and lightly coloured. This long slow cooking of the onions is vital to prevent the soup being indigestible. Add the crushed garlic and cook for 5 minutes. Pour over the brandy and flambé to burn off all the alcohol. Stir in the flour and cook for 2 minutes. Remove from the heat and stir in the wine and stock. Return to the heat and allow the soup to simmer for a further 30-40 minutes.

While the soup is cooking you can make the croûtons. Place the slices of bread on a baking tray and place into a low oven for about 15 minutes until they are crisp and dry, but not browned. Rub them all over with the cut surface of a garlic clove and brush with olive oil.

To finish the dish, ladle the soup into heated bowls. According to their size, float two or three croûtons on top of the soup (don't worry if they overhang a bit because that adds to the presentation). Now sprinkle the croûtons with grated cheese and place the bowls under the grill set to a very high temperature. The cheese should be melted and golden and the edges of the croûtons slightly blackened. I think it looks even better if a little of the cooked cheese clings to the outside of the bowls.

Bouillabaisse à la Marseillaise (French fish stew)

You really need to be in Marseilles – or at least somewhere by the Mediterranean – in order to make the authentic dish as many of the fish they use are unobtainable here. But we do have a huge variety of our own fish in England, more than enough to enable us to have a pretty good go at it. This is a dish to make when you've a full house to feed, so I'm giving here the quantities to feed 10-12 people.

3-3.5kg of mixed fish: cod, whiting, sole, red mullet, gurnard, conger eel, whole raw Dublin Bay prawns, lobster tails, a few mussels

2 large ripe tomatoes skinned, deseeded & chopped

2 onions, peeled and finely sliced

4 cloves garlic, peeled and crushed to a paste with a little sea salt

2 leeks (white part only), finely sliced

2-3 sticks celery, finely chopped

Thin strips of orange rind

About 40 twists of freshly ground black pepper

5 or 6 tablespoons of olive oil

2 bay leaves

Parsley stalks

1 tablespoon finely grated fennel

A good pinch saffron strands soaked in hot water

Splash of Pernod

Tablespoon tomato purée

2 whole French loaves

Lots of finely chopped curly-leafed parsley

Fillet all the fish, saving the heads and bones for the stock. Leave the prawns whole and thoroughly wash, scrape off any barnacles, and de-beard the mussels. Remove the flesh from the lobster tails and set aside. Save the shells for the stock. Cut the fish into chunks and place in a bowl with olive oil, crushed garlic and saffron steeped in hot water. Add a few twists of black pepper, but no salt.

Heat the oil in a large, heavy-bottomed pan and add the onions, salt and pepper. Cook for a few minutes until softened. Add the leek, garlic, tomatoes, bay leaf and fennel and cook for 2 more minutes, then add the saffron. Put all the heads and bones into the pot and cover with hot water. Bring to the boil and simmer for 20 minutes, skimming frequently. Strain the whole lot through a colander lined with muslin and discard all the debris. Add oily fish and shellfish to the pan and boil rapidly for 5 minutes. Mix together the Pernod and tomato purée and stir into the soup before adding the white fish. Cook for 5 minutes until the white fish is cooked through.

Place a slice of untoasted bread in the bottom of each pre-heated soup bowl. Strain the broth though a sieve and ladle it into the bowls, finishing each with a little chopped parsley. Float a toasted croûton topped with a teaspoon of garlic and tomato mayonnaise on each dish. Arrange the fish nicely on separate serving dishes, sprinkle with more chopped parsley and serve both plates together. Extra warm bread should be served for mopping up the soup.

Garlic and tomato mayonnaise - Aïoli

1 egg yolk

50ml olive oil

100ml sunflower oil

Touch Dijon mustard

Squeeze of lemon juice

Salt and pepper

Splash warm water

Plump clove garlic crushed

Teaspoon tomato purée

Pinch paprika

See page 75 for how to make mayonnaise. Crush the garlic to a smooth paste in a pestle and mortar. Mix in the tomato purée, seasoning, and enough of the oil to make a dripping consistency. Once the egg and oil have begun to emulsify the garlic mixture may be added to the mayonnaise.

Moules à la marinière (mussels in white wine)

There used to be a time when you needed to be very wary of mussels, which for all we knew may have been gathered by the unscrupulous from around sewerage outflows at low tide. Thankfully, today we have an almost endless supply of good mussels that have been farmed on ropes in clean waters. Even so, they are still a few precautions to take.

1   *When you get your mussels home, tip them out of their netting bag into a bowl of cold water and let them stay there for a while. Remember they are alive and will continue to siphon your clean water through their innards, helping to clean away any remaining nasties.*

2   *Check them all over thoroughly. Any that have chipped or cracked shells should be discarded. As should any that feel unusually heavy as this probably means they have sand or silt inside.*

3   *Any mussels that are open before cooking should be given a sharp tap on the sink. If they don't close, it's because they are dead. Chuck these away too.*

4   *After cooking, any that remain stubbornly closed should also be discarded.*

Follow these four rules and you'll be fine. Unless, of course, you happen to be allergic to seafood.

For 4 people

1-1.5 kg mussels	A good slug of olive oil
4 shallots, finely chopped	A little freshly ground black pepper
2 cloves of garlic, finely chopped	A good knob of unsalted butter
300ml dry white wine	A handful of finely chopped parsley

Carefully go over the mussels following the rules above, and use a blunt knife to scrape off any barnacles. Remove the beard (the coarse hairy bit they use to cling on with) by giving it a sharp tug.

Heat the oil in a very large stewpan and sauté the shallots and garlic with a little pepper for a few minutes. Tip the mussels into the pan and pour over the wine. Cover with a lid and increase the heat to maximum. After two minutes, throw in half of the chopped parsley, give the pan a good shake and cook for 2-3 more minutes. By now all the mussels should have opened. Use a slotted spoon to remove the mussels to a warmed tureen (don't forget to chuck out any that have not opened). Carefully spoon out as much of the shallots and garlic as you can and add to the mussels. Strain the liquor through a fine sieve or butter muslin to remove any grit or shell particles and pour it over the mussels. Add a knob of butter and the remaining chopped parsley and toss a few times. Serve with lots of French bread to mop up that fabulous liquor.

A flavour of Normandy

Substitute Normandy cider for the wine and proceed as above. Add a tablespoon of calvados to the cooking liquor and, at the end, substitute the butter with 150ml of double cream.

A hint of Provence

Add 4 ripe tomatoes that have been skinned, deseeded and finely chopped to the sauté of shallots and garlic. Sauté a little longer to reduce the tomatoes to a pulp before adding the mussels. This time, you cannot strain the liquor as you'll lose all the lovely tomatoes, so do not scrape the last of the sauce from the bottom of the pan. You may even enhance the flavour of the Mediterranean by adding a pinch of herbes de Provence to the cooking liquor.

Tartelettes aux l'oignon (French onion tartlets)

I always prefer to have one of these little tarts than to be presented with a slice from a big one, like a lump of quiche. Tartlet tins are easily available and cheap to buy from good quality kitchen shops. Choose 100mm diameter size for good individual servings.

Enough for 6 tartlets

For the pâte brisée (shortcrust pastry)

150g plain flour   A good pinch of salt
100g unsalted butter   A few drops of iced water
1 egg yolk

Sift the flour and salt into a bowl, then add the butter in one lump and cut it with a knife into the flour. Add the egg yolk and keep cutting into the flour until it forms lumps no bigger than a pea. Now, using only the tips of your thumbs and fingers, rub these pieces in until the whole thing looks like a pile of damp cornflakes. NOW STOP: if you go on rubbing in past this point the mixture will take on the texture of breadcrumbs, and that is going to make the pastry dense.

Wash and dry your hands and go back to the knife. Now add some iced water, just a few drops at a time, and keep cutting the mixture until it begins to bind together. Once it starts to form a homogenous lump don't be tempted to add any more water because this will make it sticky, and the resulting pastry will shrink and be tough to eat. Now, without touching directly with your hands, tip it out into the centre of a large piece of clingfilm and wrap it up. Pulling the film firmly over the dough will complete the forming together of your precious piece of dough without you having to touch it again. Refrigerate for a minimum of 1 hour before using. This pastry may be made a day in advance and refrigerated overnight.

For the filling

3 onions, peeled and finely sliced lengthways   A good splash of olive oil plus a little nut of butter
2 large eggs   Freshly grated nutmeg
250ml crème fraîche   Salt and freshly ground black pepper

Lightly brush the tartlet tins with melted butter, sprinkle with flour and shake out the excess. Divide the pastry into 6 and quickly roll into balls. Roll these out on a floured surface to make 6 circles larger than the tins. Carefully line the tins, prick the bases of the pastry a few times with a fork and refrigerate for 15 minutes. Blind bake the pastries in a moderate oven, 160°C, for 15 minutes. Remove from the oven and trim away any excess pastry to leave a neatly finished edge.

Cook the onions slowly in the butter and oil for a minimum of 30 minutes, without browning. Beat the eggs and crème fraîche together and season with salt and pepper and a good amount of freshly grated nutmeg. Off the heat, add this mixture to the onions and give it a good stir. Divide the mixture equally between the six tartlets and bake for 30 minutes at 180°C. Remove from the oven and allow to cool a little before transferring the tartlets from their tins to serving plates. Accompany with a lightly tossed green salad.

Saucisson en brioche

Unless you happen to be in France, it is very difficult to find the genuine coarse-cut, pure pork saucisson Lyonnais for this superb and highly impressive dish. However if you are on good terms with your butcher a fair approximation can be achieved by getting him to mince some shoulder of pork for you. Season the mince well with salt, pepper and nutmeg before proceeding with the recipe. As a last resort, you can even remove the skins from some good quality sausages and use the meat. Cheap, mass-produced sausages do not work because the fat content is unstable and will run out during cooking, turning the brioche into a soggy, greasy mess. And besides, we shouldn't be eating cheap, mass-produced sausages anyway.

For 6 people

About 300g best quality
coarse pork sausage meat

1 egg yolk beaten with a few drops of water

Salt and freshly ground black pepper

Freshly grated nutmeg

For the brioche

200g strong white flour

1 x 7g packet dried yeast

1/2 tablespoon white sugar

1/2 teaspoon salt

2 standard eggs well beaten

1/2 teacup warmed milk

85g unsalted butter softened to room temperature

A little extra butter fully melted

Lay out a large piece of clingfilm on your work surface. Make sure the sausage meat is well seasoned, and form it into a rough sausage shape in your hands. It should be about 40mm in diameter. Place this into one end of the clingfilm and roll up so that the film wraps the meat with at least 4 thicknesses. Twist the ends as tightly as you can and secure with string. Tightening the ends will help to improve the form of your cylinder of meat. Immerse in water at a gentle simmer and cook for about 35 minutes without letting the water boil. Remove from the water and set aside to cool, then refrigerate until needed. This may be done a day in advance.

Put the warmed milk in a bowl and sprinkle in the yeast and sugar, stirring continuously until dissolved. Leave for 5 minutes until frothy on top. Sift the flour and salt into a large mixing bowl and make a well in the middle. Pour in the yeast mixture and the eggs and work together to form a soft dough. Turn out onto a floured surface and knead well for 5-10 minutes. Grease a large bowl with melted butter and turn the ball of dough in it to coat evenly. Cover with a cloth and leave to rise until doubled in size – about 1 1/2 hours. Knock back and leave to rest for 10 minutes. Use your hand to incorporate the softened butter into the dough. Turn out onto a floured surface and knead for another 5 minutes. Return to the greased bowl, cover again, and leave for 30 minutes.

Remove the film from the sausage and wipe away any excess fat from the surface. Roll out the brioche dough about 20mm thick into a rectangle large enough to enclose the sausage. Wrap the sausage in the dough, overlapping the long edge and tucking in the ends. Lay on a greased baking sheet with the join underneath and paint liberally with eggwash. Bake in the oven at 180°C for 40 minutes until the brioche is golden. Transfer to a plate and serve in slices about 20mm thick. The perfect accompaniments are Dijon mustard and a rich brown sauce made with reduced veal stock and a reduction of sweet wine. Alternatively, the saucisson en brioche makes a wonderful picnic dish served cold with salads and pickles.

CHAPTER FIVE

WHY DID IT TAKE SO LONG?

I managed to gain a few O-level GCEs at Andrew Cains and in 1962, before my sixteenth birthday, had been offered a place at The West Sussex College of Art. I don't suppose there was ever a better time to be an art student in the UK than the early sixties. I worked hard, enjoyed my time there, and left in the Summer of '65 with a scholarship from the Royal Society of Arts. It was money, and I was allowed to choose whether I would use it to travel or to pay for work experience. I chose the latter, and went to work in a London advertising agency as what was designated a junior visualiser. I quickly discovered that junior anything wasn't what I wanted. I needed to be my own boss, to find a way of avoiding the petty politicking that exists in large organisations. Thus, after a brief time spent working for a ceramics and fabric printer, at the beginning of '67 I struck out on my own and began what was to be four decades of working in what is aptly called 'below-the-line' advertising. I was never a 'hot-shot' in the ad world, simply one of the many people in the industry trying to help businesses make the most of their marketing budget when they can't afford to go 'above-the-line' into broadcast media. There are worse ways of making a living, I had some reasonably good years, and some pretty bad ones. I lost one business, narrowly escaped bankruptcy during the recession of '89/'90, and a couple of years ago things began to get difficult again. This final crisis was a combination of two things: me getting tired of advertising, and advertising getting tired of me. It was then that I began to think about bringing together the two things I am best at to create a new and exciting career for myself. Quite simply, I wanted to combine forty years of having to come up with visually creative concepts and the words to go with them with fifty years' love and enjoyment of food and cooking. I didn't think it was such a long shot.

* * *

Back in my cabin on QE2 I was quite clear about why I was there, but the path that had led me there seemed, in retrospect, scarcely credible. I used to watch MasterChef back in the Lloyd Grossman days and often thought about how much I would enjoy entering the competition myself. But, as I've said before, there are those who do and then there are those who merely talk about it. Seeing the first series of MasterChef Goes Large was another story altogether; it really inspired me to have a go, and egged on by my wife and my step-daughter I, together with around five thousand other people, applied to get into the second series. With them, I completed the four page application, and fired it off online about half an hour before the midnight deadline on 6th June 2005. Knowing full well how many applications they would receive and well versed in the ways of the speculative pitch, I persuaded myself to expect nothing further.

Around 9.30 the following morning my mobile rang while I was driving. In those circumstances I would normally let it ring, but for some reason I answered it. 'Hello, is that Peter?' asked a young female voice. 'It's MasterChef here, I've just read your application and I'd like to ask you a few questions. Is this a convenient time for you?' 'Oh gosh!' I replied, 'Thank you for calling me, but I shouldn't be doing this, I'm driving.' 'Whoops, sorry,' said she, 'no problem, I'll call you back later this afternoon.' 'OK, thanks, bye.' Damn, I thought as I put the phone down, they probably have to make hundreds of calls, and if I couldn't even be bothered to speak to her she probably won't call back. I thought I'd blown it.

Good as her word, the young lady did call me back at 5.30 that afternoon. She said they'd been very impressed with what I written in my application, and went on to ask lots of questions about my life, my interest in food, how long I'd been cooking, who were my food heroes etc, etc. After about half an hour she said 'Great, thanks Peter, we'd like you to come up for a casting, can you make it to London tomorrow?' 'Certainly' I replied, 'When and where?' 'Give me your email address and I'll send you all the details' she said. 'Oh, and one other thing, could you bring something with you that you've cooked for our judges to taste?' With that she was gone, and sure enough an email arrived within a couple of minutes with all the information I needed. They wanted me to present myself in Notting Hill Gate at 11.45am. Which left one small problem. It was now about 6.30pm on a Tuesday evening, I live in a tiny hamlet with no shops, and the nearest town is about ten miles away. Being totally uninspired by the contents of a post-weekend fridge and store cupboard, I headed off to that town in the certain knowledge that the only place still open for food at that hour would be the Tesco supermarket.

On the drive into town I thought about what I might cook for the judges. It was early June so I wanted something light and fresh on the palate. There would be no heating facilities so it needed to be a dish that was intended to be eaten cold, that I could prepare that evening and take up to London in a cool bag the next morning. It also loomed large in my mind that this was the first really big test of the competition, and could easily be my last. Whatever I decided to cook, I had better make it good. I thought about doing a freshly smoked trout with a walnut and horseradish sauce, perhaps a salmon mousse with courgette linguini, or maybe … By 8.00pm, when I arrived at Tesco, the only fish available was in blue polystyrene trays with clingfilm wrapping; that wasn't going to be good enough to impress food judges. Then I remembered one of my favourite summertime dishes: Jambon Persillé – and I could make a lemon and Dijon mustard mayonnaise to go with it. Suddenly the shopping was easy. All I had to buy was a small corner of unsmoked gammon, a big bunch of parsley, and a bottle of fairly cheap white Burgundy. Everything else I already had at home.

Jambon persillé (jellied ham with parsley)

This wonderful old-fashioned dish has been much overlooked, but to my delight I found it on the menu of the Hotel du Vin in Brighton only a few months ago. Served with tiny new potatoes, lots of salad and home-made mayonnaise, it is the ideal main course for a summer garden party. It makes an equally impressive first course for a formal dinner.

Traditionally the jelly was achieved by adding split calves feet to the ham during boiling, but these days commercially produced gelatine is a much easier and less queasy way to produce the same results.

Like a lot of really good dishes it has to be started well in advance, but really is quite easy to make. This is the proper way to prepare this dish; on the night before my audition I had to improvise and take a few shortcuts.

For 8 people as a main dish, or up to 20 as a starter

1kg unsmoked, uncooked ham joint

3 unsmoked, uncooked ham shanks

1 packet of gelatine leaves

1 large whole onion stuck with 3 or 4 cloves

3 cloves of garlic, unpeeled

3 or 4 whole shallots, peeled

A few whole black peppercorns

A large bunch of parsley, chopped very finely

A few sprigs each of tarragon and thyme

1.5 litres of dry white wine

1/4 glass white wine vinegar

You are going to need your largest stew pan for this, and a nice big glass bowl for serving. The finished dish is so pretty that you want to be able to see it through the sides of the bowl.

The evening before, soak the ham and shanks in three or four changes of cold water. Cover and leave to soak overnight. Next day, change the water again before bringing the pan to the boil and simmering for an hour. Drain away the cooking water. Freshen the meats under cold water and return them to the pan with the vegetables, herbs and seasonings. The vinegar and parsley come much later.

Pour over all the wine, cover, bring to the boil, then simmer for 2 1/2 hours.

Remove the meats from the pan and use a couple of forks to first remove the skin and excess fat from the ham joint and the shanks. Now use the forks to break the meat away from the shank bones. Discard the skin, fat and bones. Break down all the meat by gently crushing with the forks. Arrange half the ham, packed quite tightly, into the bottom of a glass bowl. Sprinkle over a generous layer of chopped parsley then add the other half of the meat. Finish with another layer of parsley.

Triple strain the cooking liquid through 4 layers of butter muslin. Soak the gelatine leaves in a little white wine (check the maker's recommendations for number of leaves and soaking time). Whisk the gelatine into the hot, but not boiling, cooking liquid. Now add the wine vinegar and pour the whole lot over the ham. Do this carefully so as not to wash the parsley to the outer edges of the bowl.

Refrigerate until set. This dish will keep in the fridge for anything up to a week or more, so if you want it for a dinner party you can easily prepare it a couple of days beforehand.

previous page: jambon persillé

Lemon and Dijon mustard mayonnaise

Mayonnaise is so easy to make that I often wonder how the shops manage to sell so much of that sickly ready-made stuff. The whole process takes just 3 minutes, I promise. Forget the food processor, all you need is a good glass mixing bowl, a balloon whisk, and a jug with a tight pouring lip.

Makes about 150ml

1 egg yolk
150ml oil: one part extra virgin olive to three parts sunflower
1 generous teaspoon Dijon mustard
Juice of half a lemon
Salt and white pepper
A little tepid water

Separating eggs the easy way

Give the egg a little tap on the rim of a cup about two-thirds of the way up to the pointed end. Now, holding the egg upright over the cup, stick your thumbnail into the crack you've just made and peel back the top just like opening a lid. The white from the top third will just run through your fingers into the cup. Discard the top and tip the egg out of its shell into the gently cupped fingers of your other hand. Let the white slip through your fingers leaving the yolk intact in your hand. Easy eh? And it feels rather nice as well, but enough of that.

Have the oil ready in a jug from which you can pour drip by drip. Place a damp tea towel on your work surface and put the bowl on top of this to stop it moving about while you are mixing. Place the egg yolk in the bowl and add the mustard. Whisk vigorously with the balloon whisk until completely blended. Now begin to add the oil, literally one drop at a time to begin with. Drip the oil with one hand and whisk continuously with the other. If you add the oil too quickly at the beginning the mixture will not emulsify, and you'll end up with a load of horrid blobs in a sea of oil.

Gradually increase the rate at which you add the oil until it is all used up. At this stage you should have a clump of mayonnaise stuck to your whisk like over-whipped cream. Now add the seasoning and the lemon juice and whisk again. At this point the consistency will be such that it will not drop off a spoon. This is desirable for some uses, like topping avocados or adding to sandwiches, but for a softer finish add a few drops of tepid water. Transfer to a serving dish, cover with film, and refrigerate until required. It will keep in the fridge for up to two days.

* * *

Providing the trains are running on time it takes about two and a half hours to get to central London from where I live, so with an 11.45am appointment I had to catch the 9 o'clock train from Lewes. That meant leaving home by eight: clearly there was no time for anything to go wrong with my dish. I had finished the Jambon persillé by about midnight and placed it in the fridge with a prayer that it would set. The mayonnaise I made an hour before going off to catch the train.

I need not have worried. On arrival at the appointed place at the appointed time I was met by a young man who was wired for sound and offered me a very welcome drink of cold water. The door in front of me opened and a very young lady, 18 or 19, obviously a young hopeful, came out, smiled at me, and left through the door I had just entered. Inside the audition room was a man, who it transpired was the programme producer, with two of his female assistants. One announced herself as the person who I had spoken to on the phone, straight ahead of me was the lens of a digital video camera. The people were all friendly enough, and seemed to be genuinely interested in what I had to say. After excusing myself to go and wash my hands before handling the food, I did the best job I could under the circumstances of plating up my dish. With all the dignity I could muster, I presented it to them with the announcement: 'I have made you a Jambon persillé with lemon and Dijon mustard mayonnaise – I hope you like it'.

My plate did look good. I had sliced neatly through the layers of ham and parsley, laid it centrally on the plate and allowed a spoonful of my mayonnaise to drop casually over one side of the meat onto the plate. The dish was decorated with a couple of chives that I had picked from my garden that morning, and I stood back and hoped for the best. The hmmmmms and ahhhhhhs gave everything away. The producer said: 'Can you believe some idiot served me sushi at eight o'clock this morning. This is delicious, thank you'.

My pleasure, and indeed relief, was amplified when he said 'Thank you Peter, you will be in the show'. I had no time to be surprised by this pronouncement as his two female assistants, almost with one voice, said 'You can't do that. We're supposed to go away and look at the videos, then make a collective and well-measured decision.' 'My programme', said the producer: 'my decision. Peter's in.'

It was a good couple of months before I heard any more from the programme's production company. Eventually a letter arrived giving dates, times and place for my first rounds. All contestants had to work on the basis that they would get through the initial heats, and provide in advance detailed recipes and lists of ingredients and equipment required for their dishes in the second heat and quarterfinal. They have a company commissioned specifically for the purpose of ensuring that each contestant gets the ingredients and equipment they need in the right place at the right time. I had idly wondered how that all happened: I soon found that it is a very well-oiled piece of machinery.

It is hard to describe the mixed emotions on that first morning of the competition. I hate to be late for anything. To me, arriving late is rude and inconsiderate. The consequence of this belief is that I have grown accustomed to being the first person to arrive wherever I go. On this particular morning though, upon arrival at the studios just off Euston Road, there was already a considerable throng of people milling about in the yard outside the building. Most of them seemed to be wired up in some way or another, with headsets and radio microphones, power packs and portable video monitors. There were cameramen and soundmen, producer, assistant producers, director, assistant directors, and all sort of other people, all of whom appeared to be very busy and very important. I was quickly spotted by one of the young women I had met at the audition.

She ushered me past the crowd and in through a pair of glazed doors that had been emblazoned with the MasterChef logo in self-adhesive film stuck to the inside of the glass. Within, she sat me down on a rickety old chair in the tired and tatty foyer of what was a very shabby building. Two of my fellow contestants were already there, and we soon struck up conversation and friendships. It was then and there that I discovered three of the fundamental and unwavering truths about appearing in a TV competition:

1   *They never tell you anything until immediately before you are required to perform.*

2   *Just like being a patient in hospital, you give up all rights to your own body for the duration of filming. You will be accompanied at all times. You will be told when to stand up and when to sit down, when to talk and when to be silent. What time to arrive and when you may leave – you are even told when you may use a lavatory and when you may not.*

3   *There is an awful lot of time spent hanging about.*

Anyone who finds these requirements incompatible with their own beliefs and/or personality will not make it past the first day of filming. The production crew, however, are on to a winner from the start. They know that every single contestant is there because they want to prove that they are good at what they think they are good at and, more than anything, they desperately want to get through to the next round. Being treated like children in a kindergarten is tough for most people to accept, especially when those who are making the demands appear to lack even the most basic courtesies. There were considerable undercurrents of dissent among the contestants throughout much of the competition, and on occasion these feelings came very close to the surface. But with so much at stake none of us ever allowed those feelings to erupt.

Obviously there is a lot of money involved when you are making a TV programme of forty episodes, and everyone is working under such enormous pressure that a degree of discipline must be imposed. However, I still find it hard to believe that discipline cannot be achieved without resorting to ill-judged and ill-timed demands backed up with the threat of the consequences of failing to comply. Despite all this we did have lots of fun and several good old belly laughs on occasion. Sadly, precious few of these good-humoured sequences made it past the cutting room.

Pretty soon all six of us first-time hopefuls had assembled in the foyer, and it was clear that all of us passionately wanted to make it through to the second round. It would be a bitter blow indeed to fall at the first fence, but we had a lot of respect for each other and any rivalry was kept in check by a genuine feeling of goodwill. There was plenty of activity amongst the crew, but none of it involved any of us so we had time to get to know each other. Looking around at the other five in my heat one thing was already clear. I was at least twice the age of the next eldest contestant, and I wondered if this might hinder my chances.

Charles was from the Caribbean, a lovely young man who lived in Liverpool and worked for the corporation looking after the city's homeless. Charles and I hit it off immediately and we became really good mates in the two days we spent together. Anne-Sophie was an art dealer from Burgundy, now living in London after spending quite a long time in Tuscany where she had learned to add Italian dishes to her French repertoire. Hannah was a nice girl, German originally but now from the north of England. What she lacked in cooking experience she made up for with enthusiasm and a bubbly personality. Phil was a young man from the West Country who worked in insurance and dearly wanted to own and run a small bistro. Phil spent all the time he was not actually cooking poring over his well-thumbed book of Italian cookery. Finally there was Clare, a young woman in her mid-twenties who worked as a fitness instructor, but was far more passionate about food than exercise. She told us that she had written a book about the link between organic food and fitness and wanted to get on as a food writer. I felt I was in good company, but of course had no idea how good any of them were as cooks. They'd got this far, so they must have something.

Time dragged throughout that morning as each of us was taken out in turn to be interviewed about how we were feeling, why we were there, what we wanted out of the experience, and did we think we could win the competition. These same questions kept coming back with predictable regularity throughout the subsequent rounds of the contest. I didn't realise how cleverly framed the questioning was and how, through persistence, they got me to say things that could be taken out of context to mean something completely different. For example, on that first morning, I remember being asked: 'So Peter, are you going to win MasterChef?' I replied that I was among a lot of young talent and I didn't know how good my opposition was. That from 5,000 applicants just being there was an achievement in itself for me, etc, etc. 'No, no,' said the director, 'Don't be like that, let's see some real passion from you. Now; come on, are you going to win MasterChef?' This time my reply went something like this. 'I do have quite a bit of food knowledge, and at my age probably more experience than most of the other contestants. I think I am a pretty good amateur cook and just maybe, if I'm lucky and I stay focussed, there is always the possibility that *you are looking at the next MasterChef.*' The Director smiled and gave me the thumbs up. I thought this meant that he was pleased with the take. Of course what it actually meant was that he'd managed to get me to utter the words that would come back to haunt me when I heard myself saying them on TV in the very first programme of the series.

At about 2.30 we were taken downstairs to a basement kitchen that had been turned into a sort of canteen eatery. There were bowls of all sorts of pasta and salads and baskets of bread, bags of crisps, and cans of fizzy pop all lined up on a long table. We were told to eat as we'd be performing in the studio kitchens in about half an hour's time. None of us had much in the way of an appetite, and the uninspiring array of foods did little to remedy the situation.

Finally, the time had come: 'OK guys, this is it. You are going up to the studio now. I need you to follow me and be quiet on the way'. Up we went until we arrived at a landing quite unlike anywhere else in that dismal old building. Here everything was glass and bright lights, with new paintwork in cream and pink and the glazing on the doors bearing that now familiar 'M' logo. We followed the assistant producer in silence as she led us into a large room with green sofas and chrome shelves against the walls covered in cookery books and kitchenalia. 'Right, now pay attention you lot. You'll be going through those doors into the kitchens in approximately five minutes. I need you to go in through the right hand door in the order that I'll tell you in a minute. Proceed down the right hand side of the room and peel off to your designated workstation. Don't look at the cameras, because you'll look stupid if you do and we'll have to do the whole thing again until you get it right. OK, look at this diagram. Now can you see where each of you will be standing? OK, line up here and wait for me to give you the signal to go in.' I took this opportunity to wish all my fellow contestants the best of luck and was immediately told to 'Keep the noise down Peter. And ... ACTION!'

As we entered the room there were those two familiar faces of judges John Torode and Gregg Wallace staring back at us. We peeled off to our workstations as instructed, and all stood to attention waiting for something to happen. The Director called out: 'OK thanks guys, can we just try that one more time?' After the third attempt he seemed happy and the show went on. John and Gregg each did their bit and explained that this was the Invention Test. In front of us we each had an identical collection of ingredients. We could use as many or as few as we liked to create, 'one great plate of food' in just 40 minutes. 'If you're not ready when I call time, tough! OK aprons and name badges on, you'll be told when to start.'

It is worth mentioning at this point that 16th August 2005 was one of the hottest days of the year, that we were in a room with no open windows or air conditioning because the noise would ruin the recording, and that, wait for it, six ovens were on at maximum temperature. It was like Hell on a Bank Holiday in there, and we hadn't even started cooking yet.

In the corner of the room beside a water dispenser there was a large electric fan that had to be turned off as soon as cameras started rolling. For now John and Gregg were standing in front of it, each with their shirts held wide open so the cooling blast could hit their bare chests. The Director was happy that everything was ready. 'Right' said Gregg, now with his shirt rebuttoned, 'you have 40 minutes, start now and make yourselves proud.'

I had already had a pretty good look at the ingredients in front of me, and I have to say that at that precise moment it was as though I had never cooked anything in my life. My mind went a complete blank. I looked around and everybody else was busy; cutting, chopping, filling pans etc. I looked down again at the ingredients: a nice looking leg of corn-fed chicken, some sheets of fresh pasta, blue cheese, radishes, spinach, potatoes, onions, garlic, a piece of black pudding, an apple, cream, sweet white wine and an array of basics. Oils and vinegars, salt and pepper, butter, eggs, mustard and some bunches of fresh herbs tied up with string. I still didn't know what to do but I had to do something constructive. I decided to make a bowl of mayonnaise; it would take two or three minutes and hopefully impress the judges while I was making my mind up about what to cook. As I was whisking away it came to me in a flash. I'd bone out the chicken leg, season it with salt and pepper and a little garlic, then stuff it with black pudding and tie it up with the string from the herbs. Pan fry it in a little olive oil and butter, and finish it off in the oven. I would leave the Charlotte potatoes in their skins and boil and crush them. Dry fry the spinach and serve the ballotine of chicken on top, and spread out the crushed potatoes and smother them with the mayonnaise flavoured at the last minute with a little chopped fresh tarragon. Phew, I'd cracked it. All I had to do now was cook it.

All the time you are cooking John and Gregg are going around, observing, checking the way you handle things, tasting things as you are doing them, and constantly asking questions of the contestants. It's a nerve-racking experience on the first day, and it doesn't get that much better the more familiar you become with it. I had just boned out my chicken leg when Gregg appeared at my left shoulder. Picking up the bone he asked: 'So what are we going to do with this Peter?' I replied that sadly it would be going into the bin, as I didn't think I had time to use it for making stock. He smiled and nodded knowingly, then very kindly offered to put my mayonnaise into the fridge for me until I was ready to serve. I thought this a very warm and helpful gesture, and as the competition unfolded I came to learn that it was very typical of the man. It was about this time that he and John began to question me about my past and who I considered to have been the greatest influences on my cooking. I briefly mention my mother, Madam Dreyfus, Leno my Italian friend in Brighton and my erstwhile neighbour Kazume, the lady from Kashmir who taught me some of the secrets of Indian cookery. They probed deeper and asked which chefs had influenced me. I replied that much as I enjoyed experimenting with the new ways of doing things, I was still keen to perfect classic French cooking and always referred back to *Ma Cuisine* by Auguste Escoffier.

By the time two minutes was called I was well up to speed. My dish was looking good, it smelled good, and I was confident that it was well cooked and the flavours would work well together.

The tension in the room was now palpable; all six of us had made a tremendous effort. Sensing the need to lighten things up, Gregg burst into song with a rendition of one of my late father's favourite ditties:

I'm 'enery the Eighth I am, 'enery the Eighth I am I am
I got marri'd to the widder next door, she's bin marri'd seven times before
And evr'y one woz an 'enery, she wooten 'ave a Willy or a Dan
I'm 'er eighth old man named 'enery, so 'enery the Eighth I am
Cor blimey, 'enery the Eighth I am!

The fact that I couldn't resist singing along with Gregg clearly revealed my Cockney origins and, I imagine, raised doubts in the minds of the production team over their pre-conceived assumptions about me. Media professionals love to categorise and pigeonhole people; it makes it easier for them to 'package' and present you to their audience as an easily digestible cliché. One of the crew told me that whilst viewing the audition videos they'd already endowed me with a 'tag name' by referring to me as 'The Bayless'. Clearly, from my accent and demeanour, they had ascribed me as the product of a middle class upbringing with the benefits of a public school and university education. In the first round of the competition I had demonstrated that there was more to this contestant than they had previously thought.

When my turn came to present my plate to the judges I had no idea how well it would be received. They had been quite scathing to the people that had gone before me. Gregg tucked in to each part separately, then tasted them all together. 'Cor, tastes good though mate,' he said. John commented that he didn't like potatoes cooked in their skins and would have preferred an 'honest mash'. Then he blew me away completely by saying that if only I'd done something else with my potatoes they could have stopped the competition then and there, because they'd have found their MasterChef. I was flabbergasted, and didn't know what to say.

Later on in the competition I was told that when the trays of ingredients are put together for the invention test the judges already have one specific dish in mind, and that all the other ingredients are really red herrings. The judges always hope that one of the contestants will identify the 'hidden dish', and that, it seems, is exactly what I did.

Outside in the holding room the other contestants were all very nice to me but I didn't know what to feel. If the judges really meant what they said then I'd given them a high level of expectation which I would have to live up to. On the other hand, maybe they were just being kind and didn't really intend to take me any further in the competition. In the event, Charles, Anne-Sophie and I were the three selected to go through to the second heat, and thus my incredible journey towards the final began in earnest.

CHAPTER SIX

THE PRESSURE TEST

Wednesday 17th August 2005. The three of us were dressed in chef's whites, feeling very conspicuous standing in Covent Garden's Wellington Street at eight o'clock in the morning. We knew we were being thrown in at the deep end, but none of us could have imagined quite how deep it was going to be. If you have never been to the Anatolian restaurant Papageno, let me tell you that you have to see it to believe it. The seriously OTT interior décor sets it somewhere between the stage set for an opera, the Tomb of Tutankhamen, and a bric-a-brac store owned by someone with a mild penchant for pornography. The menu is equally eclectic; mostly Mediterranean, it borrows from Greece, Cyprus, France and Italy, with a smattering of Turkish and English thrown in for good measure. It is fun, it is reasonably priced, and with seating for 700 it is also very busy.

Little did Anne-Sophie, Charles and I know what was about to hit us as the owner Richard Niazi entertained us to coffee and croissants when we arrived. Once in the kitchen head chef Kurt, dressed in chef's 'blacks' and wearing a chestful of medals awarded in Turkey for his cooking, set us to work preparing vegetables for the lunchtime service. The actual cooking space in the kitchen seemed absurdly small considering the number of meals they had to produce in it. What with the real kitchen staff, the three of us plus camera man, sound man, director and a runner, it was almost impossible to move between the stoves and the pass. I finished chopping my vegetables and was put onto making pancakes for their highly popular vegetarian main dish. I soon picked up the knack of handling four pans at once, and made three trays full of pancakes. Imagine my disappointment when television only showed the one pancake that I dropped out of the pan, and none of the other six dozen or so that I'd made perfectly.

The next task was for each of us to learn and practice one main dish each from the à la carte menu. Anne-Sophie was given the vegetarian pancake with cream sauce and gratinéed cheese, Charles got the Chicken Princess with asparagus and red wine sauce, and I got the halibut with tomatoes, onions and white wine sauce. As already noted, there was so little room in there that it was impossible for any of us contestants to see what the others were doing, so we concentrated on getting our own dishes right. Chef was pleased with my attempts to emulate his presentation of the dish, and I began to feel a little more comfortable. Richard the owner came up to the pass and announced that they had a busy lunch ahead with several hundred bookings, and that the first diners would be arriving in a few minutes. It was at that moment that chef threw the three of us into complete confusion by switching the dishes he wanted each of us to prepare. I had to change from halibut to the Chicken Princess, Charles was given the vegetable pancake, and Ann-Sophie now had to do my fish dish. We were still desperately trying to brief each other on the ingredients and method for the dishes when the first orders came through. A table of 30 covers had arrived, 7 of them ordered Chicken Princess, 5 ordered halibut, and 4 ordered vegetarian pancake. Having been shown each of the dishes cooked individually in a small pan, we didn't have a clue how to go about cooking them en masse. Just as panic was beginning to set in another load of orders came in. For me there were now 7 Chicken Princess needed in five minutes, and 12 more five minutes after that.

I had given up thinking about helping the other two, and had no idea how to cope with what had suddenly become an endless stream of orders. The regular chefs were all going at full speed and dishes were flying like greased lightning over the pass. I thought that with two of the largest pans I could find I might just be able to cook six of my dish at once, but there wasn't enough room to manoeuvre and there weren't enough burners on the stoves either. The regular chefs were pushing and shoving us out of the way and the whole thing was becoming impossible. The head chef called the three of us aside. 'Now watch and learn what it is like in a real kitchen.' Chefs arrived out of nowhere with huge metal trays of the dishes we had been working on, already prepared and ready to cook. The trays went into ovens and under red-hot salamanders, and as they were doused with wine the alcohol immediately ignited in the intense heat. Within minutes not just five or six of each dish but two to three dozen were cooked and ready to plate up. I'd never seen anything like it and neither, it seemed, had Charles or Anne-Sophie. We were all disappointed. We hadn't been shown any of the mass catering techniques required to cook for such large numbers of people, and in the end only a few of the dishes we cooked made it out to paying customers in the restaurant. It was, though, a fantastic and salutary experience.

John and Gregg arrived to get the low-down on our performances from the head chef, and after being treated to a selection of Greek and Turkish mezze we headed back to the studio. We would now face the test that would determine which one of us would go through to the quarter final.

That afternoon we had just 50 minutes to prepare and cook a two-course meal for the judges. The real problem with these time constraints is not the actual cooking time, but the fact that you need to get all your preparation done within that time too. At home, before the competition started, I had thought long and hard about the dishes I would tackle on television. Anything that requires a marinade or slow-cooking or resting time is obviously out of the question, as is any dish that requires lengthy preparation. For my two-course meal I had planned to do pan-roasted sea trout with samphire and tarragon mayonnaise, followed by damson pudding and Chantilly cream. Just before handing in my recipes I had a change of heart. For starters samphire is at its best in May and June, and although still available can be very woody by mid-August. Secondly, I didn't know if the home economists working on the programme would be able to lay their hands on the fabulous sea trout that my local fishmonger gets in directly from the Shetlands. Finally, I'd made tarragon mayonnaise the day before, so that wouldn't be too clever. I decided to go for something really simple and to do it as well as I could, a genuine attempt to get as close as I could to perfection with simple ingredients. Thus I opted for pan-roasted cod with a sesame crust and garlic pea purée, a decision that almost cost me my place in the quarterfinal.

The 50 minutes went by very quickly and I was ever conscious of the divine aromas coming from Anne-Sophie's cooking and the amazing array of Caribbean ingredients that went into Charles's fantastic crab claw dish.

Both the judges thought I'd opted out of tackling a 'fine dining' dish. In their words, 'knowing that you've read Escoffier from cover to cover, why have you gone from Michelin to Auberge?' I began to suspect that they had pigeonholed me and were expecting me to stick with classic French dishes. Furthermore, I didn't know whether this was a good thing or not. Luckily they loved my pudding and I think that it saved the day for me. John even said: 'sue me if you like Peter, but that dessert is so good it's going on my menu!'

Here are the recipes for my two dishes, plus the sea trout recipe I abandoned on that occasion.

50 minute 2 course meal - quantities for two persons

Pan-roasted cod with sesame crust on a garlic pea purée

150g centre fillet loin of cod	Sunflower oil
100g podded peas (frozen petit pois are quite acceptable)	Knob of butter
	Teaspoon of sesame seeds
2 cloves garlic	A few drops of sesame oil
Sea salt and freshly ground black pepper	A few leaves of mint
Pinch or two of caster sugar	A little flour
1 rounded tablespoon of crème fraîche	

Begin by skinning the cod fillet and checking thoroughly for any pin bones that must be removed prior to cooking. Cut across into 2 similar pieces and set aside.

Pan-roasted cod with sesame crust on a garlic pea purée (cont)

Put about 300ml of water into a saucepan, add the unpeeled garlic cloves, cover and bring to the boil. Cook at a rolling boil for about 8 minutes then add the peas. Bring quickly back up to the boil and cook for about 5 minutes until the peas are tender. Strain through a sieve, but reserve the cooking liquor. Reserve a small spoonful of the cooked peas in a bowl and put the rest of them into a blender. Squeeze the garlic skins and add the delicious pulp to the peas along with a good pinch of salt, about half a teaspoon of caster sugar, and a few twists of freshly ground black pepper. Pour over two tablespoons of the cooking liquor and blitz to a smooth purée. Return the purée to the saucepan and stir in the crème fraîche. Cover and keep warm at the back of the stove.

Cut some mint leaves into fine julienne and add to the reserved peas along with a splash of sunflower oil and a drip or two of sesame oil.

Spread the sesame seeds out on a baking sheet and toast under the grill for a minute until lightly browned.

Heat a little sunflower oil in a non-stick pan until quite hot but not smoking. Dust the fillets on the skin side with a little flour and pat off the excess. Season them with salt before laying into the pan floured side down. Cook for about 3-4 minutes until nicely browned, then add a knob of butter to the pan and carefully turn over the fillets. Cook for another couple of minutes and then remove from the heat. The residual heat in the pan will complete the cooking.

To build the dish, carefully spoon a round of the purée into the centre of a warmed serving plate. Lay the cod fillet on top and spoon on a few toasted sesame seeds.

Garnish around the outside of the plate with the pea, mint and oil dressing.

Damson pudding and Chantilly cream

This dish is a culinary joke based on one of my father's favourites. Dad always liked my mother to save a piece of Yorkshire pudding from the roast beef dinner so that he could eat it cold at teatime spread thickly with jam. This dish is today's version of that childhood memory.

Damsons arrive in mid-August and with any luck remain with us well into the autumn. They are so acidic that they are usually only used for making jam or infusing in gin; this recipe however allows us to enjoy their full flavour without the acid bite.

Note: If damsons cannot be found the recipe works equally well with the tiny golden Mirabelle plums available in late summer. If Mirabelle plums are used, exchange the port for an equal quantity of Muscat dessert wine.

For the pudding	For the fruit filling	For the Chantilly cream
1 large egg	150g damsons	150ml double cream
150ml milk	2 heaped tablespoons caster sugar	1 heaped tablespoon icing sugar (plus extra for dusting)
50g plain flour	2 tablespoons ruby port	A splash of cognac
Pinch of salt	Small piece of cinnamon stick	1 vanilla pod
A few drops of sunflower oil		

Pre-heat the oven to 220°C. Begin by making the pudding batter using the 'reverse' method. Break the egg into a bowl and whisk thoroughly with the milk and a pinch of salt. Cover with a tea towel and set aside for 10-15 minutes. Place the flan tins on a baking sheet and get them really hot in the oven.

Gently heat the sugar, port and cinnamon stick in a saucepan until the sugar has dissolved. Carefully cut the damsons in half, remove the stones, and add the fruit to the saucepan with the syrup. Cover and simmer for 15-20 minutes.

Put the cream, icing sugar and cognac in a bowl. Split the vanilla pod, scrape out the seeds, and add them to the cream. Whisk to a soft peak consistency, then cover with film and refrigerate until ready to serve.

Pour a teaspoon of sunflower oil into each hot flan tin and return them to the oven to get the oil really hot. Meanwhile, give the egg and milk mixture a quick whisk before gradually sieving in the flour, whisking continuously. Remove the baking sheet with the flan tins from the oven and while still very hot pour the batter into the hot oil, filling almost to the brim. Return to the oven for about 25 minutes until cooked and well risen at the edges. If you've got it right, there should be a nice well in the centre of the puddings ready for the fruit filling.

To serve, remove a pudding from its tin and place it on a plate. Spoon in the syrupy damsons (don't forget to chuck out the cinnamon stick first). Now shower with a little dry icing sugar through a sieve and spoon a generous amount of the sweet cream alongside.

Pan-roasted sea trout with samphire and tarragon mayonnaise

A piece of centre fillet of sea trout 350-400g

Flour for dusting

Salt and freshly ground black pepper

150ml sunflower oil

50ml extra virgin olive oil, plus an extra slug for the samphire

50g unsalted butter

1 large egg

1/2 teaspoon mixed Dijon mustard

1 lemon

A few sprigs of fresh tarragon

A little warm water

250g samphire

2 medium vine-ripened tomatoes

Pinch of caster sugar

Wash and de-scale the trout fillet. Dry on kitchen paper and check thoroughly for any pin bones that must be removed with tweezers or fine pliers. Cut the trout into two equal portions and set aside. Check though the samphire and cut away any hard woody stems. (August is towards the end of the season for samphire, and it can get woody as it gets older.) Wash through a colander and set aside to drain.

To make the mayonnaise, simply place the yolk of an egg into a mixing bowl along with a dollop of Dijon mustard, a pinch of salt and a few twists from the pepper mill. Whisk together with a balloon whisk. Put the olive oil into a jug with a tight pouring lip and add to the egg yolk one drip at a time whilst continuously whisking. As the egg and oil begin to bind you may increase the rate at which you add the oil. Now gradually incorporate the sunflower oil until you have a great lump at the end of your balloon whisk. Now add the juice of half a lemon and beat in. Finely chop a few leaves of tarragon and add these to the mayonnaise. Adjust the consistency by adding a few drops of lukewarm water. Cover and refrigerate until needed.

Put the tomatoes in a bowl and cover with boiling water. Leave for 2 minutes, then plunge into cold water. This makes it easy to remove the skins. Cut open, remove and discard the seeds, and roughly chop the tomato flesh. Heat a little olive oil in the small pan, add the tomatoes with a little pinch each of salt and sugar and cook briskly for 1 minute. Plunge the samphire into boiling water and cook until tender - 3-4 minutes. Drain the samphire, toss with a little olive oil and keep warm (do not add salt as samphire is already very salty).

Heat a little sunflower oil in the large pan. Dust the skin side of the fish with flour and pat away the excess with the palm of your hand. Cook in the hot pan, skin side down, for 5-6 minutes. Do not move the fish during this time as we want the skin to become really crisp. Season the flesh side of the fish with a little salt and pepper before carefully turning over in the pan. Add a little knob of butter and turn off the heat from under the pan, allowing the residual heat in the pan to finish cooking the fish.

To serve, place a mound of samphire in the middle of a warmed plate and scatter over some of the chopped tomato. Place the fish on top with the crispy skin side up and spoon over a generous amount of tarragon mayonnaise.

* * *

I was genuinely surprised to be the one chosen to go through to the quarterfinal. In a very short space of time I had acquired an enormous amount of respect and admiration for my two fellow contestants, and I can truly say that I believe both Charles and Anne-Sophie were among the strongest of the contenders I met throughout the whole competition. Charles and I have kept in occasional contact since the competition, and when I saw the programme in which he was knocked out of the running, I was very touched by his comment 'I'm rooting for Peter now: I believe he can go all the way'. Thanks for your confidence in me, Charles.

CHAPTER SEVEN

THE FIRST SEMI-FINALIST

Thursday 18th August, and another early start at the studios. For me it was the third day running, but the other quarterfinalists had done their heats one, two, or three weeks earlier. I wasn't sure who had the advantage; me for still being on an adrenaline buzz, or them for having had a rest. We met up in the now familiar tatty foyer and soon got to know each other. Gillian was a feisty young Scot with masses of confidence in herself and her cooking ability, but a sweet smile and charming personality ran alongside. Gareth was a very intense young man who professed his passion for food and cooking. He had, it seemed, already given up his job in order to enter MasterChef, and intended to pursue a career in catering whatever the outcome of the competition. Finally there was Paul, a young graphic designer from South London; highly creative, he had a bright view of life and oozed enthusiasm. I think that on first meeting we were slightly more wary of each other than we had been of the contestants in earlier rounds, but it was getting serious now. At the close of that day one of us was going to be in the semi-finals.

All four of us had become accustomed to the first of the 'truths' about appearing in a TV programme, so it came as no surprise that we hadn't a clue where we were going as we headed off in the back a large 4x4. As it turned out, the idea was to film us doing a kind of mock version of a shopping trip. I say mock because most of the ingredients for the three-course meals that we were to prepare later in the day had already been bought. We did get to buy our own meat and fish if we were using it, but the shopkeepers had been well primed. I remember thinking that it could have been made into a real test of knowledge and skill if we'd just been sent off to really do our own shopping. But that would have broken the second absolute 'truth', that you will be accompanied at all times. No contestant is permitted to do anything unsupervised.

Of all the dishes in the world that I might have selected to cook for my main course, I chose grouse. Being just a few days after the 'Glorious Twelfth' it seemed to me very appropriate; the trouble was that Gillian had had the same idea. In the butcher's shop there were only a few 'oven-ready' grouse on display and, as they were all new season hens from the same day's shoot on the North Yorkshire Moors, I wasn't too fussed about which one I bought. Just as long as it wasn't too high and it had its liver intact I was happy. Gillian on the other hand insisted on picking them all up in turn, squeezing them, smelling their bottoms and generally looking knowledgeable before deciding which one to have. This was the first occasion that I discovered how some things seemed surprisingly unimportant to the judges. I would have thought that they would have wanted us to pluck, eviscerate and truss the birds, but no one seemed to care whether we knew how to do any of these things. On we went to the fishmonger, where again I was surprised to see people asking for their fish to be cleaned and filleted, and scallops to be already prepared. I have no wish to sound like a food snob, but I wouldn't dream of cooking a scallop that I hadn't killed and cleaned myself. How else do you know how fresh it is?

I was after mackerel for my starter, and to my mind those on display weren't quite as fresh as I would have liked. Where I live I am lucky enough to be able to get mackerel straight from the sea at Newhaven: their bodies are stiff and their glistening skins reflect every colour of the rainbow, their gills are bright and smell of the sea, and their eyes bulge and sparkle. The skate wings looked fabulous but it was too late to change my mind, the recipes had been handed in and I was committed. Funnily enough, there was a large basket of samphire on the slab. I picked up a piece and bit through the centre of the stem. It was like trying to bite through bamboo; I'd definitely made the right decision the day before.

Back at the studio once more we each had to do an ingredients recognition test. This involved identifying all the parts of a pig's innards laid out on a large platter, which presented me with no problems at all. That was followed by a collection of about ten different varieties of vinegar already decanted into little white ramekins. I found these very difficult to identify by taste and smell alone. I was told later that I'd only got about half of them right, and I am not altogether convinced that I would do much better if I tried again. Conversation in the holding room was getting intense. Paul and Gareth thought they'd both mucked the whole thing up; having never seen the insides of a pig they had been hard pressed to identify them. As for the vinegar, they just didn't know. I chatted through what I knew and admitted my doubts about the vinegar. Gillian kept her own counsel, and I thought I detected the tiniest hint of smugness in her expression.

Next came the shock that none of us had been expecting. Each of us was required to make an individual plea to the judges for our own survival in the contest. We had 15 minutes to think about it, and a minute each to make our plea. After that one of us would be going home without even getting to cook their three-course meal. The nerves jangled, the tension mounted, and the stress-factor reached previously unknown levels. It was already very hot in there, and now all four of us were red-faced and perspiring. These TV programme people certainly know how to turn up the pressure. Poor Gareth seemed to crumple. He was already convinced that he'd scored zero in the identification test, and now he said that he was useless at speaking up for himself. It was almost as if he'd given up before the fight had begun. Paul went into another room to be alone with his thoughts, while Gillian paced up and down with arms straight to her sides and fists tightly clenched. Rarely have I seen such determination.

I thought I had as good a chance as anyone, but was a long way from feeling confident of getting through as I still didn't know what the judges were looking for. If it was a broad-based knowledge of food and cooking techniques with years of experience, then maybe I had a chance. If, on the other hand, they wanted youth and malleability, someone who would learn quickly and adapt to different environments, then it probably wasn't me.

In the event Gareth had talked himself out of it and was dismissed before being given another chance to cook for the judges. He was so very passionate about changing his career and working in a professional kitchen – I do hope his dreams come true.

Now the heat was really on. Whatever had gone before was no preparation for the pressure that the three of us were under to perform and create a three-course meal of our own recipes in just 70 minutes. I put my mind into overdrive and went for it for all I was worth. The temperature was unbelievable in there. To what was already the hottest day of the year we added three ovens, twelve hot plates, and three people working harder under pressure than they'd ever worked before. Everything seemed to be going all right for me. With about five minutes to go I was up to speed and began to plate up my food. The first course looked a picture. The main course had come together beautifully, and I decided not to pour the sauce over until the very last moment to stop things going soggy. I turned to my dessert: my soft chocolate puddings weren't too soft any more. They'd carried on cooking out of the oven and sunk down a bit inside their ramekins. They looked more like cakes than soft-centred puddings. Then I grabbed my sauce from where it had been gently simmering at the back of the stove. I took a spoonful to taste for seasoning before serving it. It tasted like vinegar. I should have checked it earlier. Ah well, it's easy enough to add sugar or other sweeteners to a wine reduction if it goes a bit too acidic...

'That's it. Time's up. Put everything down and don't touch another thing!' Too late. Damn, damn, damn, damn, it was too late to do anything about the sauce. I put it down on the worktop and stood back very disappointedly.

Viewers of the MasterChef programme are probably not aware that the judging of three dishes from each of three contestants can take an hour and a half, sometimes even longer. That means that the last person to be judged will have had their food on the plates for well over an hour. Things go cold, things congeal, things can even go limp or curly at the edges, and all this is taken into account in the judging. Nothing however could mask the fact that I had failed to satisfactorily complete my wine and shallot sauce, and had therefore elected not to serve it. That moment in the judging when Gregg said 'where's your sauce Peter?' will live with me forever. In the scheme of things it wasn't really that bad an error, but the programme editors decided to make it a recurrent theme at any and every opportunity throughout the whole of the semi-finals and finals. From being initially mildly irritating, this ultimately became intensely annoying. It was used to create cheap dramatic effect, and to deliberately mislead the audience into thinking that I couldn't possibly become the winner. In truth, when you are in the programme, going through all the tests and challenges, it never occurs that any manipulation may be going on. It is only afterwards, when you see the edited versions on television, that you realise the tricks that are pulled in order to make compelling viewing – often at the expense of the protagonist. In the tension of the studio kitchens, it's a wonder to me that any of us managed to cook anything without errors.

The judges were out for a long time, and in the holding room all three of us were mentally, physically and emotionally drained. We were also soaked through with perspiration. Paul and I sat quietly on the sofa drinking from bottles of cold water, but Gillian was still pacing up and down the room. I had listened to the judge's criticisms of Paul and Gillian and I tried to assess these comments against those levelled at me. I couldn't make my mind up one way or the other, but by the time we marched in to hear the verdict I had convinced myself that my missing sauce and cakey chocolate puddings meant it was probably Gillian who would be going through to the semi-finals.

When you watch the decisions being made on television you have the advantage of hearing some of what the judges have said in their summing up of each contestant's performance. We, the performers, hear none of that, so the announcement of the winner is always a genuine surprise. The tears and the hugs may look a bit staged and corny, but I can promise you that they are very real indeed. Months later when I got to see this episode on television the judge's decision made complete sense for the first time. John said that Paul had gone right off the tracks, that nothing Gillian cooked was better than my dishes, and that her food didn't make him smile either.

What interested me though was that Paul failed for attempting to demonstrate that he had more than one string to his bow. He had come this far by cooking his own style of 'urban chic fusion food' and in the quarter-final his decision to go mainstream clearly upset the judges. My understanding of this at the time was that they were looking for someone to demonstrate that they had developed a style of their own and had the confidence to stay with it. Any thoughts I may have had before about demonstrating a broad-based knowledge of cooking styles was brushed aside for good. Rather than cook them dishes from a repertoire that includes Italian, Greek, Indian, and Chinese, if they wanted me in a box marked 'Classic Anglo-French' that was precisely where I was going to stay, and hope that proved to be a successful strategy.

Thus I became the programme's first semi-finalist. I now had to wait for three months while they searched for the five people who would be joining me. Interestingly, the final round of heats was reserved for people who had been recalled as the best of the previous year's losers. I rather fancy that Charles or Gillian, or both of them, will be reappearing next year: they certainly deserve to.

70 minute 3-course meal - quantities for two persons

First course

Seared mackerel fillet with red onion marmalade

1 whole very fresh mackerel about 400-500g
Olive oil
Maldon sea salt and freshly ground black pepper
1 lime
Small bunch of chives

For the onion marmalade

2 medium sized red onions
A small handful of seedless raisins
A dessert spoon of soft dark brown sugar
A good couple of slugs of sherry vinegar (red wine vinegar will do if sherry vinegar is unavailable)
About 25g butter plus a splash of olive oil
Maldon sea salt and freshly ground black pepper

Peel and finely slice the onions. Melt the butter with the olive oil in a saucepan and add the sliced onions, together with a good pinch of salt and a few twists of freshly ground black pepper. Cook over a medium heat for about 10 minutes, stirring occasionally until well softened and being careful not to allow them to burn or colour too much. Add the vinegar, sugar and raisins, bring to the boil, then simmer gently for 30 minutes. When the marmalade comes together as a mass turn it out into a dish and keep warm at the side of the stove.

Meanwhile wash and pat the mackerel dry with paper towels, then fillet out to give two fillets with the skin left on. Remove any pin bones, then cover and set aside until 10 minutes before serving.

Heat the frying pan to very hot, brush the fillets on both sides with a little olive oil, and lay in the pan skin side down. At this point you'll probably set the smoke alarms off - but that's what they're there for isn't it? After 3 minutes sprinkle the flesh side of the fillets with a little sea salt and freshly ground black pepper and transfer the pan to the oven at 200°C for 2-3 minutes, depending on the thickness of the fish. Cut the lime in half and then cut two thin slices away from the middle. Make a slit in each slice from the centre to the outside edge and give each slice a half twist. Finely pare a little zest from the remaining lime. Place one fillet onto each serving plate, squeeze the lime juice over, and sprinkle with a little of the zest. Place a spoonful of the onion marmalade alongside and garnish with two or three chives and the twist of lime.

Main course

Roast grouse with parsnip chips and watercress served with a rich red wine and shallot sauce

What I really love about grouse is the wonderful taste of the heather on which the birds have fed. Care should be taken not to mask this unique flavour with other over-powerful ingredients.

1 whole young oven-ready grouse - including giblets	2 whole parsnips	1 stick celery
4 rashers of fatty unsmoked streaky bacon	3 or 4 shallots	1 bay leaf
	2 large mushrooms	A few sprigs of parsley
A good quality, square-section white loaf, preferably a day old	A few sprigs of fresh thyme	The outer leaf of a leek
	1 bottle red Burgundy	A bunch of watercress
Pack of unsalted butter	1 generous glassful ruby port	A few redcurrants (optional)
Maldon sea salt and freshly ground black pepper	A little plain flour	1 litre sunflower oil
	1 carrot	Dijon mustard

Undo the trussing string and remove the giblets and the wishbone. Wipe the bird inside and out with kitchen paper. Season inside the cavity with sea salt and freshly ground black pepper and stuff with chopped mushroom and a few leaves of thyme mixed with a little butter. Wrap the bacon around the bird, being careful to cover the breast and legs. Secure with string. Place on a rack in a roasting dish and place in the centre of the oven at 200°C for 20-25 minutes depending on the size of the bird. Remove the bacon from the bird for the last five minutes roasting time. Leave the bacon in the oven to go really crispy. Remove the grouse and bacon from the oven and allow to rest for 5-10 minutes before serving.

Set aside the liver, but transfer the other giblets to a saucepan, cover with water, season with salt and pepper, and add a bouquet garni made by tying the carrot, celery, bay leaf, thyme and parsley into the outer leaf of a leek. Bring to the boil and simmer at the back of the stove.

Finely slice the shallots and sweat in a little butter until well softened. Add half a bottle of Burgundy and a glass of port and reduce until thick enough to coat the back of a spoon. Now strain the giblet stock and boil rapidly to reduce to about a quarter. Add this to the wine reduction, strain again, and keep warm at the back of the stove.

Cut two thick slices of bread (about 20mm thick) and remove the crusts. Place on a baking tray and put in the oven until dry and well browned. Break up some more of the white bread and grind to breadcrumbs. Fry the breadcrumbs in butter until golden brown, drain on kitchen paper, and set aside.

Heat the sunflower oil in a deep saucepan until it reaches the temperature when a small piece of bread will instantly begin to brown and have little bubbles all around it. Peel the parsnip and cut across into very thin slices. Fry these chips in the hot oil until crisp. Drain on kitchen paper and set aside. Fry the grouse liver in butter until well cooked. Pound the liver with more butter to which you have added a touch of Dijon mustard. Spread this paté onto the 'toasts'.

Remove the string from the bird, cut off the legs (if the thigh meat is too rare you can return the legs to the oven for a few minutes while you build the rest of the dish). Carefully fillet off the breasts, keeping them whole.

To build the dish place a croûton on a well heated serving plate, paté side up. Cover with a little of the mushroom stuffing, then one breast and one leg of the grouse. Place a bunch of watercress alongside and a stack of parsnip chips to the other side. Crumble the bacon over the watercress, coat the grouse with the red wine sauce, sprinkle with fried breadcrumbs and serve immediately. If available, a small sprig of redcurrants makes a very attractive garnish.

Dessert course
Soft-centred chocolate pudding with greengage compote

I live in East Sussex not five miles from the Firle Estate, where an enlightened forebear of the present Lord Gage was responsible for the introduction to this country of the 'Green Gage', known in France as the Reines-Claude. This unique and delicious fruit is only in season during August and September, so the timing of this part of the show was just right for its use, served here with a warm, soft and gooey chocolate pudding.

60g good quality dark chocolate
1 egg, plus one extra egg yolk
1 teaspoon flour, plus extra for dusting
60g butter, plus extra to butter the ramekins
2 tablespoons caster sugar

To make the chocolate puddings begin by painting the inside of the ramekins with plenty of melted butter. Chill in the fridge before giving them a second coat, then dust them well with flour.

Break the chocolate into a bowl, add the butter and set the bowl over a saucepan of simmering water (make sure the bottom of the bowl does not touch the hot water). When the chocolate and butter are melted together remove the bowl from the heat.

Use an electric whisk to beat together the egg, egg yolk and caster sugar to a soft peak consistency. Pour into the warm chocolate and sieve over the flour. Gently fold these ingredients together and spoon into the prepared ramekins. Place into a pre-heated oven at 220°C for 9-10 minutes. Remove and allow them to cool a little before serving just warm.

Greengage compote

150g greengages
150ml water
The juice of one lemon
100g caster sugar

Put 150ml of water and sugar with the lemon juice in a saucepan over the heat and stir until the sugar has dissolved. Allow this to simmer gently for a few minutes before adding the halved and stoned greengages. Simmer in the syrup for about 4 minutes until cooked through, but retaining a bite. Allow this to cool a little before serving warm alongside the chocolate pudding. Garnish with a little lemon zest.

CHAPTER EIGHT

FILMING DATES

Life returned to normal after the quarter-final, and nothing much happened for the next three months until a letter arrived early in November providing dates for filming the semi-finals and finals. If I hadn't been aware before, I could now see that if I got through to the final MasterChef was going to be taking over my life for a large part of the two months leading up to Christmas.

The run up to the first day's filming on 15th November was a strange time. I was looking forward to it, but at the same time aware that I would be up against some serious competition and worried that I might not be up to their standard. Menus had to be written, with detailed lists of ingredients and recipes. To make matters even more difficult there is no hot water provided in the studio kitchens, which means that you can't do any washing-up. So every piece of equipment you are going to need in order to prepare and cook your dishes has to be listed, down to the last spoon and balloon whisk. Not easy, if you think about it, and usually means you end up with enormous lists that include as many as six frying pans and ten mixing bowls! Despite all the recipes I carry around in my head, or how often I go into the kitchen and just make something up on the spur of the moment, I was finding it very tricky deciding on dishes that met the criteria as I understood them. Time constraints ruled out many dishes that one might have liked to offer the judges. Whatever one chose needed to be creative, well executed, and provide that indefinable 'WOW' factor. I also wanted to cook dishes that would demonstrate a good knowledge of how to put colours, flavours, and textures together and show that I had mastered many basic and advanced cooking techniques. Common sense told me that I shouldn't tackle dishes that I had never cooked before, but at the same time I instinctively knew that there would be times when it would become a case of 'who dares wins'. I laboured long and hard over my menus, constantly changing, updating and adding new ingredients or accompaniments, until at last I emailed them off to the production company. The information pack advised that apart from menus for the pre-known challenges we should also have at least another two 3-course menus and two or three outstanding single dishes up our sleeves. I couldn't help thinking this was a bit odd, as I imagined that the six semi-finalists would have several hundred other dishes 'up their sleeves'. Further information set the mind racing. I would need to bring my passport, I would need cold weather clothing, and they wanted me to affirm that I didn't suffer from air or motion sickness. There was, of course, no mention of where we might be going or for how long. Remember the first and second absolute truths about being in a TV programme?

Soft-centred chocolate pudding with greengage compote

I was staying in Fulham again for the first few days of the semi-finals, without knowing whether I would be in the competition for the rest of November or going home after just two days. To arrive at the studios by 8.30am I reckoned I should leave the flat at around 7.00: the journey was straightforward, with a single change at Edgware Road, and I felt sure this would give me time for a coffee and croissant at Pret à Manger on the way in. It took almost an hour just to reach Edgware Road. The eastbound platform was very crowded, and I soon found out that due to some incident on the line eastbound services were cancelled until further notice. I felt sure that I could find my way to the studio on foot, but didn't have the faintest idea how long it would take. It is actually a fair step from Edgware Road tube to Onsnaburgh Street and time was getting on. Now you know that I hate to be late for anything, and this was the first day of the semi-finals. By the time I got to Baker Street I had broken into a run. A bit hot and somewhat out of breath I rounded into the yard outside the studio at 8.30 on the dot. And that was when 'absolute truth' number three kicked in – they get you there early for their own convenience, just to know you are there. You then have to hang about for a couple of hours or so while nothing happens.

As on my first day at the studios there were loads of people milling about outside, a few I remembered from earlier rounds plus a number of new faces. One of the cameramen was the first to recognise me and congratulate me on getting this far in the competition. A very open-faced young lady with big brown eyes and flashing white teeth jumped up from where she had been sitting on the wall. She stretched out her hand and in a Southern States accent said: 'Hi, I'm Becky, pleased to meet you. You must be one of the other semi-finalists – none of the others have arrived yet'.

Inside, the tatty old foyer looked exactly as I had remembered it, and I thought about the 132 hopefuls who had all been through those doors. Now there were only six of us left in the competition. Next to arrive was a jolly, bubbly young teacher called Fiona, followed by a young man called Patrick who talked very knowledgeably about food and whom I suspected of knowing what he was talking about. Next came Dean, a slender young man from Bristol who looked like he might have just stepped out of the picture on the front of a 'boy-band' album. The five of us chatted away happily enough until at length the sixth semi-finalist appeared. Daksha was a bit flustered because delays on the Northern line had made her late. She need not have worried, as it was ages before any of us had to actually do anything – 'absolute truth' number three was hard at work. As Daksha introduced herself to the rest of us I had the feeling that she looked vaguely familiar. Not surprising really, because she had competed the previous year and had been invited back to try again. On the previous occasion Daksha made it as far as the quarter-finals: this time she was adamant that she meant to go all the way.

It seemed to take forever to film all the individual interviews, and when it came to my turn I soon discovered that the same old questions were being asked. How did I feel having got this far? What would getting through to the next round mean to me? Did I still think I could win the title? This last question I thought completely pointless. The idea of winning had always been a distant dream, now made even more remote as I had no knowledge whatsoever of the capabilities of the other five semi-finalists.

After about four hours we were taken down to the old basement canteen where a meal, even more gruesome than I had remembered from the previous rounds, was laid out for us. More interviews followed, asking much the same questions over again, and finally we got to run through our lists of ingredients for the dishes that we were to prepare the next day. This was an interesting challenge: one whole chicken plus whatever other ingredients we asked for, one oven, two hobs, and one and a half hours in which to create 'one great plate of food'. Patrick caused a huge furore by requesting a white truffle in his list of ingredients. I don't believe that he did it for effect, I think he genuinely wanted to create a sublime dish; but it was an outrageously extravagant request for him to make and one that ultimately did him no favours at all.

As day one of the semi-finals staggered limply to a close we hadn't been anywhere near a kitchen, or any food for that matter; the word can hardly be attributed to the stuff we had been offered to eat in the basement canteen.

Next morning everyone was at the studio bright and early and raring to go. Aprons and name badges on we were marched into the studio kitchens just as before. We all thought we would be cooking our chicken dishes, but before that the producer had another little trick up his sleeve. In front of each of us was a whole (dead) lobster, some cream, milk, flour, bayleaf, peppercorns, thyme, eggs, brandy, butter, onion, clove, cayenne pepper and Parmesan cheese. No prizes for guessing what was going to be the dish of the day, but at as it turned out only Becky and I had identified the ingredients for a lobster thermidor.

Not for the first time in the competition I was surprised by the things we were not required to do. We didn't have to kill the lobsters, because they'd already been boiled, and we didn't have to use knowledge or initiative to create a dish. All they wanted was to discover how well we could follow a step by step recipe, in this case written by Michelin-starred chef John Burton-Race. John Torode asked whether any of us had cooked a lobster thermidor before. I replied that I had, but not to that recipe. I didn't want to say any more for fear of sounding like a know-all, but as far as I was concerned it is in a lobster Newberg that the lobster is flamed with brandy. not in a thermidor. Still, eminent chefs create their own versions of the classics all the time so I was more than happy to follow instructions.

Just my luck; I got the hen lobster, absolutely stuffed full of dark green slimy coral that took a lot of cleaning before I could start cooking. Forty minutes later there were six versions of Chef Burton-Race's lobster thermidor for the judges to taste. As will always happen when different people cook to the same recipe with similar ingredients, six different dishes were prepared. I was reasonably happy with mine for its presentation and quality of cooking, but I didn't like the taste. For me it was over-rich, with cream, egg yolks and Parmesan added to the béchamel sauce, and the effect of flaming in brandy and adding cayenne pepper added too many strong flavours, overpowering the delicate lobster flesh. Becky was no stranger to cooking with lobster and handled the dish with consummate ease.

One thing that was very interesting was how well both Daksha and Dean had done in this test. Both admitted that they had never handled a lobster before, yet both produced first rate dishes. This ability to follow instructions and imitate what they had been shown was going to become a great asset to them as the contest progressed. I suppose it does take a little longer to teach an old dog new tricks, and I kept thinking about how much I preferred my own recipe for lobster thermidor.

Lobster thermidor for two people

2 live lobsters each weighing 350g

1.5 litres court bouillon

250ml thick béchamel sauce

1/2 teaspoon English mustard

1 dessertspoon thick double cream (optional)

A pinch each of sea salt and ground paprika

A little melted butter

For the court bouillon

1.5 litres water

125ml dry white wine

4 shallots, finely sliced

1 carrot, finely sliced

Juice of half a lemon

Teaspoon of salt

A few black peppercorns

Bouquet garni: sprig of thyme, bayleaf, and a few parsley stalks tied into the outer leaf of a leek

For the béchamel sauce

25g plain flour

25g butter

250ml milk

Half an onion, peeled and stuck with a whole clove

Salt and freshly ground white pepper

A pinch of freshly grated nutmeg

A bouquet garni: tie together a bay leaf and a sprig each of thyme and parsley

103

Put all the ingredients for the court bouillon except the peppercorns into a pan, bring to the boil, and simmer for 1 hour adding the peppercorns for the final 10-12 minutes. Strain through muslin.

For the béchamel sauce, melt the butter in a pan and stir in the flour. Keep stirring while you cook out the flour over a moderate heat to a pale buff colour. Remove from the heat and cool a little before whisking in the milk. Bring back to the boil, then add the seasoning, onion and bouquet. Simmer gently for 20 minutes. Strain through a very fine sieve.

Kill the lobsters in your preferred fashion, then plunge them into the boiling court bouillon and boil gently for ten minutes. Remove, drain and allow to cool a little. Split the lobsters in half lengthways and remove the stomach bag from inside the head and the intestine (the black line running down the tail). Brush the flesh with melted butter, season with a little salt and paprika, then place flesh side down in a hot pan. Cook for 4 minutes.

Stir the mustard and cream (if using) into the béchamel sauce together with the 'cuisson', the juices from the pan in which the lobster was cooked. Remove and cut the meat from the tail into generous scallops. Chop up the head and claw meat and mix with half the béchamel. Divide this mixture between the four cleaned and trimmed lobster shells. Carefully arrange the tail scallops (rounded side up) on top and coat with the remaining béchamel. Sprinkle with a little melted butter and glaze under a very hot grill.

Following the lobster recipe had been an interesting exercise, but as none of us mucked it up I don't think it actually established much in the way of a pecking order.

After a short lunch break the real test of the day began; the one where we had the opportunity to be creative and to really demonstrate what we were capable of.

Gregg: 'One whole chicken, one and a half hours, go!' John: 'Two of you are going home after this so make it good, make it the very best you can do.'

* * *

Ballotine of chicken with mustard velouté
served with potato cake and wild rocket and watercress

For two people

2 whole breasts of chicken

Olive oil

Unsalted butter

Salt and freshly ground
black pepper

Chicken and wild mushroom
mousseline

Chicken velouté

Whole grain mustard

For the mousseline

1 leg and thigh of chicken

Salt and freshly ground
white pepper

The white of one large egg

2 small closed cap mushrooms,
very finely chopped

Double cream

Sprig fresh tarragon

Sprig fresh parsley

Cup of milk

Handful of stale breadcrumbs

For the velouté

Shallots

Unsalted butter

Plain flour

Salt and freshly ground
white pepper

Glass dry white wine

Glass Noilly Prat

Cup of 'quick' chicken stock *

Half cup double cream

Half cup single cream

For the accompaniments

Desiree or Maris Piper potatoes

Salt and freshly ground
black pepper

Unsalted better

Olive oil

Bunch each
wild rocket and watercress

* For the 'quick' chicken stock

Chicken bones from leg above
plus a couple of wing joints

Olive oil

Stick of celery

1 leek

1 carrot

1 onion

2 cloves garlic

Large sprig of thyme

1 bay leaf

Water

Splash of white wine

Remove the wishbone from the chicken and fillet off the two breasts. Remove one leg and both wings and save the remainder of the chicken for another dish. Remove the skin from the breasts and remove the small underside fillets. Cut through the breasts horizontally about three quarters of the way through to form a pocket. Season inside the pocket, cover, and set aside.

Make a handful of white breadcrumbs, place in a small saucepan, cover with milk, and set aside. When the crumbs have absorbed the milk, place the pan over the heat and stir until the paste leaves the sides of the pan. Remove from the heat and cool. This is the bread panada.

De-bone the leg and thigh and remove and discard the skin. Roughly chop the leg meat and add it to the food processor along with the reserved underside breast fillets. Add a little salt and white pepper and blitz for a few seconds. Scrape down with a spatula and blitz again. Scrape down again and add the egg white and a spoonful of the bread panada. Blitz again, and again scrape down before adding a splash of double cream. Blitz again, and with the motor running gradually add more cream. Finally rub the mix through a fine sieve into a bowl set over ice. When well chilled, stir in the finely chopped mushroom and a little finely chopped tarragon and parsley. Stuff the mousseline into the pockets in the chicken breasts and roll up tightly. Secure into several layers of clingfilm, tie off at the ends, and chill in the freezer for 10 minutes.

Put the leg bones and wing joints in a saucepan along with a splash of olive oil and cook gently for a few minutes. Chop up the celery, leek, onion and carrot and add to the saucepan along with 2 cloves of garlic (unpeeled), a sprig of thyme and a bay leaf. Cook for a couple of minutes then add a good slug of white wine. Cook until the wine has all but gone, then cover the contents of the pan with boiling water. Keep at a brisk boil for 15 minutes. Strain into a bowl and discard all the debris.

Peel the potatoes and slice across into rounds about 3mm thick. Cook in boiling salted water for two minutes and drain through a colander. Put the blanched potatoes in a bowl and toss in olive oil and melted butter. Season with salt and pepper, then press them down into ring moulds. Place in the centre of a pre-heated oven (180°C) for 20 minutes. Remove from the oven and press them down again with the back of a spoon. Add a little more melted butter and put back in the oven for a further 20 minutes. The tops should be golden brown.

Bring a saucepan of water to the boil and drop in the chicken ballotines, then place an empty pan on top to keep the ballotines submerged. Keep at a gentle simmer for 12 minutes, then remove the chicken from the water, snip one end off the clingfilm sausages and slide the ballotines out onto a plate. Set aside to cool while you make the velouté.

Cook the finely chopped shallots in a little butter until soft but not coloured. Add the wine and the Noilly Prat and boil hard to reduce by a half to two thirds. Add the chicken stock and boil hard again to reduce to half. Stir in the single and double creams and cook gently to achieve a smooth creamy sauce. Strain through muslin, return to the heat and beat in a few of knobs of kneaded butter to thicken to the required consistency. Now season with salt and pepper.

Melt some butter in frying pan and when frothing add the chicken ballotines. Cook gently on all sides until nicely golden.

To assemble the dish first trim off the ends of the ballotines, then cut them in half at an angle of 45 degrees. Present the halves alongside the potato cake. Stir a teaspoonful of wholegrain mustard into the velouté just before serving to the side of the plate.

Place a small bunch of watercress and rocket to the other side of the plate, and drizzle with olive oil, a twist of black pepper and a drop or two of lemon juice.

* * *

I really enjoyed this challenge because I was cooking my kind of food, without having to follow someone else's recipe or having to make my dish look the way someone else told me it should look. I didn't think much of the ovens or the black glass hobs that seemed impossible to control, but we were all in the same boat so I just had to grin and bear it. I looked around at what everyone else had done and listened carefully to all the praise and criticism from John and Gregg. When they got to me John accused me of 'playing safe' and 'taking the easy option'. I didn't agree at all and for the first time felt confident enough to say so. I told him that I had purposely tackled three quite separate and quite difficult techniques in my dish. Making the mousseline, stuffing, rolling and poaching the chicken, and making the velouté sauce and my 'Pommes de terre Anna' were not exactly easy either. John complained that my potatoes were not seasoned enough and then said that he thought that grain mustard was 'girly' and not nearly hot enough. Again, I didn't agree. What would be the point of going to all the trouble of making a delicate chicken ballotine with a subtle filling, then smothering it with hot mustard sauce? I couldn't be sure, but just for a moment I thought that he might have been pulling my leg. I was encouraged in this observation by the fact that Gregg seemed to be very impressed with the whole dish.

Now all six of us were back in the holding room waiting for the judges' ruling on which two of us would be going home. As if that wasn't stressful enough, we also had to contend with cameras and microphones being thrust into our faces and having to answer another barrage of questions. How did we think we'd done in there? Had we done enough to get through? How would we feel if we were sent home now? Bloody silly question, anyone would be mortified to be sent home after putting so much of themselves into a competition like that. All the while of course the cameras kept rolling, so I was constantly on my guard, constantly trying to remain upbeat in my responses no matter how crass or inane the questioning appeared to be.

After what seemed like an eternity we were finally called back into the studio kitchens to hear the verdict. We had only spent a relatively short time together, and the fact remained that we were in competition with each other, but already we had formed close friendships and a genuine feeling of goodwill towards each other. The programme makers tried their best to set us against each other, presumably because angst and backbiting make for 'good television', but it didn't work; they made everything so hard for us that fraternity grew out of common adversity.

Patrick and Fiona were sent home. I couldn't work out why, and I couldn't grasp the criteria by which they had been judged to be failures.

Ballotine of chicken with mustard velouté
served with potato cake and wild rocket and watercress

CHAPTER NINE

'YOU FOUR ARE GOING ON AN INCREDIBLE JOURNEY'

Back to the holding room, and Patrick and Fiona had already been seen off the premises before we'd had a chance to say goodbye – no room for sentimentality, then? Without the chance to even catch a breath we were then thrown into a maelstrom of activity. The crew were packing up cases full of cameras and sound equipment, people were running around with clipboards shouting instructions, and in the middle of it all we four were being issued with outfits designed to withstand the coldest of weather conditions.

Thermal undershirt and long-johns, one of each
Thermal socks, two pairs
Thermal gloves, one pair
Long sleeved, zip-up fleece jacket, one
Heavy-duty, ski-style over jacket, one
Heavy, thick, mountain-style boots, one pair
Woolly ski hat, one

Cooks for the use of.

I remembered what my Father had told me years ago about kit issued to him during the War. The RAF gave him tropical clothing, and he ended up being posted to Iceland! Careless talk cost lives in those days, and clearly our programme producer was operating under a similar set of rules. We had absolutely no idea where we were going, and nobody was going to let us in on the secret. Perhaps, as they had issued cold weather gear, we were really going to the Sahara? Absolute truths numbers one and two reared their heads again.

Together with a handful of the crew we headed off into the night in the direction of Heathrow. It was now well after 9.00pm and we had been under constant pressure for over thirteen hours. The elation of having made it to the final four was mixed with the tiredness that comes when you suddenly switch off after an intense period of work. Add to that the excitement and anticipation of the moment, tinged with anxiety and the irritation of once again being treated like schoolchildren, and you will have some idea of how I was feeling on that leg of the journey. Our driver didn't know how to find the hotel in Uxbridge where we were to stay for the night, so after a few stops to consult the A-Z, large format version, we eventually arrived at about

10.30. Aside from a desultory peck at the dismal lunchtime 'nosh' in the basement canteen, none of us had eaten anything that day. Inside the hotel we were given ten minutes to dump our belongings in our rooms before making it back to the dining room by last orders at 11 o'clock. We ate a reasonable hotel-type meal and downed a few glasses of wine, and by about one in the morning we were just beginning to feel a little more mellow. That was when they told us that our cars would be leaving for the airport at 4.30am - and still we didn't know where we were going.

I fixed my alarm call for 4.00 but needn't have bothered. Despite being tired, I had so much on my mind that sleep did not come easily. I drifted in and out of fitful naps and rose again at 3.55, showered, shaved and went downstairs with my travel bag. Considering how early it was the hotel lobby was quite a hive of industry. Members of our crew were directing operations by organising the loading into cars of the vast amounts of luggage and equipment that had to accompany us on our journey. I volunteered to lend a hand, but was firmly rebuked and informed that I should rest as we had a very long day ahead of us. Some mistake, I thought; surely you mean another very long day?

Next down was Becky, looking just as bright as she had done when she retired less than four hours earlier. Then came Daksha, clearly a little weary, but keen as mustard and up for whatever they were going to throw at us. Dean sauntered in, hands in pockets and head buried inside his hoodie. He didn't look too happy to be there at that time in the morning, but there was no power on earth that could have stopped him from competing.

At the airport we met up with the rest of our party – about seventeen in all counting us four plus the judges, cameramen and soundmen, producer, director, assistants, researcher, runners, etc – and a veritable mountain of luggage and equipment. Still we didn't know where we were going, and still we were being kept under constant surveillance. We couldn't even go to the loo unaccompanied. The demand for us to hand over our passports met with no resistance as we checked in at the SAS desk. It wasn't until we were queuing at the entrance to the departure lounge that our passports were returned to us ready for inspection, and at last we were given our boarding cards. Lakselv, via Oslo and Tromso! Where in the world is Lakselv?

The crew, and in particular the producer and judges, thought it hilarious that we four had come all this way without knowing where we were going. They found it even more hilarious when I told them that my wife, who was in Cape Town at a conference organised by the company she works for, was going out of her mind with worry not knowing where I was going or for how long. By then it was too late to call and tell her, because her conference had started. I wouldn't be able to call her again until much later in the day, by which time I would be almost at the opposite end of Planet Earth. I thought Gregg was going to choke with laughter, but there was no malice in it and even through my concern I could see the funny side of the situation.

Once into the departure lounge we contestants headed straight for the first bookshop. Dean grabbed a big atlas and quickly discovered that Lakselv sits on the northernmost tip of mainland Norway, well inside the Arctic Circle. I found a travel guide to Norway and discovered that Lakselv is famous for the quality of its salmon fishing, so that during the season anglers travel there from all over the world to catch the king of fishes. I also noted that during winter months temperatures can be among the lowest anywhere on earth, and daylight is down to a mere three hours a day. Still, if we were lucky we might get to see the Aurora Borealis or the odd polar bear.

Despite such an early start, it was already late afternoon and quite dark by the time we boarded our third flight of the day for the last leg of the journey to Lakselv. Although we now knew where we were going, we still had no idea what we would be doing when we got there. Spirits remained high, however, amongst everyone except our soundmen, who were pondering the consequences of having lost their boom poles. For some reason best known to themselves the airport officials at Tromso had felt it necessary to confiscate these items, that had been accepted as hand luggage on the previous two flights of the day. Unless the poles turned up again at Lakselv airport our soundmen had a serious problem, because a soundman without a boom pole is about as much use as a colander without holes.

The steward aboard our flight was the most friendly and obliging member of aircrew I have ever encountered. and took all the moving about and filming well within his stride. Nothing it seemed could bother him. Until, that is, he received a message from our Captain. Lakselv was in the grip of a blizzard, with winds gusting at over a hundred miles an hour. It was impossible for our plane to land in those conditions, so we would have to be diverted and land at Alta. The terminal building at Alta turned out to be not much more than a centrally heated concrete shed: outside, everything was ice and snow, pitch dark and very, very cold. By now we were starting to share the soundmen's gloomy outlook on life. We'd been travelling all day after hardly any sleep the night before. We had eaten a snack at Oslo airport, but that was hours earlier, and Alta didn't have a café or a bar or even a vending machine. Furthermore we were still 200 kilometres from Lakselv, and a ridiculous rumour was going around that the airline was laying on a bus to take us there by road.

The bus took three hours to get us to Lakselv. When we arrived we were cold and tired, hungry and thirsty, but above all relieved to have survived the journey. I don't know how they train the bus drivers in northern Norway, but somehow our heroic driver managed to keep that huge vehicle on the road, driving it through blizzard conditions with nothing more than compacted ice for a road surface. It was a remarkable achievement that he seemed to take for granted, but I for one would never wish to undertake a journey like that again. At the entrance to Lakselv airport the evidence of our eyes gave us an inkling of what lay in store for us. Lined up very neatly in the snow were a collection of camouflage-painted military trucks and Land Rovers, and in front of them, also very neatly lined up, were a camouflage-clothed section of the Royal Marine Commandos.

'So you're the cooks are you? Well, you'd better be bloody good.' Such was our greeting from a fearsome looking moustachioed Colour Sergeant, who stood about 6ft 10ins in his highly polished boots. 'Right you lot, get into that white bus over there before you all freeze to bloody death.' In the minibus we were all squashed together, sitting with our bags across our knees. I'd made the mistake of putting my bag down on the frozen ground outside, and once inside the warm vehicle the ice that had gathered on its base was now melting and soaking through my trousers. The day was a long way from being over, and arriving at a military base we were first shown to our quarters. Dean and I were sharing a small barrack room with two sets of bunk beds, a table and chairs and a pair of wash basins in the corner: the girls, Becky and Daksha, were given similar accommodation across the corridor. The Royal Marines had been most particular in their signage of facilities for the duration of our stay. The Commandos don't get too many women doing four months' extreme weather training in the Arctic Circle, so Becky and Daksha plus the female members of our crew had been given their own ablution facilities that were marked strictly 'out-of-bounds' to the male contingent.

The next task was to get us fed. We fought our way through the snow and icy blast across the half-mile of parade ground to the canteen, where the Sergeant IC catering and his two Corporals had remained on duty to feed us. We soon discovered that these three men were responsible for feeding the entire camp of some 250 officers and men.

Next up was a trip to the other side of the camp where we were treated to a lecture (with slide show) on how to survive in extreme low temperatures and how to identify the first signs of frostbite on our colleagues' faces. We were also shown slides of what first, second, and third degree or 'deep' frostbite looks like. I am not sure that I would care to watch a repeat performance of that particular sequence. We men were instructed not to shave in the morning as it tightens the skin and weakens its resistance to the effects of the cold. This was followed by a demonstration of how to dress for the weather we were about to face. With the ladies present this turned into something approaching vaudeville, particularly by the time the young Royal Marine who was acting as mannequin got down to his thermal underpants.

Then it was back out into the cold again to yet another corner of the camp, the Quartermaster's Stores. The four of us were lined up in front of the officers – and our crew and the cameras – with a huge array of kit neatly laid out on the floor in front of us. I couldn't believe it. They were actually going to film us getting dressed up in this gear, and it was at this point that I noticed that our soundmen clearly hadn't been reunited with their boom poles They'd lashed their big fluffy microphones to the ends of a couple of end-to-end broomsticks, which themselves were lashed together with gaffer tape. They looked pretty Heath Robinson, but seemed to work OK. The whole thing was hilarious, and became even more so as we tried to struggle into our kit. It is almost impossible to don over-trousers and over-boots when you are standing on one leg and before long all four of us had fallen to the ground where, if we'd had any sense, we would have started from in the first place.

Kit finally stowed away in kitbags we were all more than ready for bed, but the Commanding Officer told us that it was compulsory to join him in the Mess along with the other officers for a night-cap before turning in. We stayed for a couple of drinks and finally got to bed around 2.30 in the morning. It certainly had been another long day, and just before retiring we'd been told that we must be in the canteen for breakfast by 6.30 at the very latest. As Dean and I turned in and switched out the lights, our last words to each other went something like: 'What the fuck do you suppose they've got in store for us tomorrow?' 'Dunno, but you can bet your life it'll be a fucking long, cold day. Good night.' 'Yeah, good night.'

CHAPTER TEN

THE FROZEN LAKE, AND OTHER JOYS OF LIFE WITH THE ROYAL MARINE COMMANDOS

Getting dressed for breakfast was a thoroughly chaotic affair. Neither Dean nor I had the time or the inclination to go downstairs to the communal showers, so we made do with a quick splash of hands, face and armpits at the basins in the corner of our room. The sleeping quarters are kept at a very high temperature, and we couldn't open the windows because the temperature outside was about –15°C. Pulling on thermal long johns and long-sleeved vests had the effect of making me perspire even before any other layers went on. At this point I hit a problem, and began to suspect skulduggery. My Royal Marines' issue thermal vest was about four sizes too small. I couldn't get an arm through a sleeve or the neck over my head. Being of very slim build compared to me, Dean kindly volunteered to swap his loose-fitting one for mine, but it turned out that mine was too small even for him. Luckily I had packed the thermals that I had been given back at the studio. Next came my special roll-necked shirt, and again this might have fitted a thirteen-year-old boy. I made do with my own thick cotton shirt with a field cravat at the neck. My zip-up fleece was also very tight fitting, but I did just about manage to get into it. My combat trousers and jacket were all right, but they had seen better days and didn't feel comfortable at all. Hat and gloves were OK, but my snow boots were a complete disaster. These boots have been specially designed to keep your feet warm in the coldest of conditions. They have cleated plastic soles and thick Goretex uppers that are held up just below the knee with a drawstring. We had been instructed to wear two pairs of extra thick woollen socks under our boots, and to ensure that the special thermal insoles were in place to form an insulating barrier against the cold. I had no insoles in my kit, which meant that my snow boots were useless. Remembering my Boy Scout training, I put on one pair of my own cotton socks followed by one pair of the Marines' woolly socks and pulled on the mountain boots provided back in London. I wasn't properly kitted out, but it would have to do. One last thing for both of us was to fix a reflective band around the leg below the knee. In a land where it is dark for 20 hours of the day this is worn so that drivers can see you in their headlights. Apparently local law states that if you get run over by a vehicle when not wearing one of these bands the accident is deemed to be your fault and you have no recourse to compensation, always supposing you live long enough to attempt to claim it.

Out on the parade ground on our way to breakfast Dean and the others looked for all the world like Royal Marine Commandos on extreme weather exercises. I, on the other hand, looked and felt a bit of a ragbag. I wasn't too happy about this until I saw Gregg that morning. He was wearing about fifteen layers of his own clothes, plus a balaclava helmet and a huge scarf. The unkind but entirely accurate observation offered by one of the crew that he looked like 'a bag lady' sent howls of laughter throughout the whole camp.

After a huge high-calorie breakfast we learned our fate. We were to be taken out to a field kitchen set up beside a frozen lake, where we would cook for 100 Royal Marine Commandos who had been bivouacking out on manoeuvres in the sub-zero temperatures. The result of our efforts would be the first hot food these men had eaten for several days. This whole exercise was highly time-critical. Commencing at 1200hrs, sections of ten men at a time would be arriving at the feeding station at approximately ten-minute intervals. As one section left, another would arrive. There could be no delays as the men had to be on their way immediately after eating, and the food eaten by the last section had to be as good and as hot as that eaten by the first. The whole performance – preparation, cooking and serving – also had to take place inside the four-hour window during which there was enough light for filming.

It was about 7.30am when we climbed aboard the Norwegian Army Snow-Cat vehicles that took us out to the frozen lakeside. The vehicle's headlights illuminated a path through an eerily beautiful frozen wasteland, and after about an hour we arrived at our destination. I remember thinking that we had about three and a half hours before the first section was due. Knowing how much time the director and crew can use up doing take after take while we are left hanging around, I was anxious to get started as soon as possible.

Two open-fronted tents were erected side by side, each set up as a field kitchen with butane gas burning rings and a field oven, trestle tables, pots and pans, and an assortment of other cooking equipment. The sergeant lined the four us up outside. 'Right youse lot, listen in. For this exercise I'm dividing youse up into two teams. Becky and Peter will be in Kitchen A right here behind me. Daksha and Dean will be in Kitchen B to the right. This is not about fancy nancy food, this is about survival. This is about getting these fighting men fed with good wholesome hot food. They need high-carb, high calorie scran and they haven't got time to hang about waiting for it. Make no mistake these are hard men, and they are on a very hard exercise. Get it right and they'll be happy. Get it wrong and they won't be backward in letting youse know what they think. I am expecting youse to come up with a hot tasty meal of at least three components. Plus a hot duff, warm bread and a hot wet. My Corporals are here to answer questions and help with unfamiliar equipment, but they will not step in to help with the cooking unless it looks like youse are going to fail. Understood? Good. Go to it, and good luck.'

If we had been able to 'go to it' there and then it would have made our task a lot easier than it turned out to be. Instead it took ages to do take after take of the Sergeant's instructions. Then we had to climb back up the hill to the vehicles and be filmed walking down to the kitchens another three or four times. By the time we actually got into our kitchens it was gone half past nine.

Becky and I were really excited by the experience. It was a tremendous challenge, and not something that was ever likely to occur again in our lives. We hadn't a clue about what might be going on in the tent next door, and it wasn't until the programme was televised that a few things came to light. Certainly the programme makers were having a bit of fun at the expense of Becky and me. They made it look as though we were completely out of our depths, that we might not even get the food ready on time. Nothing could have been further from the truth.

We had field ration boxes that contained dried foods and cans without labels, the contents of which had to be identified before we could decide on a menu. There were a few fresh provisions and we thought it important to make sure we made use of them. We had cans of meat and cans of beans and cans of tomatoes, and we had packs of chilli seasoning and herbs and both dried and fresh onions. Chilli con carne was an obvious choice. We didn't have rice, but we did have lots of other carbohydrates in the form of pasta and both dried and fresh potatoes. The main course was under way:

CHILLI CON CARNE
SPICED BEANS
PASTA
FRESH HERBY POTATO AND ONION SAUTÉ
DRIED POTATO MASH WITH A CHEESY TOPPING

Becky had uncovered bags of flour, sugar and oatmeal, packs of margarine, and tins of peaches, apricots and apples. We found milk powder and custard powder, so the dessert course – or 'hot duff' as it's referred to by the Royal Marines – was:

BAKED FRUIT OAT CRUMBLE WITH CUSTARD

Add to that a huge billy can full of hot tea, some lovely crusty bread that we defrosted and warmed on top of the oven, bars of chocolate and bags of sweets, and we felt we had it cracked. Becky and I had no problems about division of labour, we just fell into a natural pattern of working together. We both seemed to instinctively know what the other was doing and there was never a moment of panic or dissent between us. With about ten minutes to go before the first section of men were due to arrive the Sergeant appeared: 'Right, how's my Kitchen A team doing?' 'Very well thanks Sergeant' replied Becky. 'Peter and I work really well together and we're about ready, just keeping things hot 'til the boys arrive.' 'Talk me through the main course Peter ... Very good' said he, after seeing and tasting everything. 'What about their hot duff?' Becky showed him the trays of nicely browned fruit crumble in the field oven, and I was stirring the custard. 'Good again. What about their hot wet?' 'All done sergeant. I've made tea in the hot billy can', I answered. 'Right, I see youse've laid out the chocolate and sweets, don't put anything else outside until me or the Corporal gives youse the signal. It'll get frozen in no time outside the tent. It's brass monkeys out there, and getting colder by the minute. I bet youse've forgotten that the bread is frozen.' Becky and I both laughed; we had already sliced the loaves into generous chunks, wrapped them in foil, and placed them on top of the field oven. 'Good, well done youse two in here, I'm glad to see someone's got it sorted. Next door haven't stopped fucking arguing yet.'

Our Corporal appeared at the entrance to the tent. 'OK, first section coming in now. You'll be feeding them, then the next section will go next door and we'll alternate like that until they've all been through. Don't forget as soon as you've served the lads, get your food covered up and back on the heat at the double. Its –15°C out there and the wind chill is taking down it much lower. Good luck. I'll be here if you need me.'

Becky and I gave each other a big thumbs up and decided that as there was a competition running between the two kitchens she should go out front and serve the men their food, while I did the running in and out of the kitchen. Those men wouldn't have seen a woman for days, let alone one as pretty as Becky. If you've got a secret weapon its silly not to use it!

Our first service went very well, and for me it was a very moving experience. Watching the men skiing in across the frozen lake towing sledges of equipment behind them was an extraordinary sight, and their white hooded anoraks and overtrousers made them look like players from the movie 'Where Eagles Dare.' But this was no movie, this was the real thing, or at least as close to the real thing as I am ever likely to get. These are the young men who voluntarily offer their lives to protect our freedoms. These are very special people indeed.

One of the men from the first section came back to our tent to offer his thanks. Becky and I were thrilled; the Sergeant, who had overheard, told us that what he wanted to hear was praise from the last section, not just the first. As luck would have it the Sergeant was standing close by when two men from the last section we fed came back to thank us. The Sergeant didn't say anything, but he did give us a wink and a knowing smile.

Despite the lack of sleep and the extreme cold this was not the hardest challenge in the quest to become MasterChef. It was, however, an emotion-charged experience, and a high point not only of the competition but also of my life. An experience that had a profound effect upon me and one that will stay with me for a very long time.

Back at base we went in to the canteen for some lunch, and just when we thought it was safe to relax John Torode hit us with the big one. 'OK you guys, if you thought this morning was tough you ain't seen nothin' yet. There are 200 officers and men in this camp at present and all them, including the Officer Commanding and his wife, will be dining in here this evening – and you are going to be cooking for them. The doors open at 6.30, so you've got just over three and a half hours. Follow the Sergeant into the kitchens, and good luck. You're going to need it.'

At this point I was the only one capable of raising a wry smile. I had mentally prepared myself for the worst, and that is exactly what they threw at us. Dean looked thoroughly 'pissed off', Daksha looked tired and irritable, and Becky looked pale and close to tears. I said to the producer that what were undergoing was a test of mental and physical strength and stamina, rather than a quest to find the best cook. He told me I was free to chuck in the towel any time I wanted, but he knew I would never have done that.

In kitchens the size of a football pitch, with vast industrial cooking equipment, this was a really daunting task for all four of us. The Sergeant gave us the evening's menu and did a double-quick demonstration of the heavy cooking gear, and an even quicker run through of the cold and dry produce stores. The four of us had to cook from scratch enough of the following dishes for over 200 people, making the assumption that each of the three main dishes should serve 80 covers.

COTTAGE PIES
BAKED HADDOCK FILLETS WITH PARSLEY SAUCE
STIR-FRIED TURKEY WITH VEGETABLES AND NOODLES
BOILED POTATOES
ROAST POTATOES
CHIPS
GREENS
CARROTS
COURGETTES
GRAVY

The staff had already taken care of the sweet course, but this was still a very tall order. The Sergeant was not in a good mood, telling us that we should have started two hours ago and would now have to do everything at the double. Understandably there was a bit of panic and rushing about at that point, and we quickly discovered that our outdoor boots were no match for the slippery kitchen floor. It was like trying to balance on a skating rink. Becky was the first casualty to go flying when she lost her footing. She hit the ground with a frightful bump, but got herself up again and soldiered on bravely.

We had a hurried conversation about recipes, and it transpired that it was a good thing that I carry recipes for things like cottage pie and stir-fries around in my head because clearly no one else did. Time was marching on and we were all going flat out. I am not sure how it happened but I ended up being responsible for the stir-fry. Thus it was that I found myself once more in front of a brat pan big enough to boil a horse, only this time I was cooking the meat that I had stripped from three whole turkeys plus bucket loads of chopped vegetables and noodles. I don't know quite how we did it, but we did get all the food ready and laid out over the bain marie at the servery ready for the Royal Marines to eat at 6.30. All the dishes were very well received, and several people asked if we would come back to cook for them again, which I took as a compliment. My stir-fry was going down very quickly so I hurried through to the kitchen to replenish stocks from the warming ovens. Big mistake: as my leading foot hit the slippery floor I went flying, and crashed to the ground. I thought I had escaped injury. apart from a slight numbness in my right hand,. In fact I had broken a small bone in my middle finger, and had to continue with this impediment throughout the rest of the competition.

There was a lovely moment later when the CO called the four of us out in front of the men and asked them to show their appreciation. The wolf whistles and loudest cheers were meant for Becky, but we were all very pleased that The Royal Marine Commandos had enjoyed the food we cooked for them. Back in the kitchen John and Gregg asked the Sergeant which one of the four of us he would choose to join him in the Royal Marines. No prizes for guessing which one he chose: it wouldn't be a pretty young woman, it wouldn't be a man aged 59, and neither would it be a mother of two in her mid forties. Gregg said: 'Well done Dean, take a bow, you've certainly impressed the Royal Marines'.

When eventually I saw this episode I thought at first that the editors had made a mistake. Gregg said his bit about take a bow Dean, and then they showed the 200 Royal Marines cheering and applauding as if for Dean. As the series unfolded so this piece of crafty conflation was used over and over again to build the case for Dean to be seen as the probable winner. This sequence became a source of intense irritation to me, and was repeated almost as many times as 'Where's your sauce Peter?' Dean didn't need bolstering up with misleading imagery, he did well enough all by himself. I would also have preferred not to have been made to look quite so foolish.

We were due to leave the camp at around noon the following day, and the Royal Marine Commandos were determined to give us a night to remember before we left them. The 'Party' in the Officer's Mess would commence at 2100hrs and our presence was demanded rather than requested. I had a good hour to spare so decided on a good long hot shower to soak away the aches and pains of the day. I found my way down to the communal showers, then encountered a problem that afflicts all who wear spectacles. You have to leave your spectacles with your clothes in the dry room then find your way through to the wet room where the showers are fitted. Problem number one is to negotiate your way past all the benches and other obstacles in the dry room without falling over something, and problem number two is working out how to operate one of the showers when you can't read the dials without your specs on. After failing miserably on the first count and only succeeding on the second after much fumbling, I decided that it was a good thing I did not have to spend any longer than that night in a military camp.

The Officers' Mess was full of cheer, with a blazing log fire in the grate and faces glowing with booze, heat, or both. The men, including the NCOs who were in there by special dispensation, all looked quite different in their 'civvies', and I doubt that you would give them a second look if you passed them in the street. Apart that is from the 6ft 10ins moustachioed Colour Sergeant, who had a ramrod for a backbone and a voice that always sounded like he was giving orders. They started us off with a pint each of Moose Milk – a revolting concoction of whisky, Baileys and warm milk. Then it was on to whatever else one might choose to get drunk on. They are a splendid group of men who go around the world clearing up the messes that other people leave behind. It wouldn't do to probe too deeply into what they sometimes have to do, but if anyone deserves the right to let their hair down on occasion, these men certainly do. Twenty years ago I would have joined in their drinking games, but these days it doesn't do me any good to drink too much. I enjoyed their company, had a few drinks and left them all to it at about one in the morning. Apparently they carried on until 5.00am and I met a few of them in the canteen at 7.30am, shaved, uniformed and eating breakfast. Some of their voices were a bit croaky, though.

Back in our barrack room my youthful roommate was still sending up the zeds. I thought it would be prudent to leave him to it, so packed our 'extreme weather kit' back into its bags and headed out to the far corner of the camp to return them to the Quartermaster's Stores. Outside it was snowing heavily again, and through the sound-dulling atmosphere I could just make out the rattle and roar of diesel engines being fired up and orders being barked at another platoon of young Marine Commandos who were going off to practice survival in that unforgiving land. I never did get to see the Aurora Borealis or any polar bears, but I did get to see a part of the world that made me ask questions of myself, and found when I answered them a degree of steadfastness that had previously been almost completely obscured.

CHAPTER ELEVEN

UNDERNEATH THE ARCHES

Twelve hours later, standing outside Heathrow Airport waiting for our cars to arrive, I overheard people complaining of the cold. It was probably about 3 or 4°C in London that night, and I wondered what they would have thought of the weather we'd just left behind in Lakselv. That was Saturday evening, and with the next filming scheduled to begin at 8.00am on Monday there wasn't a lot of time to recover from the sleep deprivation of the previous four days. I needed to get home to Sussex, not just for my sanity but also to get some clean clothes organised for the coming week of trials, so it was past midnight by the time I finally locked my own front door.

Monday 21st November, and the second week of semi-finals, kicked off with another load of filmed interviews. Much the same sort of questions as before, but by now we were old hands at reacting to the questions and giving the sort of answers they were looking for. The morning's test was pretty straightforward; pot-roasted pheasant with chestnuts, cabbage, and bacon, and potato, celeriac and apple mash. I was in my element; this was exactly my kind of autumn/winter food. I used to do quite a lot of shooting, and over the years have devised a good number of recipes for pheasant, partridge, woodcock and grouse.

Becky knew how to handle game birds but for the other two this was a completely new experience, and both admitted as much to the judges. Not for the first time in the competition I was surprised by the gaps in knowledge and experience that were revealed in my fellow competitors. And again I was frustrated that the judges had not asked us to demonstrate that we knew how to pluck, eviscerate and truss a bird.

Gregg approached me. 'This is a walk in the park for you, isn't it Peter? I bet you've done this a thousand times.' 'Yes, just a few.' I replied, 'but it would be even more of a walk in the park if I was using my own recipe rather than trying to exactly follow the one you've given us.' Gregg just smiled and walked away. I am not sure whose recipe we were given, but it worked well enough. The judges let us know that everything we did was being marked, even to the extent of naming a pecking order at the end of each task. On this occasion Daksha's lack of knowledge of European foods let her down badly, and Becky didn't really shine either. Dean's plate of food looked a terrible mess, and he was very disappointed that his lack of experience was to blame. Gregg made some remark about wanting to look at my dish while he ate Dean's. I am not sure what he meant by that because, at the risk of sounding immodest, I was confident that on that occasion my dish was well ahead of my competitors' attempts.

Pheasant is perhaps the most common and readily available of all the game birds, and although in season only from 1st October to 1st February frozen pheasant may be on sale well outside these dates. Pheasant is like chicken but with a lot more flavour, so may be used in almost any of your favourite chicken recipes. Hen birds are plump with succulent flesh, providing enough meat for up to four people. Cock birds are usually larger and more slender, their meat somewhat tougher and stronger in flavour.

Various different views are put around about how long a pheasant should be hung before eating. Some say 6-7 days, whilst others insist on 14 days. There is no absolute right or wrong about this because it depends on many varying factors. Both where you hang the bird and the ambient temperature can speed up or slow down the rate of decay. Then there is personal taste; some like their pheasant to be mild in flavour, whilst others prefer it be 'high' and consequently very 'gamey'. I tend to be somewhere in the middle of these two extremes. Pheasant needs a little hanging to ensure that meat is tender and flavoursome, but I certainly don't like it to be so high that its almost gangrenous before I cook it. I used to hang pheasants from the rafters in the garage where there was no heating and the draughts blew through the eaves. Even so, the hanging times varied enormously. During mild autumnal weather, 2-3 days was ample, but when the frosts set in it would take a week or more to achieve the same results. All this is academic if you only ever buy pheasant from a game dealer, as the oven-ready birds will have been prepared to his, rather than your, preference.

Some supermarkets stock frozen oven ready pheasants, usually hen birds, which although a welcome change from chicken are never quite as tasty as fresh ones.

You would normally choose a hen bird for roasting and either pot-roast or casserole the cock birds. That said, for a special occasion two brace of pheasant (ie two hens and two cocks) roasted on a bed of vegetables and presented at table with their tail feathers tucked back into the rear trussing string is a sensational sight. The combination of the buttery hen's meat with the slightly stronger and darker meat of the cock makes a splendid meal worthy of being offered as an alternative Christmas lunch.

* * *

Roast brace of pheasant

Like most game birds pheasant is inclined to dry out during roasting, so it's always necessary to cover them well with fatty streaky bacon before cooking. It is also a good idea to roast the birds on a bed of vegetables to help keep them moist.

For 4-6 people

1 brace of pheasant (1 cock and 1 hen)

8 rashers streaky bacon

8 closed cap mushrooms,
cleaned and quartered

4 carrots, peeled
and roughly chopped into chunks

3 sticks of celery, cut into chunks

2 onions, peeled and quartered

4 juniper berries, slightly bruised with a pestle

2 tablespoon of butter

A few sprigs of thyme

Salt and freshly ground black pepper

1 glass of port

1 dessertspoon redcurrant jelly

600ml chicken or game stock

Undo the trussing string and remove the wishbone., then wipe the birds inside and out with a clean, damp cloth. Season inside the birds with salt and pepper and stuff them with the mushrooms and thyme. Pull the crop skin down over the back of the bird and secure to the wings with string. Cross the string over the backbone and bring under the legs to secure the ends of the drumsticks together. Finally, tie the drumsticks to the parson's nose. Smear butter over the birds and season again with salt and pepper.

Melt the remaining butter in a roasting pan. Sear the birds all over, being sure to get a good colour on the breast skin. Add the vegetables and juniper berries and give everything a good toss in the butter. Now lay the birds breast side down among the vegetables and roast in the oven at 200°C for 30 minutes. Turn the birds to breast side up and drape with the streaky bacon. Turn the oven down to 180 and roast for a further hour. Remove the pheasants to a serving dish and cover with a cloth. Leave to rest for 15 minutes while you make the sauce.

Fish out and discard the juniper berries. Put the roasting pan with the vegetables on top of the stove and stir in 1 tablespoon of flour. Cook for a couple of minutes, then pour over the port to deglaze the pan. Be sure to scrape up all the residues from the bottom of the pan. Remove from the heat while you stir in 600ml of good chicken or game stock, then return to the heat and simmer for 10 minutes. Strain through a sieve into a jug or gravy boat and stir in the redcurrant jelly.

Place the birds on your finest serving dish and, if you have them, stick the tail feathers back into the rear trussing string. Remember that the long and beautifully coloured feathers belong to the cock, whilst the rather shorter drab ones belong to the hen. Surround with potatoes and parsnips that have been roasted in duck fat and garnish with sprigs of watercress. Serve with a tureen of a dark green vegetable – cabbage, greens, broccoli, or kale – with the crispy bacon crumbled over it. Serve the sauce separately. Bread sauce makes an excellent additional accompaniment.

Pot-roast pheasant with gin and juniper for 4 people

Juniper is an ideal flavouring for pheasant, lightening the gameyness and also imparting a hint of perfume. Gin is already flavoured with juniper berries, and the addition of two more berries in this recipe intensifies the flavour.

1 large cock pheasant
1 whole head of celery
2 juniper berries, bruised with a pestle
1 glass (100ml) gin
300ml chicken stock
1 tablespoon of unsalted butter
Salt and freshly ground black pepper

Untie the trussing string and cut out the wishbone. Wipe the pheasant inside and out with a clean damp cloth. Season inside with salt and pepper.

Melt the butter in an enamelled cast iron casserole and thoroughly brown the bird all over for about 10 minutes. Remove and set aside. Top and tail the celery and cut into chunks about 40mm long. Toss the celery in the hot butter and place the pheasant on top. Add the juniper berries and pour over the gin and stock. Cover tightly and bring to the boil before transferring to the oven at 160°C. Cook for two and a half hours. Carefully remove the pheasant to a dish and drain the celery through a sieve over a saucepan. Arrange the celery on a serving dish and place the pheasant on top. Place the dish in the bottom of the oven with the heat turned off.

Thicken the sauce with beurre manié and serve separately. Creamed mashed potatoes and whole flat field mushrooms sautéed in butter complete this dish.

Pheasant and raisin casserole for 4 people

1 large pheasant, cock or hen	A bowl of flour seasoned with salt, pepper and a good pinch of ground cinnamon (or an inch long stick if you are lucky enough to have one)	11/2 tablespoons unsalted butter
1 large onion, peeled and finely chopped		1 glass red or white wine
120g seedless raisins		600ml meat stock
3 tablespoons brandy		

Put the raisins in a dish and pour over the brandy. Cover and leave to macerate for 15-20 minutes.Joint the pheasant and toss the pieces well in seasoned flour.

Melt the butter in an enamelled cast iron casserole and cook the onions until they begin to take on a little colour. Remove with a slotted spoon and set aside.

Sauté the floured pheasant pieces in the hot butter until well browned all over. Drain the raisins, add the brandy to the pot, and flambé. Now return the onions to the pot and add the raisins, wine and stock. Stir well and cover with the lid. Bring to the boil before transferring to the oven at 160°C. Cook for two and a half hours.

Serve the casserole with a mixture of boiled white long grain and red Camargue rice, topped with caramelised onions: slice up an onion and slowly cook in butter with 2 teaspoons of soft brown sugar and a pinch of salt, cook until brown and syrupy, and spoon on top of the rice.

Later that afternoon we were treated to a masterclass from the Michelin starred Latvian Viking himself, the truly inspirational Martin Blunos. With him we did a step-by-step copy of one of his signature dishes 'A Partridge in a Pear Tree'. This is a sensational dish of roasted and jointed partridge served with a glazed and roasted pear and a rich wine jus. I believe we all made quite a good job of this dish, but with a teacher like Martin there was no excuse not to. I would not dare to give you Martin's recipe so here are a couple of my own.

* * *

With a season from 1st September to 1st February, once we get into December it's time to stop roasting partridge and pop them in the pot instead. Generally speaking one partridge, either grey or red-leg, is enough for two people.

Roast partridge with black olives

For 4 people

2 young partridges.
6 rashers unsmoked streaky bacon
Butter
Salt and freshly ground black pepper

For the black olive sauce
100g pitted black olives
1 onion or 2 shallots, peeled and finely sliced
2 rashers unsmoked streaky bacon, cut across into thin lardons
200ml good meat stock
1 glass robust red wine
1 large tomato, skinned, deseeded and chopped
A knob of butter

Heat the butter in a saucepan and add the sliced onion (or shallots) and bacon lardons. Cook for a few minutes until beginning to colour, then add the chopped tomato and olives. Cook a little longer before adding the wine then bubble away fiercely to reduce the wine by about a half. Pour over the stock and reduce the heat to a simmer while you roast the partridges.

As with all game birds, start by removing the wishbone. Season inside with salt and pepper, smear the breast and legs with butter, and 'lard" with rashers of streaky bacon tied around with string to keep them in place. Roast for 20 minutes at 200°C, then check that the meat where the thigh meets the breast is cooked through. If you like the breast meat slightly pink, it is acceptable to cut off the legs and return them to the oven for a few more minutes. Allow the cooked birds to rest under a cloth for 10 minutes. Split in half, remove and discard the backbones, and keep warm.

Place half a partridge on each warmed plate and spoon over the olive sauce. Serve with sautéed potatoes and steamed shredded cabbage.

Pot-roasted partridge with white cabbage and pork

For 4 people

2 old partridges, ie shot December or January
2 shallots, peeled and thinly sliced
2 sticks of celery, cut into thin crescents
2 carrots, peeled and cut into rounds
250ml chicken stock
1 glass dry white wine
A knob of butter
A couple of sprigs of thyme and parsley tied up in muslin
Salt and freshly ground black pepper

1 large white cabbage
200g sliced belly of pork
2 onions, peeled and thinly sliced
A knob of butter
250ml dry white wine
1 dessert spoon whole grain mustard
1/2 teaspoon salt

Undo the trussing string, remove the wishbones and wipe the bird's insides with a clean damp cloth. Melt the butter in an enamelled cast iron casserole and brown the birds all over. Remove and set aside. Add a little more butter and fry the shallots until just beginning to colour. Add the celery and carrots and cook for a couple more minutes. Place the birds on top of the vegetables, pour over the wine and stock, add the herbs and season with salt and pepper. Cover and bring to the boil. Transfer to the oven at 180°C for one and a half hours. Remove the lid for the last 10 minutes.

Cut the cabbage into quarters and cut away and discard the hard core. Use a large chef's knife to shred the cabbage as finely as you can. Heat the butter in a large saucepan and fry the onion with a little salt until tender but not coloured. Add the shredded cabbage and stir and cook for a couple of minutes before pouring over the wine. Cover tightly and cook over a very low heat for about 45 minutes.

Meanwhile, cut the sliced pork across into pieces about 20mm wide. Fry the pork gently in a little butter for about 15 minutes until well browned all over. Add the pork to the cabbage and cook for another 15 minutes. Stir in the whole grain mustard just before arranging the cabbage and pork on a large serving dish. Retrieve the partridges and place them whole, side by side, on top of the cabbage and pork.

Quickly reduce the sauce in the pot over a fierce heat, strain, and serve separately.

All we had been told about Tuesday's trial was that we would each be required to cook a dessert of our own creation, to be served to 10 people as part of a British fine dining menu. We were required to hand in our recipes by the weekend prior to the test, but before doing so I made enquiries about the other courses that would be served as they would affect my decision about what the dessert should be. To say that I was fobbed off would be an understatement, and I wasn't the only semi-finalist to gain the impression that our desserts were going to be just a small part of a very much bigger story.

The whole picture was revealed to us when we arrived at the premises of Jalapeño, a very up-market outside catering company. The truth was that we were going to cook the whole meal for a dinner party hosted by the Chairman of the English Heritage Foundation. Among his guests were Lord Hambro and other notables, plus the celebrities Griff Rees-Jones and Stephen Fry. To make life even more difficult, the venue for the party was a room over the Wellington Arch just below Hyde Park Corner. We had to prepare everything in the professional kitchens of Jalapeño, then transport the whole meal, in various stages of completion, for finishing off and serving from the tiny kitchen at the Arch.

Jalapeño is no stranger to the demands of fine dining. It is a company that has earned an enviable reputation by maintaining the very highest standards, and as such has become the frequent choice of caterer for parties held by film, pop and sports stars as well as the aristocracy and royalty. The guests that night would be expecting the very best, and we had to attempt to live up to their expectations and to meet the standards set by Jalapeño's head chef.

As in Norway we were divided into teams, only this time I was paired up with Daksha and Becky with Dean. Jalapeño had devised a really complicated menu that required both an enormous amount of preparation and the use of catering techniques quite unfamiliar to us.

The hors d'oeuvres had to be made from scratch, and were terrifyingly complex. We had to make Parmesan pastry biscuits, miniature bagels, tiny risotto balls, savoury tuiles etc, all with fillings and toppings that required the most delicate handling of the finest ingredients. Assembly of these morsels would take place on site, but the advance preparations took up far too much of our allotted time. Becky and Dean were given the two starters to prepare, while Daksha and I had the two main courses plus the vegetarian option, all the vegetables, and two different sauces. It seemed to us that we'd pulled the short straw, but there was nothing for it but to soldier on.

With only an hour to go before the vehicles had to leave for the Wellington Arch we finally began to prepare our own desserts. Given an hour and the kitchen to ourselves, I believe that each one of us would have had no difficulty producing our 10 portions of dessert. As it was we were falling over each other, running out of pots and pans, and in my case having to cope with no space left on the cooker. Instead of slowly poaching my pears in a saucepan, I had to cook them under a paper cartouche in a roasting dish in the oven.

The Wellington Arch is one of London's most famous examples of monumental architecture. Originally commissioned by George IV as the grand entrance to Buckingham Palace, it has stood on its present site since 1882. Every day tens of thousands of people drive past this landmark, and I would wager that few of them have ever suspected that the rooms within may be hired for private functions. Everything we brought with us had to be carried from the vans below into a tiny lift, then manhandled into position on the second and third floors over the Arch. The main room, just below the balconies from which one may view the great bronze statue of the Angel of Peace, was adorned with flowers and beautifully laid out as the dining room for the evening. Off in the wings, Daksha and I found our place in the tiny kitchen. Inside there was a worktop, a commercial oven, two measly hotplates, and hardly enough room to swing a cat, let alone accommodate two people cooking plus the chef shouting instructions and the now customary crew of cameraman, soundman, director and assistant. We were already beginning to feel nervous.

On the floor beneath us, Dean and Becky had plenty of room to lay out the components of the canapés and calmly set to work assembling them. Their two first courses were fillet of sea bass on a julienne of vegetables, and roasted goat's cheese on rocket salad with balsamic vinegar dressing. With no cooking facilities on their floor, their two major components, the sea bass and goat's cheese, had to be sent up to us for cooking. As if preparing tournedos of beef topped with portobello mushroom stuffed with savoury cous-cous, served on a bed of turnip and swede purée with baby carrots and snow peas, all finished with a rich veal and red wine sauce, plus breast of guinea fowl with sautéed potatoes, a selection of vegetables and a delicate sauce with fresh cranberries wasn't enough! As well as that, Daksha and I also had to prepare eight portions of the vegetarian option of Mediterranean vegetables stuffed with cous-cous flavoured with raisins and pine nuts, served with torn and toasted Mozzarella, just in case anyone ordered it. Now we had to cook the other team's dishes as well.

Viewers of this programme were treated to images of Dean and Becky looking every bit the cool 'dream team', while Daksha and I appeared flustered, hurried, and harried by the chef.

Both of the starters and main courses went down well with the diners, and they complimented each team in turn for their performances. Now came the big one – the menu featured a choice from our four offerings of dessert. Several went for Dean's soft chocolate pudding with pistachio shortbreads; just one chose Becky's pear poached in red wine with Stilton and crème fraîche; one opted for Daksha's chocolate mousse; and two opted for my pain perdu with pear and rhubarb sauce.

Even before we served these desserts I knew that my pain perdu had gone a bit stodgy after sitting around for a good two hours. Dean's chocolate puds looked like they'd gone 'cakey', Becky's dessert looked wonderful, but Daksha had obviously cracked it. Her chocolate dessert was soft, smooth, comforting and very seductive. It was a lovely moment for her, and truly deserved when the diners voted hers the finest dessert of the evening. Here are the instructions I sent to the production company prior to the event.

Dessert for British fine dining dinner party of 10 people: to be prepared in 40 minutes

Eggy bread (pain perdu) with poached pear and rhubarb sauce

For the pears	For the pain perdu	For the rhubarb sauce
10 Williams or Comice pears	1 day old uncut white sandwich loaf	800g good pink rhubarb
400g caster sugar	6 large eggs	50g caster sugar
1 litre dry rosé wine	150g caster sugar	50g icing sugar plus extra for dusting
	300ml full cream milk	
	A few drops of finest quality vanilla extract	
	A splash of eau de vie de poire (or calvados or cognac)	
	175g unsalted butter	
	A few mint leaves	

Begin by putting the wine and sugar into a large saucepan. Leave to stand while you carefully peel the pears, leaving the stalks on. Place the saucepan over the heat, bring up to boiling and carefully stand the pears down into the liquid. Cover and simmer for 10-15 minutes until the pears are tender (the exact time will depend upon how ripe the pears are). Remove the pears with a slotted spoon and stand up in a dish to allow them to cool down. Meanwhile, rapidly boil the sauce to reduce to a thick syrup.

Mix the eggs with the sugar in a large mixing bowl to dissolve the sugar. Gradually mix in the milk, vanilla extract and eau de vie de poire (or calvados or cognac). Divide this mixture between two large dishes.

Cut the crusts off the loaf and cut 5 slices about 2cm thick. Divide these in half diagonally, and place all ten pieces into the egg mixture. Leave for 5 minutes, then carefully turn each piece over and leave for a further 5 minutes.

Heat a large knob of butter in the frying pan and when foaming begin to fry the slices a few at a time. Allow two minutes per side before turning over. Each piece should be a good rich golden brown. Remove the slices with a fish slice and place on a baking tray. Repeat this process until all the slices are cooked, remembering to wipe out the pan between each batch to avoid the butter blackening. The baking trays of pain perdu can now go in the oven at 160°C for 5-6 minutes.

Cut the rhubarb into lengths of about 25mm and place in a saucepan with the sugar and a couple of tablespoons of water. Cook for 3 minutes, then use a slotted spoon to remove a small quantity of the 'just cooked' rhubarb and place this to one side while the remainder of the rhubarb cooks almost to a pulp – about another 5 minutes. Pass the contents through a sieve into a bowl standing in cold water. When cooled, whisk in the icing sugar and add the reserved solid pieces of rhubarb.

For transportation, the pain perdu may be covered with upside down roasting dishes and on arrival quickly flashed under the grill prior to serving. The pears will probably be safest standing up in the saucepan in which they were cooked; the two sauces should be carried in suitable containers.

To build the dish, place one pear on each plate beside a pain perdu. Spoon some of the pear syrup over the pears and spoon the rhubarb sauce alongside, allowing some to fall over the pain perdu. Cut the mint leaves into very fine shreds and sprinkle a few on each serving. Dust with icing sugar.

* * *

It was an exhausting day that didn't finish until about 1 o'clock the following morning, but at least we then had a few days to recover before the next challenge on Monday 21 November.

CHAPTER TWELVE

EVERYDAY SEASONING, JERK CHICKEN, AND 50 LITRES OF CURRIED GOAT

The MasterChef programme makers have a real thing about media catch-phrases, about 'team-players' and 'comfort zones'. The Norwegian episode was designed to take us 'outside of our comfort zones,' as indeed was the challenge to cook for the English Heritage dinner party. I found the constant reference to my 'comfort zone' intensely irritating, as the whole experience of taking part in the programme was way beyond anything I had ever undergone before. I may feel 'comfortable' cooking roast beef and Yorkshire pudding, but ask me to do it in a strange environment, using unfamiliar equipment, within a specified time limit and in front of cameras and judges, and suddenly it is no longer very comfortable at all. Throughout the championship I believed it was important to stamp my mark, so to speak, on any and every dish I was asked to prepare. Whilst I kept my mind open to learn from new experiences and great teachers, I wanted to demonstrate that I did have a style of my own, which is not at all the same thing as staying within a 'comfort zone'.

The next challenge was announced to us by Gregg. 'This test is specifically designed to take you way outside your own comfort zone. Each of you is going to be cooking in a professional restaurant kitchen in a style of cuisine that is completely unfamiliar to you.' Thus it was that Dean was sent to a new-wave Asia/Pacific restaurant, Becky to a traditional English restaurant and Daksha to a classic French restaurant. 'As for Peter' said Gregg with a fiendish smile on his face, 'it was a bit more difficult to find a cuisine that is completely unknown to you, but we've found one. Tomorrow you are going to spend the day cooking in a Caribbean restaurant!' Well they certainly got that right. Unlike many people I have never been to the Caribbean and had never cooked Caribbean food. In fact I had never even eaten Caribbean food, but I was looking forward to it very much.

Early next morning, dressed in chef's whites and feeling just a little nervous, I was being filmed walking up Kentish Town Road towards The Mango Room, Camden's famous Caribbean restaurant. Established, owned and run by the ebullient, fun-loving and eminently likeable Derek – who, I hope he will forgive me for saying, looks exactly like a young Bob Marley – The Mango Room serves traditional and modern dishes to new-comers as well as a large group of faithful devotees of genuine Caribbean cuisine. Derek and his head chef Jo, who is actually Brazilian but before coming to England studied and practised in some of the top hotels in Jamaica, told me that Caribbean food has evolved from Africa under the influences of Britain, Spain, Portugal and France. The sweet and colourful fruits and vegetables that are indigenous to the region combine with its soft cane sugar and spices from the southern hemisphere to create a unique range of flavours and textures. I liked the place and I liked the people, and from the moment I entered their door I was made to feel welcome and comfortable. Sorry MasterChef: you may have taken me into the unfamiliar, but you didn't succeed in taking me out of my comfort zone. On the contrary, just one day spent working in that restaurant has opened my eyes to a whole new cuisine, and I have spent a lot of time since attempting to emulate what I learned there.

Inside the small but very well equipped kitchen the staff were already busy preparing for the lunch service, due to start in about three hours. My immediate impression was quite different from that gained in other professional kitchens. The background reggae music seemed to add to an already laid back atmosphere, and busy though they all were everyone seemed to be relaxed and happy. If that's what is meant by the expression 'being cool', then I subscribe to it wholeheartedly.

Curried goat is one of the Mango Room's most popular dishes, and one that requires long, slow cooking on day one followed by a second cooking on day two prior to service. That made complete sense to me, because all the Indian curry dishes I know benefit from being twice-cooked in the same way. My first task then was to prepare a huge vat of curried goat. It's a very simple dish to make at home, and as my local butcher doesn't stock goat meat I have successfully recreated it using lamb instead. This is not a precise recipe, but it goes something like this.

Curried goat

Adjust the quantities to suit the number of servings: this is for 8-10

2kg meat cut into cubes
2 dessertspoons crushed garlic
2 dessertspoons curry powder
2 dessertspoons Caribbean Everyday Seasoning
4 dessertspoons soft dark brown sugar
1 finely chopped red chilli, Jalapeno or Scotch Bonnet

Put the meat into a large bowl. Add the curry powder, Everyday seasoning, garlic and chilli. Use your hands to mix everything together thoroughly, making sure that all the meat is evenly coated with the seasonings. Cover and leave aside for at least an hour, or up to 24 hours in the fridge.

Curried goat (cont)

Heat the sugar in a large saucepan. When the sugar has dissolved, add the meat mixture and stir thoroughly. Cover with a lid and simmer gently for four hours. Keep checking that the meat is not catching on the bottom of the pan, and give the mixture a good stir every so often. If the curry seems to be drying out, add a little water to loosen the texture. Remove from the heat and set aside to cool down. Next day, bring the curry up to a gentle boil and simmer with the lid off. Serve with 'rice and peas' (plain boiled rice mixed with cooked black-eyed peas) and sprinkle with chopped fresh coriander leaves.

My baptism into the ways of curried goat making involved being up to my elbows in a vast bowl of chopped up meat, stirring it all around in the spices. In this kitchen, the goat meat is chopped up with a cleaver, bones and all, and they say that cooking it with the bones in gives it its unique flavour and texture. I am sure they're correct, but I did manage to cut myself a few times on sharp pieces of bone, and diners need to be warned in case they swallow a piece.

I then got involved in filleting fresh snapper and cleaning whole sea bream. These I put into marinades prior to cooking at lunchtime. There were marinades to be made for the chicken breasts for the jerk chicken, and fish and chicken stocks to be got ready for the sauces to accompany the main dishes. Jo explained that the secrets of Caribbean cooking lay in the quality of the ingredients, the marinades, and the sauces. Lunch service seemed to be upon us in no time, and I was impressed with how quickly beautiful plates of food were going out over the pass without anyone appearing to rush or get flustered.

Lunch service wound down, and I'd had a wonderful time getting involved in pretty well every task in the kitchen, including grilling the meat and fish over hot coals and deep frying the slices of plantain and yams. For a short period Jo even let me take over managing the pass.

No time for rest, because now I had to create a two course meal using ingredients and techniques learned at the Mango Room. The following day these dishes had to be cooked in the studio kitchens and served to the judges, but first I had to cook them in the Mango Room for Derek and Jo and get their opinions. With some helpful advice and suggestions from Jo, this was my menu:

RED SNAPPER WITH MANGO AND GREEN PEPPERCORN SAUCE followed by
JERK CHICKEN WITH FRIED PLANTAIN AND SWEET POTATO CRISPS

I cooked these while the chefs around me were prepping up for the evening's service, and was very pleased with the praise I received from both Derek and Jo. Derek said that the mango sauce could have done with a bit more 'fire', maybe a touch of Scotch Bonnet, but Jo didn't agree. He said that there was enough heat in the jerk sauce, and that adding more chilli to the mango sauce would kill the subtlety of the fish. I left the Mango Room feeling that I had learnt a lot in a very short space of time, and made some new friends too.

Pan-roasted fillet of red snapper with a julienne of vegetables served with mango and green peppercorn sauce

1 kg red snapper
Mango sauce *
1 leek
1 carrot
1 each red, green & yellow peppers
A bunch of spring onions
A fistful of chives
A bunch of coriander

For the marinade

Half an onion, finely sliced
A few spring onions, slivered
Everyday seasoning
1/2 teaspoon crushed garlic
A bunch of coriander stalks, chopped
Zest and juice of half a lime
Vegetable oil

* Mango and green peppercorn sauce

1/2 mango, diced
A few chopped spring onions
1/2 teaspoon crushed garlic
1 teaspoon green peppercorns
Splash of white wine
Cup of reduced fish stock **
1/2 teaspoon sugar
1/2 mango pulped
A squidge of tomato paste (or ketchup)

** For the fish stock

Head and bones of the red snapper, washed and gills removed
1/2 an onion, finely sliced
White part of a leek, sliced
Stick of celery chopped
Sprig of thyme
Splash of white wine

133

Wash, descale and fillet the fish. Place the head and bones in a saucepan along with the other ingredients for making the stock. Cover with water and bring to the boil then simmer gently, skimming off any scum that rises to the surface. After twenty minutes strain through a fine sieve into a clean pan and cook fiercely to reduce by half.

In a bowl, mix together all the ingredients for the marinade. Carefully cut diagonal slashes through the skin of the fish fillets before placing them into the marinade. Turn the fillets over a few times to ensure they are well covered.

Prepare the julienne of vegetable by very finely slicing the leek, carrot, red, green and yellow peppers and spring onions. Try to keep them all the same length.

To make the sauce first sweat the mango, spring onions, green peppercorns and garlic for 2 minutes in a little oil. Add the sugar and stir, then add a splash of white wine and cook off the alcohol. Add the tomato sauce, mango pulp, juice and zest of lime. Stir in a cupful of fish stock and simmer gently until required.

Heat a non-stick pan to very high, shake the marinade off the snapper fillets, and place them into the hot pan skin side down. Cook for two minutes until the skin is crisp and well browned, then turn the fillets over and remove the pan from the heat. The residual heat will finish the cooking. Place a little fish stock in another pan and when bubbling quickly blanch the julienne of vegetables. Remove from the pan, drain and stack the vegetables in the centre of pre-heated serving plates. Spoon mango sauce over the vegetables and around the plate before carefully laying the fish fillet on top of the vegetables, skin side up. Garnish with chives and fresh coriander leaves and a slice of lime.

Jerk chicken with jerk sauce, fried plantain and sweet potato crisps for 2

Two chicken breasts
wing bone attached

Jerk sauce *

1 plantain

1 sweet potato

1 each
red, green & yellow pepers

A bunch of spring onions

A fistful of chives

A bunch of coriander

Marinade

1/2 teaspoon
Everyday seasoning

1/2 teaspoon jerk seasoning

1/2 teaspoon crushed garlic

Vegetable oil

Sprigs of thyme

* Jerk sauce

A few chopped spring onions

Some chopped leek

1/2 teaspoon crushed garlic

Some chopped celery

Thyme leaves
stripped from stems

Cup of reduced
chicken stock **

1 teaspoon sugar

1 teaspoon tomato paste

1 teaspoon
Everyday seasoning

1 teaspoon jerk seasoning

** Chicken stock

Chicken carcass, chopped

1/2 onion, finely sliced

Some chopped carrot,
leek, and celery

Sprig of thyme

Clove of garlic

Fry the chopped chicken carcass in a little oil until coloured all over, then add the onion, carrot, celery, leek thyme and garlic and continue to cook for a few minutes. Cover with water and bring to the boil, skimming off any scum that rises to the surface. Simmer gently for 40 minutes. Strain through a fine sieve into a clean pan and then boil hard to reduce by half.

Put all the marinade ingredients in a bowl and mix well. Remove the skin from the chicken and make diagonal slashes in the flesh. Place the chicken in the marinade and turn over to coat thoroughly with the mixture. Set aside for 20 minutes. Finely slice the red, green and yellow peppers.

To make the jerk sauce, first sweat the leek, celery, spring onion, garlic and thyme in a little oil. After two minutes add the jerk seasoning, Everyday seasoning, sugar and tomato paste and cook for two more minutes. Add a cupful of chicken stock and simmer for 10 minutes. If the sauce appears too thin, thicken it with a teaspoon of cornflour dissolved in a little cold water.

Heat a non-stick pan to very high, shake the marinade off the chicken breasts, and place them in the hot pan skin side down. Cook for 4 minutes until well browned. Turn the chicken over and cook for a further 4 minutes. Now place the pan into a hot oven for a further 4 minutes. Allow the chicken to relax out of the oven for a few minutes before serving. Before serving, pull the suprême away from the underside of the chicken breasts and slice the breasts in half lengthways. This gives three pieces of chicken per serving. Place a little chicken stock in another pan and when bubbling hot quickly blanch the strips of peppers.

Cut the unskinned plantain into diagonal slices approximately 1cm thick and deep fry in hot oil for a few minutes until the flesh appears golden. Remove from the oil and drain on kitchen paper. Use a vegetable peeler to trim long paper-thin slices from the sweet potato. Fry these in the hot oil for a few seconds until crisp.

Place a mound of the blanched peppers in the centre of the pre-heated serving plates. Cover with a chicken supreme and then build up the two halves of breast to form a pyramid. Surround with slices of fried plantain and carefully spoon the jerk sauce over the chicken. Balance some sweet potato crisps on top of the chicken and garnish with coriander leaves, snipped chives, and finely shredded strips of spring onion.

Next day, trying to recreate these dishes in the studio kitchens under the watchful eyes of the judges, I realised how impossibly hard it is to cook professionally on a domestic cooker. That said I was reasonably pleased with the results, and I think Derek and Jo would have been proud of me. When subsequently I saw this episode on television I was bitterly disappointed that they didn't even show my jerk chicken, just Gregg complaining that the mango sauce on my fish wasn't powerful enough for him. Maybe I should have followed Derek's recommendation and whacked in the Scotch Bonnet?

CHAPTER THIRTEEN

"THEY SHOOT HORSES, DON'T THEY?"

I doubt if those restaurant critics will ever know the pain and anguish they caused us. And if they do, I further doubt that the knowledge will cause them a moment's pause. They had been invited along to the MasterChef studios to give their professional opinions on the dishes cooked by four amateurs, and the one thing you can always rely on critics to do is criticise. After all, there wouldn't be much point in them being there if they merely said that everything was very nice, thank you (and whom do I see about the cheque?).

On the morning of Wednesday 30th November I'd gone along to the studios feeling reasonably comfortable about having to cook for the critics, but we all knew that after they'd had their say one of the four of us would be going home. Only three people could go forward into the finals. The day began, like most other days in the competition, with seemingly endless rounds of interviews on camera: How did we feel today? Were we frightened by the thought of cooking for three of the country's most eminent food critics? Did we think we were good enough to make it through to the finals? And in my case: 'Peter, you've had a pretty bad time in these semi-finals haven't you? Do you think you've got what it takes to pull something out of the bag today?' I was a bit taken aback by this; I didn't think I'd done that badly in the previous rounds. With the cameras rolling I was aware that I had to keep my cool and answered in a very non-committal sort of way.

At about 11 o'clock the producer came through to the holding room, which had been dressed up for the day as the dining room for our critical guests. He explained the plan for the afternoon. Each of us had two hours in which to cook and serve our two dishes. The first person would commence cooking at 1.00pm, with the rest starting at half-hourly intervals. The first person would serve their first course to the critics at 3.00pm and all subsequent dishes were to be served at 15-minute intervals thereafter. So far so good I thought. The producer then gave us our running order: Becky first, Daksha second, me third, and Dean last. As there were a couple of hours spare until Becky was due to start we decided we might as well get out of the studio and relax in a coffee bar. At this point none of us had yet had the opportunity to check our ingredients or our equipment, but the producer assured us that there would be plenty of time for that later; so off we wandered to Starbucks further down the Euston Road. Naturally we were accompanied, another blast of 'absolute truths' numbers two and three.

I have always known that laughter and tears are highly contagious, but it wasn't until that moment that I realised that anxiety can be the single most contagious of all human emotions. Without any of us trying we somehow managed to wind each other up to fever pitch. By twelve o'clock I was feeling sick with nerves, and I wasn't the only one. We had come to the realisation that for one of us this was it. One of us would not get through, and the more we tried not to think about it the worse we all felt. Once more that strange and unexpected phenomenon occurred: we were competing with each other, yet no-one wanted to see anyone else fail. We'd been through too much together, and this extra concern only served to make us feel even worse. At about 12.30 Becky suggested going back to the studio. She was scheduled to cook first, and hadn't yet checked her ingredients. With nothing else to do I volunteered to walk back with her and we got to the studio about ten minutes later. Becky went straight through to the kitchen to check her things, and I sat in the corridor with the Times crossword while I waited my turn. About ten minutes later the producer appeared and said: 'We've had to change things round a bit Peter. You're going on first. You start in ten minutes'.

Already nervous, I was now gripped with abject terror. I protested that I hadn't yet had the opportunity to check through my ingredients or my equipment, that I really wasn't ready to start. 'Well you'd better get a move on then, hadn't you?' was all the answer I received.

In the kitchen nothing was ready for me, and Becky, who was doing her final checking of ingredients, hadn't even been told about the change of plan. My ingredients began to arrive at my workstation in an ad hoc kind of fashion, as did the equipment. I checked my watch: already past one o'clock, and I was nowhere near ready to begin cooking. I was checking against my copy of the list, and items were missing. Contestants aren't permitted inside the staff kitchen, so it wasn't as if I could fetch the missing items for myself. Time was moving on, and by now the other contestants had arrived in the kitchens to check off their ingredients. I was in a state of panic before I even got to chop my first shallot.

In the event I didn't begin preparing my dishes until 20 minutes into my allotted two hours, and my agitated state would be no help in making up for lost time. Both my dishes were complicated, intentionally so: I'd wanted to pull off something really special for the Critic's meal, now the main concern was whether I'd even get them finished. I had cooked both dishes many times before, and the previous week had tried cooking them both together against the clock. In my own kitchen I'd managed to be ready to serve just inside 1 hour and 50 minutes; now, in the studio kitchen with the naff hobs that I had trouble regulating, I needed to knock a massive ten minutes off this personal best.

With four ovens and sixteen hobs on the go it was incredibly hot in the kitchens and that, combined with my state of panic and attempt to do everything at the double, resulted in me doing a good impersonation of a swamp. 3 o'clock arrived and I wasn't quite ready. John came over to me. 'Peter, there's only one way to save the day. Go in and tell them that you're running late. Better to be late than serve food that's badly cooked.'

I must have looked ridiculous standing in front of three food critics with sweat pouring down my face as I pleaded for ten more minutes. I heard Matthew Fort mutter something about hoping it was going to be worth waiting for.

Inside the 'dragon's den' I served my first course of roasted squash and walnut ravioli with sage butter and Parmesan shavings. At her first sight of the clarified butter Kate Spicer said: 'my God, I hope that's not sweat'. I didn't react, and on my way back into the kitchen overheard her say 'yuk, I just loathe Parmesan cheese, smells like sick'. Poor woman, I hope she doesn't have to eat in Italy too often.

My main course was a bit of fun really. I called it steak and 'kidney pie': in fact, it was 'steak' as in fillet steak stuffed with duxelles and sautéed garlic, served with a 'kidney pie.' I love this dish so much. The pie is actually a gougère or savoury choux bun that's filled with sliced kidneys in a cream sauce. There's curly kale for colour and to provide a bitter edge to offset the cream, and the dish is finished with a sauce Bercy made with wine and shallots.

Still trying to make up for lost time, I misjudged the minutes that my steaks spent in the oven and they ended up more like medium to well done rather than the rare to medium I had intended. I served my first course at 3.10 and my second at 3.25, so even though I'd managed to make up ten of the twenty minutes I'd lost I still succeeded in making the other three contestants ten minutes late with their dishes. To be completely honest I hated that afternoon. I have no idea why they felt it necessary to throw me off track by suddenly changing the running order, and I remain convinced that even if I had delivered on time and not slightly overcooked my steaks, I would still have suffered at the hands of those three critics. I absolutely loathed watching the edited version on television, and thought that Kate Spicer's comment that Becky's sorrel sauce was like 'poison' was a despicable remark to make about an amateur who had tried her level best to please. As to their accusation that my food was 'pretentious': of course it was, there's no point being self-effacing when you are trying to win.

These are the notes that I sent in to the production crew prior to the challenge.

Programme 36: the Critic's Meal. Two-course meal for 3 Critics plus 2 Judges. Quantities for 5 people to be prepared in 2 hours.

Note to Beth: 3 ingredients will be brought from home:
Chicken stock, Brown stock, Mushroom pâté (duxelles)

First Course: Ravioli of walnut and roasted squash with sage butter
Main Course: Steak and 'kidney pie'

First course

Ravioli of walnut and roasted squash with sage butter

For the pasta

200g Tipo '00' pasta flour plus extra for dusting

1 large free-range egg (plus one extra just in case the pasta is too stiff)

2 large free-range egg yolks

Pinch salt

Splash of olive oil

For the filling

225g squash cut into segments and de-seeded

115g (shelled weight) peeled and finely chopped walnuts

1 clove garlic

50g freshly grated Parmesan plus a bit extra for topping the finished dish

Salt and freshly ground black pepper

A handful of dry breadcrumbs

1 large free-range egg

A few leaves marjoram or thyme

Olive oil

For the sage butter

A bunch of fresh sage

175g unsalted butter

Salt and freshly ground black pepper

To make the pasta, pulse all the ingredients in a processor until well mixed. Pull together into a ball of dough, then wrap in clingfilm and refrigerate for 20 minutes.

Season the segments of squash with plenty of salt and pepper, lay on a baking sheet and drizzle with olive oil. Scatter with marjoram leaves and roast in a hot oven (200°C) for about 20 minutes until tender and beginning to brown in places. Remove and cool before blitzing in a food processor to a smooth paste. Turn the paste out into a bowl and add the finely chopped walnuts, breadcrumbs, grated Parmesan, marjoram, salt and pepper. Crush the garlic to a smooth paste and stir well into the mixture along with one lightly beaten egg.

Roll out the pasta ending up with manageable lengths the width of the machine and rolled to the finest setting. Place each length on a floured surface and put heaped teaspoons of the filling at approx 80mm intervals down the middle. Lightly dampen along the outer edges of the pasta and between each mound with a damp pastry brush. Fold the pasta over the filling and press around each mound with your fingertips. Cut out the individual pieces with a zig-zag pasta wheel. Lay out on a floured tray to dry a little.

Gently melt a little of the butter in a saucepan, add the sage leaves, and fry until almost crisp. Remove the leaves and drain on kitchen paper. Discard the butter and wipe out the pan. Gently melt the main block of butter and mix in the sage leaves.

Bring a large saucepan of water to the boil and add a generous pinch of salt. Cook the ravioli in the hot water, in batches if necessary. Three minutes at a gentle simmer should be sufficient. Remove with a slotted spoon and carefully drain on a clean tea towel. Serve on warmed plates with the sage butter and a sprinkling of freshly grated Parmesan.

Main course

Steak and 'kidney pie'

For the steaks

5 well hung fillet steaks about 100g each

5 rashers smoked streaky bacon, rinded

1 whole bulb of garlic

Mushroom pâté

At least 20 extra button mushrooms

Extra butter

Olive oil

3 shallots

Cup of white wine

500ml brown stock

Beurre manié (unsalted butter & plain flour)

Salt and freshly ground black pepper

Tablespoon chopped parsley

For the kidney filling

2 fresh pig's kidneys (approx 250g)

125ml milk

Small onion, finely chopped

2 rashers unsmoked streaky bacon cut into small lardons

Seasoned flour

250ml light stock

A sprig of thyme

1 bay leaf

Splash white wine vinegar

2 tablespoons crème fraîche

Knob of butter

For the gougère (choux paste)

2 1/2 tablespoons plain flour

2 tablespoons butter cut into small cubes

2 eggs lightly beaten

Pinch of salt

150ml water

Vegetables

300-400g curly kale

Minimum 25 small baby carrots with their green tops

Knob of unsalted butter

Use a very sharp knife to cut the white cores out of the kidneys before slicing them through into rounds about 3mm thick. Place these in a bowl, cover with milk, and set aside for 30 minutes.

To make the choux pastry sift the flour and salt onto a sheet of paper and bring the water and butter cubes to the boil in a saucepan. When the butter has completely melted into the water remove the pan from the heat and tip in the flour all at once. Beat thoroughly with a wooden spoon and return the pan to a moderate heat to 'cook out' the flour. Stir continuously until it leaves the sides of the pan and the paste glistens - about 2 minutes. Remove from the heat and leave for another 2 minutes. Add the lightly beaten eggs a little at a time, beating well into the paste between each addition. Cover a baking tray with baking parchment and drop on neat spoonfuls of the paste, leaving plenty of room between each to allow for expansion during cooking.

Place in a 200°C oven and cook for about 30 minutes until well puffed up and golden brown. Remove from the oven, make a slit in the side of each gougère and paint the top with a little reserved beaten egg mixed with a few drops of water, then return to the oven for another 5-7 minutes. When finally cooked and glossy on top, leave them on a wire rack to cool.

To make the kidney filling first drain off and discard the milk the kidneys have been soaking in. Melt some butter in a sauté pan and cook the onion and bacon lardons together for a few minutes; don't let the onion colour too much. Remove the onion and bacon with a slotted spoon and set aside. Toss the kidney slices in seasoned flour, shake off the excess, and sauté until well browned all over. Add more butter as necessary. Return the onions and bacon to the pan with the kidneys, add a splash of white wine vinegar, and cook until the vinegar evaporates. Add the stock, thyme and bay leaf. Cover the pan, reduce the heat, and simmer for 40 minutes until the kidneys are meltingly tender. The 'kidney pies' are assembled at the very last moment before service to prevent the choux pastry from going soggy. Remove the thyme and bay leaf

Steak and 'kidney pie' (cont)

and stir in the crème fraîche over the heat. Keep warm at the side of the stove while you reheat the gougères. Place one gougère on each warmed serving plate, hinge back the top through the slit already made and place a spoonful of the kidney mixture inside. Let the top down gently so that it is just gaping open.

For the sauce Bercy, (so named after the Quai de Bercy on the right bank of the Seine in Paris, which used to be the landing point for the barges carrying wine into the capital) place the shallots in a saucepan and add the wine. Boil and reduce the wine to about a tablespoon. Add three quarters of the stock and bring back to the boil. Simmer for a few minutes before whisking in a few pea-sized pieces of beurre manié, just enough so that the sauce covers the back of a spoon. Check for seasoning and adjust if necessary. This sauce may now wait until the steaks are cooked.

Make an incision through the side of each steak and make a small pocket in the centre. Stuff each steak with mushroom pâté and one well-blanched and peeled clove of garlic that has been sautéed in butter for three minutes. Tie a rasher of streaky bacon around each steak, smear with olive oil and season with salt and pepper. Sear the steaks in a very hot griddle pan for 2 minutes on the presentation side and 1 minute on the other. Set aside on a tray covered with baking parchment. To finish, place the steaks into a hot oven for 6-8 minutes. Let the steaks rest for 5-10 minutes before service. To complete the dish, add the reserved stock to the pan and boil. Stir to dissolve and incorporate the pan juices. Add this to the shallot sauce. Bring back to the boil and finally stir in the finely chopped parsley. The steak is topped with 2 or three sautéed mushrooms and presented on the plate alongside the 'kidney pie'. Accompany with a little steamed and lightly buttered curly kale and a small fan of baby carrots. Pour a little of the sauce Bercy over the steak and on the plate, but try to avoid it coming into contact with the kidney pie.

* * *

By the time the critics had tasted the final dish of the afternoon all four of us were in a state of collapse. We had given our all, and were now mentally, physically, and emotionally drained. As the judges conferred with the critics we waited impotently outside for their verdict. There was a tremendous sense of camaraderie, and all of us were close to tears as we wished each other the best of luck. Still we had to suffer those intrusive cameras, and yet more of the same prying questions. 'Have you done enough today?' 'Will the critics be impressed with your dishes or will they think you were being pretentious?' 'Do you think that running late and therefore making everyone else late has cost you your place in the final?' Once again all this had far more to do with taking people to the limit to make 'good television' than with trying to find the best cook among us.

At least a couple of hours had gone by since the judges went into deliberation. At last we were called in to hear their decision: one final handshake all round, one last group hug, and in we marched as directed.

Both John and Gregg stood motionless, their inscrutable expressions heightening the tension of the moment. I told myself not to worry, that I had already done well to come this far, but still my breathing became heavy and my heart began to pound.

First a little pep talk from John who told us that we should all be very proud of ourselves and that it had been very difficult for them to choose which one of us to send home. He told us about how much he cared for us. By now I had resigned myself to the conclusion that they would get rid of the 'old man' and take the others through to the finals. Gregg spoke next: 'All four of you are special people, all four of you are very fine cooks, but one of you has to go. This is one of the hardest decisions we've ever had to make. When I call out your name, I want you to come and stand over here. Dean, come over here please.'

What did this mean? Were they sending Dean home or was this yet another turn of the screw? 'Peter, we couldn't let you go home yet, could we? Come and stand next to Dean please. You two are staying.'

I was too numbed by the experience to feel elated, and felt myself shaking as I looked over at the two girls. Which one were they going to choose?

'Daksha, come over here and join the others. Sorry Becky.' There were more hugs and more tears, and as Becky said her farewells and gave her thanks to the judges, both of them were reduced to tears also. We witnessed sides to the characters of each of them that were never meant to make it into the public domain.

Later on, I mentioned to the producer that I was surprised that the judges chose Daksha over Becky. This was not because Daksha specialised in Gujurati cuisine, but because she seemed to lack some of the basic skills, for example carving meat, jointing poultry, filleting fish. There is no reason why the exponent of any style of cooking should not be voted MasterChef, but I do think that they should demonstrate the mastery of a broad range of basic skills. I did not receive the answer I expected. He told me that it had not been a question of choosing between Daksha and Becky. Daksha, he said, was brilliant, and there had never been any doubt about her going through. The judges' decision, he said, had been between Becky and me - and as far as the critics were concerned, I should have been sent home long ago. I was dumbfounded: this did not seem to fit with anything that had gone before, and his words left a strange and bitter taste in my mouth. Clearly, if I thought that I had even begun to work out what this programme was all about I had better start thinking again. Maybe all the compliments and words of encouragement I received from the judges were in reality no more than a wind-up. Was it perhaps merely a gimmick to keep a man of almost sixty in the finals?

CHAPTER FOURTEEN

WE'RE IN THE FINALS NOW

There was hardly time to draw breath between the end of the semi-finals and the beginning of the finals, and the judges had promised us a journey even more incredible than what had gone before. During the two days' break between filming I began to wonder how it was that I had become one of only three people left in a competition that originally attracted over 5,500 applicants. I began to think about how the three of us might be 'packaged' before being presented to the viewing public, particularly in light of what I had learned about what goes on behind the scenes in TV productions. The more I thought about it, the more I felt that the programme makers had either struck lucky or been very clever. I couldn't believe then, and I still don't, that there had been any collusion between the judges and the producer, and yet they would have been hard-pressed to find three more disparate characters as finalists.

An irrepressible and energetic Indian lady in her mid-forties, a handsome young university graduate who'd got a bit lost and ended up driving a JCB, and a 59 year old man who was fed up with trying to make a living in advertising. What we all shared was a love of food and cooking and desire to change our lives and do something new and challenging. I knew that we ought to make for fascinating viewing, but at that time had not fully considered the effect of the way we would be packaged and how this would alter the way the viewing public would perceive us.

* * *

Saturday 3rd December, and I was standing at my workstation back in the studio kitchen suffering from the strangest of feelings. Smiling back at me from the front of the room was the unmistakable face of Michel Roux Jr. MasterChef certainly kicked off the finals on a high note. Hero-worship is something one normally associates with little girls and pop stars, or perhaps adolescent boys and premier league footballers; but I can confirm that in certain circumstances it's an emotion that affects us all. I was totally in awe of Michel, an awe that showed itself by a heady mix of excitement and nerves. Michel is not a large man – a strict regime of exercise and training for marathons ensures that he remains physically lithe and slender – but he carries with him an aura that commands attention and respect. There are so many celebrity chefs around these days, but few of them have taken the culinary arts to the heights achieved by Michel. Few restaurants have secured the reputation for excellence that Le Gavroche has maintained since he took it over in 1994 from his equally famed father and uncle.

This was our Master Class, and the subject was Îles flottantes ou Oeufs à la neige – poached meringues coated with caramel and floating in a pool of custard. This is a classic dish traditionally cooked by French mothers as a special treat for their children. The apparent extravagance of ingredients is mitigated by the fact that the egg whites are used for the meringues, whilst the yolks are used up in the custard, (crème à l'anglaise), while the vanilla flavoured milk required for poaching liquid is also used in making the custard.

I should confess that I am generally better at savoury dishes than sweet ones, but with Michel Roux Jr for a teacher, I couldn't go wrong. Or could I? The poached meringues, or 'snow eggs' as I know them, presented me with no problems. They are quite a favourite of mine and I have cooked them many times before, but crème à l'anglaise is another matter altogether. Michel came and chatted to me while I was making the meringues. He asked me if I had ever made this dish before. I said that I had, but was a little concerned not to overcook the eggs while cooking out the crème à l'anglaise. 'You talk the talk Peter, let's see if you can walk the walk.' That made me even more nervous, and I cursed my stupidity for saying that I'd cooked the dish before. Now he was expecting great things of me, and giving far more help and attention to Daksha and Dean who had both admitted that the dish was completely new to them. In the event, while none of us did particularly well with this dish there is no doubt whatsoever that mine was by far the worst. I'd cooked my custard to just beyond the point where it starts to become scrambled egg, and my caramel needed a hammer and chisel to break through it. Michel confirmed what I already knew, that there was no way that my dish would be served at Le Gavroche.

Michel left us to return to lunch service at his restaurant, and I was bitterly disappointed to have made such a hash of things during his Master Class. He left behind a recipe and a further challenge for us to face that afternoon.

Gâteau Saint-Honoré. To prepare this gâteau is a test of skill even for the professional pâtissier, so for us it was going to present enormous problems. I had heard of this famous pastry gâteau before, but never attempted to bake it. Honoré is the patron saint of bakers and pâtissiers, and serving this wonderful gâteau on St Honoré's Day commemorates the anniversary of the saint's death on 16th May AD600. It is generally believed that a renowned Parisian pâtissier called Chiboust was responsible for creating the recipe some time in the mid-eighteen hundreds. This probably explains why the gâteau is traditionally filled with crème Chiboust, another of his creations (otherwise known as crème Saint-Honoré). The finished gâteau looks a bit like a crown, and around the outside rim are thirteen 'jewels', small cream-filled and caramel-topped choux buns. It may be that the number thirteen is to do with Christ and his twelve disciples, then again it may just refer to a baker's dozen. Who knows? Whatever the reason this is a delicious gâteau, and well worth the trouble to make at home on May 16th, or any other day for that matter. We all struggled with this challenge, but in the end the judges voted mine the best, and I was really quite pleased with it myself.

Gâteau Saint-Honoré

Essentially there are only four main components in a Gâteau Saint-Honoré but each one of them is in itself a demonstration of the craft of the master pâtissier: puff pastry, choux pastry, crème pâtissière, and caramel.

The base is a disc of puff pastry, approximately 25cm in diameter and 6-7mm thick. This should be placed on a baking sheet that has been covered with baking paper. Fit a piping bag with a plain 12mm nozzle and fill with choux paste. Hold the nozzle close to the pastry base so that the piping is flattened. Starting from the centre of the circular base, pipe a contiguous spiral towards the outer edge. Stop short leaving a border of about 35mm. Refill the piping bag and build up three layers of choux paste around this outer edge.

Line a second baking tray with baking paper and pipe thirteen small buns of exactly the same size onto the paper. Leave enough space between each to allow for expansion during cooking. Place both trays into a pre-heated oven, 220°C, for 10 minutes, then turn the temperature down to 180 for a further 10 minutes. Remove the buns from the oven, make a hole in the bottom of each, and set them on a wire rack. If the insides are still soft and doughy, return them to the oven for a few minutes to dry out thoroughly. Check the gâteau base, and if it is rising unevenly turn it through 180 degrees in the oven. Your eyes will tell you when the base is cooked, probably about 30 minutes total baking time. Miraculously both the choux pastry and the puff pastry will cook through in the same amount of time. Remove the base from the oven and transfer to a wire rack to cool.

Meanwhile make the crème pâtissière (see page 182) and allow it to cool. There are two different ways to turn your crème pâtissière into crème Honoré. The first is to fold in stiffly beaten egg whites while the crème pâtissière is still warm. In hot weather it is better to employ the second method and fold whipped cream into the cooled crème pâtissière in place of the egg whites. It is perfectly acceptable to flavour the crème Honoré to taste, for example with praline, chocolate, coffee, orange zest, vanilla, or liqueurs.

Use a second piping bag fitted with either a star or round nozzle and fill the choux buns with the cream, allowing a little to squidge out of the hole in their bottoms. This will help to 'glue' them to the rim of the gateau. Melt the sugar in a pan, and when it has turned to nut-brown caramel remove from the heat and place in a bowl of cold water to prevent any further cooking. Carefully dip the top of the filled buns into the caramel, then sit them around the rim of the gâteau caramel side up. If you have done the job properly, the thirteen buns should just fit. Finally, pipe the crème Honoré into the centre of the gâteau in your preferred pattern. That is the traditional Gâteau Saint-Honoré, but today many pâtissiers add other things, such as fruits and chocolate, to the basic recipe.

CHAPTER FIFTEEN

PUTTING ON THE RITZ

Piccadilly is unusually quiet at 7 o'clock on a Sunday morning, and apart from the odd black cab passing by nothing much was happening outside the Ritz as the three of us were filmed making our way down the draughty colonnade towards the hotel's main entrance. On this particular occasion we knew exactly what was in store for us. The judges had told us the night before that we were to spend the day in the kitchens of the world famous Ritz Hotel, where we would be preparing a grand dinner to be served that evening to the General Manager and his guests, who just happened to be seven of the country's most eminent chefs.

Just after we arrived there was a slight delay while a security net tightened around the Ritz in order that Bill Clinton and his entourage could leave discreetly. As soon as that was over we were shown down to the kitchens, where we were met by Maître Chef de Cuisine John Williams. John is a no-nonsense Geordie who in his toque blanche towered above all he surveyed and, like a Disney cartoon chef, displayed a girth to match his stature. John is a gentleman and a gentle man. He is quietly spoken yet firm, commanding the respect of every single member of staff in those vast kitchens from where thousands of meals a day are served to some of the world's most discerning diners. It was still early morning, and room service breakfast trolleys were going out past us bearing the most wonderful foods presented on the finest porcelain, silver cutlery and crystal glass gleaming on crisp beds of fine pink linen.

John began by telling us that he was making no allowance for the fact that we were amateurs, and that he was expecting us to prepare dishes that matched the standards expected by guests of The Ritz Hotel. We would be working with some of the world's finest ingredients, and second best was not an option that would be open to us. He didn't need to tell us that it was an honour to be working at the Ritz, we knew that already. The menu for the evening was as follows:

CANAPÉS
EGG FABERGÉ
TOURNEDOS OF BEEF WITH FOIE GRAS RAVIOLI AND RED WINE SAUCE
SOUFFLÉ ROTHSCHILD

Dean was to produce the first course, Daksha the dessert, and I was given the main course. All three of us would have to prepare the canapés. It didn't sound too daunting at first. A small preparation area just off the main kitchens had been set aside for us to work in, and once in there the sheer size of our task began to become apparent. With the assistance of Sous Chef Mark, we did a run-through of the most incredible collection of ingredients I have ever seen in one place at one time. There before us were live lobsters, crabs and langoustines, a whole side of smoked salmon, a large pot of Sevruga caviar, a whole foie gras, black truffles, and baskets full of wild mushrooms; pied de mouton, girolles, morels, chanterelles and ceps. There were trays of vegetables and fruits; great bunches of herbs, and two whole, well-hung fillets of Aberdeen Angus beef. There were mountains of dry goods and dairy products, an impressive array of wines and liqueurs, even a book full of real gold leaf to be used for decorating the dessert. I honestly don't think any of us had a clue where to start. John returned to prioritise our tasks, and the ingredients not needed until later in the day were returned to the cold store.

My first task was to make the tuile paste for the canapés; 'Cornets of Smoked Salmon Moscovite'. The paste is a mixture of flour, sugar, salt, butter and egg whites, and when thoroughly smooth it should be covered and rested in a refrigerator for 24 hours. I asked Chef about this resting time: he put a hand on my shoulder and said 'Well done Peter, the paste you'll be using is in the cold store, it was made yesterday. I just wanted to see that you could make it properly and you've passed that test. What are you planning to do next?' I replied that I thought it would be a good idea to get the pasta dough made and out of the way before prepping up all my vegetables. He seemed pretty pleased with me and said: 'I know you've got a lot to do, but don't forget that your colleagues may need a hand too. You're going to need to work as a team to make this all come together at the right time.'

All three of us were going flat out. Dean was rushing about with live crustacea in his hands, and admitted that he'd never killed anything before. Daksha was chopping and mixing and whisking, and at that point there wasn't a lot that any of us could do for the others. For obvious reasons I can't provide the recipes for John Williams' dishes, but I can at least give a list of the tasks I still had to perform.

Clean and trim the mushrooms and chop them to appropriate sizes for both the onion and mushroom dressing and the duxelles for the ravioli. Finely chop the shallots and herbs. Trim the beef of all fat and sinews leaving just the centre fillets. Cook the duxelles made with a brunoise of wild mushrooms and shallots cooked in butter and cream, then spread them out on greaseproof paper and chill. Prepare the foie gras; remove the veins, slice with a hot blade and cut into medallions. Seal for 20 seconds on each side in a hot pan and chill. Make a purée of white grapes cooked with Sauternes. Prepare a dish of button onions cooked in butter and sugar until thickly glazed. Sear the steaks to caramelise the surfaces, then chill. Prepare the fillings for the canapés: hand chopped smoked salmon with cream and freshly grated horseradish made ready in a piping bag. Make the red wine sauce from scratch, a job that took about four hours of careful cooking and constant checking and tasting to ensure the quality of the end result. This is a real chef's sauce, and the reason why gravy at home never tastes as good. The process involves cooking pieces of veal with the trimmings from the beef and the foie gras until they are deeply caramelised. Shallots, bacon, mushrooms and garlic are then added and also caramelised. Over this go two whole bottles of claret and half a bottle of ruby port with a bay leaf and a sprig of thyme. This is then cooked to reduce right down to thick syrup. In goes about a litre of reduced veal stock, which simmers away for about an hour, with constant skimming for impurities. Finally the sauce is strained through 3 layers of butter muslin then checked for seasoning. It is then kept warm without further boiling, and just before service about half a pound of finest butter is whisked in. There were other jobs to do during the afternoon, but Chef decided that as I had everything under control I should go through to the Pastry kitchen and make the tuile cornets for the canapés. This was a wonderful experience, and I considered myself very fortunate as I was the only one of us to have the opportunity of working under the Chef Pâtissier. I saw the most wonderful gâteaux being made, along with hundreds of beautiful little tartes au framboises and tartes au fraises that would be served later that day on the menu of the world famous 'Tea at The Ritz'.

Using a palette knife, the tuile paste has to be scraped across a stencil laid out on a flexible baking sheet, then sprinkled with black poppy seeds. The stencil is carefully lifted away leaving behind the thinnest possible deposit of paste. Just two minutes in the baker's oven and they are done, but you have to work quickly to form the fan shapes into tiny cones. They only remain malleable for a couple of seconds, after which they go crisp and shatter if you try to bend them. After a couple of attempts and a demonstration by the Chef Pâtissier of how to do it properly, I managed to make up a tray full of these delicate, paper thin cones. Chef John Williams returned to see how I was getting on. 'Well done Peter', he said, looking at the result of my efforts. 'Looking at these you've made me very happy this afternoon.' Praise indeed, and I can tell you that his remark made me very happy too.

Back in our work area I had the time to help Dean with the Eggs Fabergé, one of Chef John Williams's signature dishes. It is the most outrageously extravagant but truly wonderful dish. An eggshell is first decorated on the inside with eight slivers of ribbed macaroni tubes that have been filled with black truffle. The shell is then half filled with lobster mousse, into which goes a softly boiled quail's egg. The shell is then filled to the top with lobster mousse before being cooked in a steamer. After that the shell is carefully broken away to reveal the cooked mousse with its decoration à la Fabergé on top. To complete the dish the Egg Fabergé is sat in a nest of cucumber spaghetti, surrounded by langoustine tails, and finished with a truffle nage and slices of truffle round the outside. It is a fantastic dish that I doubt I will ever see the like of again, but it was a privilege to work with such ingredients and I was so pleased to be able to assist in its creation.

The foie gras ravioli had to be made up next, and this proved to be very tricky. The pasta had been rolled too thin, and with the generous filling of duxelle and medallion of foie gras the ravioli were splitting. The pasta needed to be re-rolled through the machine on a thicker setting, but someone had made off with the machine. Not for the first time that day I suspected that someone may have been

151

playing games with us. This was a case of all hands to the pump, and when the pasta machine finally reappeared both Daksha and Dean stepped in to help me put the ravioli together.

The final stages of my dish could not be done until immediately prior to service, so at this point I lent a hand to Daksha and made balls from the beautiful vanilla ice cream she had made earlier in the day. Just as I was finishing them the producer appeared, and informed me that the guests had arrived and I was needed upstairs to welcome them and to announce their menu for the evening. Someone grabbed the ice-cream balls from me and I was ushered off. Chef caught sight of me and called me back. 'You're not going upstairs at the Ritz looking like that. Come with me and get some clean clothes.' During the afternoon one of the chefs in the kitchen had accidentally sprayed me with red wine, and I'd been so busy that I'd completely forgotten about it. John Williams fitted me up with a clean white chef's jacket, and instead of the junior's skullcap he gave me a real toque blanche to wear.

I was led up through the labyrinth to the grand dining room, then on to the private Marie Antoinette Suite where the guests had gathered. If you remember my 'absolute truth' number two, it will come as no surprise that I was told to wait outside, told when to go in, and told when to leave. Inside the celebrity chefs were all standing, sipping pink champagne and eating the canapés we'd made earlier. My eyes alighted on the very familiar faces of Brian Turner and Richard Shepherd. They all appeared very friendly and gave my announcement a warm reception, especially when I mentioned that we'd had the audacity to attempt one of John Williams's signature dishes.

Back in the kitchen things were hotting up, and all three of us went to work on the first course. Dean looked after his centrepiece eggs, while Daksha made the cucumber spaghetti and I finished off the truffle nage and warmed the langoustines. All three of us assembled the dishes on the pass, and they looked absolutely immaculate before being covered with their silver domes for transportation up to the dining room. Dean was called upstairs to meet the guests and to receive their congratulations for pulling off the most difficult of dishes. It is essential that the yolk of the quail's eggs should remain soft inside, and every single one of them was perfect.

Now it was my turn. The steaks needed 6-8 minutes in the oven, the ravioli 3 minutes to boil, and the mushrooms with shallots and garlic just a minute or two to sauté before adding to the glazed baby onions. The grape purée was ready, the red wine sauce only needed finishing with butter and we would be there. Just like the first course, all three of us worked together at the pass, and the main course was going out looking every bit as good as the starter had.

We did a bit of clearing down and then began to help Daksha to build her complicated Soufflé Rothschild. Into the half-filled mould go sponge fingers that have first been soaked in stock syrup and Goldwasser before being topped up with soufflé mixture and baked in the oven at 180°C for 20 minutes. Halfway through this I was called away to go upstairs to hear what the diners had to say about my main course.

Once again I was told to wait outside until called in by the director. I was to approach the guests, answer any questions they might ask, and leave immediately on being given the signal. The guests were extremely courteous, and I was humbled by the praises heaped upon me by such an eminent group of chefs. Brian Turner asked me if I would have done anything differently if it had been my dish instead of John Williams'. I replied that given the choice I would have preferred to serve some greens with the steak and foie gras, and suggested spinach. He replied that he would rather have cabbage, but everyone agreed with the observation. The director gave me the nod and I excused myself from the guests.

Back in the kitchen the soufflés were in the oven and we all set about putting together the accompaniments, a salad of exotic fruits soaked in eau de vie de Danzig and ice cream balls decorated with vanilla pod, fresh mint, and gold leaf. As the soufflés came out of the oven we all knew that Daksha had a success on her hands. While Daksha was upstairs receiving her praise Dean and I tasted the spare Eggs Fabergé; they were truly sublime, and the yolks were still soft inside.

After we had cleaned down the work surfaces and put everything away we were all invited back upstairs to join the guests for champagne and an informal chat. It was the perfect end to what had been a wonderful day. There had been moments when it looked like things might go wrong, but in the end we pulled it all together and thanks to the inspirational John Williams we produced an outstandingly good meal that we could all be proud of. So it was disappointing to see this episode on television. I was made to look as though I had purposely dallied with the guests upstairs, leaving my colleagues in a state of panic in the kitchen. It also appeared that I had done nothing to help the others, and again this was not the case. As for the ice cream balls that appeared to cause Daksha so much grief, all I can say is that they were perfectly formed when I was called away from them to go upstairs.

153

CHAPTER SIXTEEN

THEY'LL HAVE TO GO SOME
TO TOP THAT

The day at the Ritz was so special that I couldn't begin to imagine what the programme makers might come up with next. As it happened there were experiences lined up for us that were arguably even greater, but before that we had trials to get through that were slightly more 'ordinary'.

They gave us the Monday off, a day of rest before the onslaught of the last two weeks of filming, but early on Tuesday we were treated to our next Master Class. This time it was fritto misto de mare, literally 'mixed fried fish', and celebrated Chef Andrew Newman was there to show us how to do it. Each of us was given a platter of the most spectacular array of fresh seafood. King prawns, langoustines, squid, flat fish, round fish, red fish; the whole point of this exercise was to give lessons in cleaning, descaling, filleting, skinning and generally handling seafood. At this point I have a couple of admissions to make. Between the ages of eleven and sixteen I spent almost every Saturday working for our village fishmonger and poulterer, and have been handling my own seafood, poultry, and game ever since. Secondly, without trying too hard I could think of at least a hundred better ways to treat the delicious looking seafood that was in front of us than dunking it all into batter and deep frying it. In my opinion, fritto misto de mare is a complete waste of all those different flavours and textures, as everything ends up tasting of the oil, the batter, and the lemon or dipping sauces that go with it. Plus the pieces of fish are too small to retain their individual flavours and textures. I suppose it's different if you are in a little Italian fishing village and the fish has come straight off the boats and into the hot oil. Then you get to eat it with freshly baked olive focaccia and a tomato and basil salad, with a glass or two of well-chilled Verdiccio to wash it all down. But I digress: I've said it before and I'll say it again, if I am going to batter and deep fry fish, for me nothing beats British fish and chips. The fish has to be a thick, white, flaking fillet of cod or haddock, and it has to be fried in beef dripping.

Back to the Master Class. Andrew Newman very deliberately took us through each technique, ending up with an immaculate plate of raw seafood, all clean, minus skin and bones, and cut to size so that everything would fry to perfection in the same amount of time. Back at my workstation I made short work of a similar preparation of my seafood whilst my colleagues were tackling the jobs for the first time in their lives. Andrew Newman told me that if the chefs who worked in his kitchen could handle a filleting knife like me they would make him a very happy man. It was at moments like that, just as I was beginning to believe that I really might win the competition, that both Daksha and Dean would turn up trumps again. I saw how well they both performed when shown how to do something new.

In the afternoon, John and Gregg carried on with the Italian theme and had us all making potato gnocchi with Tallegio and speck. It was good to get back to basics and cook a really simple dish. I didn't feel stressed for a change, and was looking forward to enjoying the afternoon. Perhaps I was just getting more used to being put under pressure, because I knew for sure that the simpler the dish and the more basic the ingredients, the fewer are the places to hide. When they are properly made potato gnocchi should be soft and light little pillows of pasta, with deep grooves made with the back of a fork so that they hold plenty of sauce. One of the golden rules for making potato gnocchi also applies to short crust pastry; the less you handle it, the lighter it will be. The point at which the cooked potato is added to the flour and egg yolk is crucial, and needs to be done quickly with the lightest of touches. Knead it too much and the gnocchi will be heavy and doughy and thoroughly unpalatable. I have also found that it helps to let the finished pasta rest in the fridge for an hour or so before boiling it.

The judges had plenty to say about this dish. Daksha's they said was too messy and too big a plateful. Dean kneaded his dough like he was making bread, and the resulting gnocchi was as heavy as lead. As for me, all they could find to criticise was my presentation. According to Gregg the essence of Italian pasta dishes is that everything should be mixed together on the plate, with no attempt to make it look attractive. I disagreed, and was more than ready to speak up for myself. I said that Italian or any other food should attract the eye before it seduces the palate, and that there was never a case for making a plate of food look like something the dog left on the back doorstep. John laughed, while Gregg shook his head and cried, 'No, no, no. Not with Italian food, not in a thousand years'. In the end I think we agreed to differ. I still believe that presenting my gnocchi slightly raised in the middle of the plate then topping it with whole fried sage leaves and strips of speck fried to a crisp finish not only made the dish more visually appealing, it also added another dimension in texture.

Potato gnocchi

Enough for 4 portions

300g cooked floury potato (Maris Piper, King Edward, Desiree)
100g '00' pasta flour
The yolk of one large free range egg

Place the unpeeled potatoes (you'll need about 350g to start with) in a large pan of unsalted cold water. Bring to the boil and cook until tender. The time will depend on the size of the potatoes, but 20 minutes should be about right. Avoid prodding them with a knife or skewer as breaking the skin allows water into the potato. Drain the potatoes and peel them while still hot.

Sift the flour onto a work surface, make a well in the middle, and put the egg into the well. Put the peeled potatoes through a mouli or potato ricer, weigh out 300g, and add to the well in the flour. Use your fingertips to gradually work the potato flesh into the egg and flour to form a dough. It is important that the potato is still hot at this stage.

Roll out pieces of the dough into sausages about 15mm thick. Use a floured knife to cut these into cylinders approximately 30mm long. Use the back of a fork to bend each piece round the end of your thumb. The fork indents will be on the outside curve and your thumb indent on the inside. Set the finished pieces aside on a floured tray. When they are all done, cover the tray loosely with clingfilm and refrigerate for an hour.

Bring a large pan of salted water to the boil and tip in the gnocchi. When they float to the surface they are ready. Remove with a slotted spoon and drain before adding to your preferred sauce.

The simplest sauce is melted clarified butter with sage leaves, but classic Italian sauces such as garlic with chilli and olive oil, tomato and basil, cream and melted cheese, or meat ragù all work very well with potato gnocchi.

Note: The potato gnocchi may be cooked in advance and preserved in iced water. When ready to serve, tip them back into boiling water and again wait for them to rise to the surface before draining and adding to the sauce.

Gnocchi have been around in Italy a lot longer than the potato, which only found its way into Europe from the New World in the 16th Century courtesy of the Spanish conquistadors. Long before this gnocchi was made with semolina, and this simple and nourishing dish is well worth adding to a modern repertoire.

Gnocchi di semolino

Enough for 4 portions

150g semolina
600ml milk
2 eggs, lightly beaten
75g grated Parmesan
Salt and freshly milled black pepper
Freshly grated nutmeg

Put the milk, salt, pepper and a generous grating of nutmeg in a saucepan. Stir in the semolina and bring to the boil over a moderate heat, stirring constantly. Keep the mixture at boiling point for 4-5 minutes, stirring until a very thick consistency is obtained. Remove from the heat and stir in the grated Parmesan and the lightly beaten eggs. Line a baking tray with oiled greaseproof paper and pour in the semolina, spreading it out into a layer about 8-10mm thick. Allow the mixture to cool, then cover and refrigerate overnight. Next day cut the gnocchi into your preferred shapes, ie circles, squares, diamonds, triangles. Lay these shapes overlapping in a well-buttered ovenproof dish. Dot with more butter and bake at 200°C, for 10-15 minutes. Remove from the oven, cover with your preferred sauce, and return to the oven for another 10-15 minutes.

157

CHAPTER SEVENTEEN

IF I'D WANTED TO WORK IN A CARAVAN I'D HAVE GOT A JOB IN A HOLIDAY CAMP

Wednesday 7th December and a very early start, or so I had been told the night before. 'A car will pick you and Dean up from your apartments at 0615hrs tomorrow. Don't be late, because you've got a big day ahead. You need to be wearing your whites, and if I were you I'd put some warm underclothes on as you'll be outside for most of the day.' 0610hrs and Dean and I were completely in the dark, both physically and metaphorically. True to form we had no idea where we were going or what we'd be doing when we arrived. We were standing in the cold outside the apartment block by Marylebone railway station where the production company had rented rooms for us during that part of the competition. Ten minutes passed, then fifteen, then twenty. At 0635hrs I rang the producer's mobile. It went straight through to his voice mail where I left a message. I tried calling one of his assistants and got through. 'Your car's on its way', she said. 'It had to pick Daksha up from NW9 first, it should be with you in a few minutes. We are running late already.' I tried to explain that we could have walked to the studio in a little over 10 minutes, but she was gone before I had a chance to finish. A message came through on my phone. It was the producer, trying to get back to me. 'Look, you guys are only 10 minutes from the studio, you could walk in couldn't you?'

The day had not started well. By now it was almost seven, and we hadn't moved off our front doorstep. By mutual agreement, we decided to walk to the studio and arrived just as Daksha's car was pulling up outside: the driver knew nothing about picking us up as well. At least all three of us were now there, but it was getting on for another hour before we finally left for our undisclosed destination. We headed out of central London on the Westway, and between bouts of being filmed and asked more silly questions in the back of the people carrier, we played the game of attempting to guess where we were going. Daksha knew the area well and suggested we might be going to Ealing. Ealing, I thought, they still have film studios in Ealing, so it was possible that we would be cooking for a film crew. We all concurred with this idea, but also gave some credibility to the suggestion that they may have lined us up with burger and hot dog wagons at the side of the road.

We were right the first time. Our vehicle pulled into the car park of a large sixties style building with signage from the days of the GLC. Once at the back of the building everything began to fall into place. We were confronted by a large caravan that described itself in large blue lettering as the 'location catering specialists'. Alongside was a small mobile cold store, where we were met by John and Gregg who introduced us to a young man in his early twenties who it turned out usually does all the cooking by himself. We were on the set of the television series Silent Witness, and we were going to cook lunch for the eighty or so people that comprised the cast, the managers, and the crew.

As at the Ritz I thought at first it didn't sound too bad, but before long it had turned into the hardest and most trying day of the whole competition. The judges told us to elect a team leader for the day. We did this in true democratic fashion. Each person had one vote but could not vote for himself or herself. I voted for Dean, Dean voted for me and Daksha voted for Dean. The decision was made, and I was perfectly happy with the outcome. Dean had already shown himself to be very good at adapting to unfamiliar surroundings, and he had plenty of energy and enthusiasm. Everything might have been just fine, but it was ages before we could get going and our patience was being tried to the limit. For starters we'd been up and about since 0530, it was now getting on for 10.30, and not only had we not yet begun cooking, we hadn't even got out of the holding room. Our young resident chef was telling us that the first people would be expecting to eat at around noon. To be honest I felt utterly demoralised, and this was the one and only time during all those challenges and throughout all the days and days of filming when I felt like throwing in the towel. We hadn't seen the cooking facilities, we had no idea what foodstuffs were available, and here was this guy telling us that we had to feed 80 odd people in an hour and a half's time. I felt terrible, because we were going to fail. I even thought that maybe they wanted us to fail to give the viewers some negatives to talk about. Whatever the reason I was very unhappy about the whole thing. Daksha and Dean felt pretty much the same, but after all we'd already been through we knew that at least we had to give it a go.

Outside, the young chef gave us our instructions. Whatever we decided to cook, the menu of the day had to be written up on the blackboard outside. There had to be three choices of hot main meals with a whole selection of vegetables, plus a vegetarian option, a hot dessert and a cold dessert, and a few other things that he'd tell us about on the way. He had expected us to bring our own knives, which we hadn't; worse than that, there was only one cooker and one sink. Basically, in a workspace designed for one person, we had to attempt to cook with the three of us plus the chef to keep an eye on things, a cameraman, a soundman, a director and an assistant. One thing was for sure, there was no possibility of the judges getting in there as well.

Once we'd seen the available foodstuffs we very quickly decided on a menu. It was far too ambitious, but we doggedly went for it. We were working flat out, constantly having to force our way past cameras and crew and step over equipment to get from one place to another. Our chef reminded us that we needed to think about the dessert course. Everyone fell silent until I volunteered bread and butter pudding. 'Great' said the chef, 'they'll love that on a cold day like this. Do you know how to make it?' Just as in Norway, it was a good thing that I carry around in my head the recipes for all these basic dishes. But what I didn't know was that the dreadful old oven apparently had only two settings, full on or off. The top of the bread got a bit overdone, but we did manage to salvage the majority of it and top it up with more eggs and milk.

We soldiered on, getting closer and closer to our deadline and further and further away from meeting it, when suddenly it was announced that the film crew were overrunning and we now had an extra hour before service. Frankly, I didn't believe it. I was convinced that the original noon deadline had been nothing more than a wind-up.

The whole thing was frantic, but we did manage to serve:

ESCALOPE OF VEAL MILANESE WITH SPAGHETTI POMODORO
VEGETABLE CURRY AND RICE
LAMB BOLOGNESE WITH PASTA OR RICE
BOILED POTATOES
CHIPS
SWEET GLAZED CARROTS
BRAISED CABBAGE
PEAS
SPICED BREAD AND BUTTER PUDDING
CUSTARD
BANANA SPLIT WITH CHOCOLATE SAUCE*

Plus one meal especially for the man who only eats sausages and mash with onion gravy, every single day of his life!

* *The astute observer of the programme will recall that the banana split should have been served with a butterscotch sauce. Allow me to explain. About five minutes before service the chef demanded to know what was going to be served with the banana split. Dean was team leader, but so busy with other things that he was unable to respond. Like an idiot I said, 'How about a butterscotch sauce?' Now when you make this sauce you need half as much butter as sugar and equal measures of sugar and golden syrup, plus some cream and vanilla essence to pop in at the end. There was no syrup, but I'd made it at home without so thought it worth a try. As there wasn't enough space on the stove I couldn't get it on the heat until after the main course was served, which meant there wasn't enough time for the sugar to melt before the sauce was needed. The result was that I unwittingly played right into the hands of a producer who was enjoying showing me to be apparently incapable of making a decent sauce. Fool, I should have kept my mouth shut and let someone else try to do it.*

In the end, all the cast and crew of Silent Witness got fed within their allotted time slot, and we received a good few compliments too. My veal dish went down very well, as did Daksha's curry, even if a few people thought it was too hot for lunchtime! As for the bread and butter pudding, there was none of it left for the judges to taste, so I guess it wasn't that bad.

When we'd washed up and cleaned down the surfaces our young chef admitted that he thought we'd done really well. 'After all' he said, 'I'd normally start at 4.00am for a 1 o'clock lunch service, and I've been doing it for three years.'

It was quite late by the time we arrived back at the studio, but we had to stick around because the producer had a very special announcement to make before we could go home.

'Tomorrow each of you will be cooking at a two Michelin starred restaurant. Daksha, you are going to Le Champignon Sauvage in the Cotswolds where you will be working with David Everett-Matthias. Dean you are going to Midsummer House in Cambridge to work under Daniel Clifford; and Peter, you are going to Le Manoir aux Quat' Saisons. You will of course be working with the legendary Raymond Blanc.' I am not sure if my chin actually hit the floor, but it certainly felt like it. Whatever else MasterChef did or did not do for me, the programme makers could not have given me a better gift than to spend a day working with Raymond Blanc. After hitting an all-time low with the location catering fiasco, now MasterChef was giving me the opportunity to fulfil a dream.

CHAPTER EIGHTEEN

BLANC MANGE

"Le Manoir aux Quat' Saisons is the fulfilment of a personal vision, a dream that one day I would create a hotel and restaurant in harmony where my guests would find perfection in food, comfort, service and welcome."

So said Raymond Blanc, Chef Patron of Le Manoir aux Quat' Saisons since he opened its doors in 1984 and where he has maintained a coveted Michelin two star rating continuously for the past 21 years. Of course I was aware of the status of the man and of the realisation of his dream. I knew him to be one of the finest and most highly respected chefs in the land. I had read his books, seen him on countless television appearances, and empathised with his holistic approach to food and dining. But I never expected to find myself working under his personal tuition, or to be walking with him in his gardens and greenhouses where we picked fresh vegetables and herbs together. And I certainly could not have imagined that one day I would be preparing one of his signature dishes in his kitchens before serving it for him to eat in his own dining room at Le Manoir aux Quat' Saisons.

It was quite a squeeze in the car for five of us plus all the equipment as we headed up the M40 early in the morning of 8th December. The show's producer wanted to art direct this particular day's shoot himself, so journeyed with us to ensure that he didn't miss a moment of the action. Along with cameraman, soundman, researcher/runner and myself we must have made a slightly odd-looking group as we arrived at the beautiful manor house in Great Milton. The original building dates back to the time of Richard II in the 13th Century, although much of what we see today is the result of re-building in the 17th, together with a major programme of extensions undertaken in the early 20th Century and more recently by Raymond himself.

As I had come to expect, there was a lot of hanging about before I could get to meet the man and get to work. I was dressed in nothing more than chef's whites, and outdoors it was freezing cold. The crew filmed me walking up the path from the gardens to the house, down the path from the house to the gardens, going into the main entrance, coming out of the main entrance, walking into shot from off-camera right and walking out of shot to off-camera left. Eventually I got to go inside into the warm, and to experience for the first time the remarkable ambience of the place. The interior is an object lesson in tasteful contemporary style. Nothing seems to be high-tech or jarring on the eyes or senses, but absolutely everything appears light, right and dedicated to comfort. I was shown into a small lounge bar off to the right of the foyer, where a log fire glowed in the grate and a small group of bit-part actors had gathered waiting for their instructions. It transpired that they were to be the diners for the purpose of filming so that Monsieur Blanc could protect both the decorum of his establishment and the privacy of his guests.

Eventually I was called to go into the kitchen to meet Raymond and his Executive Head Chef, Gary Jones. Originally a protégé of Raymond, Gary has subsequently become a Michelin-starred chef in his own right. He rejoined Raymond in 1999, and since then has worked alongside him, adding his own flair, originality and expertise to the team at Le Manoir.

Meeting a great and charismatic person for the first time is a strange, almost surreal experience. On the one hand one is in awe, but because of their frequent media appearances they often seem as familiar as old friends. Raymond was utterly charming and warmly welcomed me into his domain. The kitchens were immaculate, and extensively equipped to the very highest possible standards of hygiene and efficiency. I was just about to get my first Master Class from Gary when, with almost childlike excitement, Raymond called me outside to meet his fishmonger. In true Gallic fashion the two men greeted each other with a hug and a kiss on each cheek. Raymond introduced his fishmonger to me as 'one of the most important people at Le Manoir; he has been supplying me with the finest seafood for over twenty years'. From the back of his van the fishmonger produced boxes of oysters, cockles, clams, and mussels, and a huge tray full of hand picked scallops. To collect these, divers go down to the seabed and gather each scallop by hand. Raymond would never buy dredged up scallops because they contain mud and sand from the seabed and, more importantly, because a dredger cannot select what to bring up and what to leave behind for later. Worse still, dredging disturbs the very habitat on which the shellfish rely for their survival. This was my first clue as to what it is that makes Raymond such an extraordinary chef. He has complete respect for the ingredients he works with, and demands that his staff and suppliers share that respect. Next out of the van came the 'pièce de résistance' of the day; the most remarkable Cornish turbot I have ever seen. Weighing in at about 14 kilograms, at £20 per kilo this magnificent beast was worth almost £300. Raymond told me that a fish this size would be 18 to 20 years old. 'Just imagine, Peter' he said, 'when this fish was hatched you and I were young men. Now we are going to cook it, and we have to make sure that the dishes we prepare with it are a celebration of its life. The good does not interest us here, we are only interested in the sublime.'

Two such turbot were carried through to the kitchen store along with halibut, bass, langoustines, and all the shellfish I had seen earlier. There is an area of the kitchen specifically designed for the preparation of fish and seafood, and it was here that I enjoyed a Master Class from not one but two Masters. Both Raymond and Head Chef Gary took me through opening oysters with care to preserve their precious natural juices, and showed me how to remove the coral and skirt (or flange) of a scallop in one swift movement. I confess that in the past I have been guilty of throwing away the scallop's skirt, but Raymond told me that it is a valuable ingredient for adding flavour to a sauce, bouillon or braisage. Next came the turbot, and while I have filleted and skinned many a flatfish I had never dealt with anything of that magnitude or value. Gary made swift work of the first one, ending up with four immaculate white fillets with the carcass and trimmings reserved for the stockpot. Now it was my turn. Never have I been so pleased to have some previous experience to fall back on. Although much larger than any other fish I had ever filleted the technique is the same, and I too soon had four white skinless fillets to place on the tray beside Gary's. The 'Bravo, très bon!' from Raymond said it all.

I had been so engrossed in the morning's work that I had completely forgotten about the cameras, or indeed that the reason we were there was to make a television programme. It was past 12.30 and the producer was determined that I should work at the pass during lunch service. Raymond thought that what I was doing was far more important than working at the pass, but eventually acceded to the producer's wishes. The kitchens were buzzing with activity, and something like half of Raymond's fifty kitchen staff were working away with quiet efficiency. No one was rushing about, while the noise level was remarkably low amongst so much activity. The only raised voice I could hear was Gary calling out the orders at the pass. I was introduced to Sous Chef Craig, a bright young man with Gary Rhodes styled hair. Craig showed me to the end of the pass where starter courses of astounding beauty and complexity were being assembled by a group of very young but highly skilled kitchen staff. My task was going to be assembling the 'Special' starter of the day, and Craig promised to remain by my side throughout service. Raymond was sweeping up and down the pass, allowing nothing to escape his scrutiny. Only after his or Gary's approval would front of house staff be permitted to take dishes through to the diners in the restaurant.

Gary demonstrated my dish to me. On an oblong plate about 14 inches by 5 inches he created a masterpiece of abstract art. Two type of foie gras, a medallion and a parfait; two types of quince, marinated dice and a 'purée de ciongs'; and a host of other ingredients including salads with dressings, finely chopped hazelnuts, and balsamic reduction, the whole thing decorated with micro herbs. Even the salt and black pepper had to be placed by hand into a pair of inch long stripes to one end of the plate. I believe that I counted seventeen items on the plate, and every single one of them had to be placed in exactly the prescribed place and relationship to its neighbour. With Raymond watching my every move, this was pressure stuff indeed. After a couple of hashed attempts I found my stride, but now the orders were coming in thick and fast. Every plateful had to be completed immediately prior to going out so that the freshly picked and just dressed leaves would arrive at the tables within the shortest possible amount of time. By the time lunch service was over something like forty of the day's special starters had been served, and I freely admit that I could not have done it without the assistance of Craig. But he did tell me that he would have needed assistance himself with such a complex dish.

The irrepressible Raymond told me that my day would now start to get really exciting. He handed me a large basket and together we headed off into the gardens. Over two acres of grounds and greenhouses at Le Manoir are dedicated to cultivating something like 90 varieties of vegetable and more than 70 different herbs, and Raymond takes delight in every single plant and seedling. Many of the herbs are picked as tiny seedlings only a few millimetres high. Raymond calls these 'micro-herbs', and uses them not merely to adorn his dishes but also to add a multitude of tiny but intense flavours that explode in the mouth and tantalise the palate. Beyond the greenhouses Raymond showed me a deep grassy ditch beneath a line of trees, perhaps an ancient ha-ha. With great enthusiasm he explained that he has commissioned a specialist supplier called The Humungous Fungus Company to sow fungus spores in order to create his own beds of wild mushrooms. 'It may not work', he said. 'But we must keep striving for perfection.'

We dug up some Jerusalem artichokes, picked some lemon verbena and lemongrass, then mibuna leaf (Asian greens), bok choi and kai lan (Chinese broccoli), then finally a whole selection of micro herbs - and all from a garden in Oxfordshire in the middle of December. Walking back to the kitchen we were deep in conversation about how vegetables lose flavour from the second they are taken from the ground, and how important it is to get them to the kitchen with the minimum of delay. Raymond said: 'This morning you prepared the fish, now you have the fresh vegetables and herbs. Let us go and cook.'

At a quiet end of the kitchens we found Raymond's own area, the place where he creates new dishes and tests his alterations and additions to classics. Along the back of the work surface it was the epitome of 'mis en place' (to put in place). A vast array of ingredients had been prepared, cleaned, chopped, sliced, or diced. The cold items kept cool, and the warmed items kept warm. Raymond was in his element. As he picked up a small copper service pan and a spoon he said 'Watch closely Peter, I am going to make a Filet de Turbot braise; Bouillon de Fruits de Mer et Citronnelle. This dish has been on my menu for 17 years, it is very popular, but it can only be made to order. I will show you only once, then you will make the dish for Gary and me, OK?' I nodded my acceptance of his challenge and watched the maestro go to work. I have since calculated that there are thirty three ingredients in this dish, and Raymond had it cooked and plated up with its garnish of Oscietra caviar and micro herbs in just over four minutes. 'Voila!' he cried. 'Now it is your turn. When you are ready, you bring your dish through to Gary and me in the small dining room through there.' With that he was gone, and so too was Gary who had been standing close by until now watching proceedings. No, I was definitely on my own, with only the cameraman and sound man to keep me company. I stopped and thought for a moment: this really was the ultimate test. After this not only MasterChef, but perhaps more importantly I, would know for sure whether or not I was really any good in the kitchen.

For obvious reasons I cannot give here the recipe for this spectacular Blanc creation, but suffice to say that it requires keeping several pans on the go at once. It also requires spot on timing when cooking ingredients that may take only a minute or, in the case of some of the leaves, mere seconds to become overcooked. I stopped and checked the list of ingredients I'd scribbled down whilst Raymond was cooking and explaining to me how the dish goes together. Just prior to the garnish one native oyster should go on top of the scallop and turbot, but I didn't remember seeing Raymond place the oyster on his rendition of the dish. I had taken just over seven minutes to complete what Raymond had done in only four, but I was pleased with the result. Raymond popped back into the kitchen to check how I was doing and I took the opportunity to ask: 'Excuse me Chef, but is it possible that you forgot the oyster?' Raymond clasped a cupped hand to his mouth, sunk his neck into his shoulders and ran out of the kitchen.

I was just finishing my presentation of the dish with a touch of Oscietra caviar and a sprinkling of micro herbs when John and Gregg appeared across the pass. 'Please don't speak to me now,' I pleaded. 'The dish is ready, and if I don't serve it immediately it will carry on cooking in the hot braisage and be spoiled.' Being the 'pros' that they are they nodded and disappeared from my view. I wiped the rim of my plate with a clean cloth dampened with lemon juice to remove any finger marks, placed the cover over the dish, and made my way through to the dining room. At the entrance to the room the producer held out his hand to stop me. 'We're not ready, we haven't got the camera angles worked out yet. You'll have to wait.' 'But it can't wait,' I replied. 'If I don't serve it now it will be ruined.' He looked back at me with an expression of exasperation. 'Look,' he said, 'If I don't get the shot then it's a bloody waste of time us being here. You'll have to wait.' I looked beyond him to where Raymond and Gary were sitting. Raymond saw me and gave that shrug of the shoulders with palms upturned that only the French can give so much meaning.

Young Craig, the Sous Chef who had worked alongside me during the lunch service, was now standing just behind me. 'Peter, you are the Chef, you have to shout at them, throw a tantrum. If you don't serve your food to RB right away it will be ruined.' I looked back at him helplessly. I knew that any protestations on my part would be useless. We were staring 'absolute truth' number two in the face, and there was nothing I could do about it.

I served my dish to Raymond and Gary apologetically, knowing that the turbot would be overcooked because of the delay. Both assured me that they would take the delay into account, and in the event the turbot wasn't quite as spoilt as I had feared it would be. 'These television people, what do they know? Huh, in these circumstances you have done brilliantly.' These words from Raymond were all I needed to hear to make my day complete, but there was more to come later. After Raymond and Gary had been quizzed by the judges over my performance I was invited to join the two of them in a taste test to establish the ideal wine to accompany my dish. They had already selected two white wines, a dry and highly perfumed Gewürztraminer from Alsace and a Chassagne-Montrachet, the divine Burgundy that manages to be dry without a trace of hardness. Raymond poured each of us a glass of the Alsace, swirled his glass, held it up to the light, then to his nose, and breathed in its bouquet. 'Can you smell the scent of flowers Peter? Take a little of the food and then some wine. Tell me what you think.' I did as suggested, and was amazed by the flavour of the food I had just cooked. I had tasted the braisage as I was cooking it, but this was the first time I tasted all the components together. I'd never tasted anything quite so 'sublime' in my life. The Gewürztraminer on its own didn't do much for me. I've never been keen on wines from the Alsace, which are always a bit too acidic for me and tend to give me the sensation of indigestion. After a glass of water to clear the palate Raymond handed me a glass of the golden Montrachet. It, like the food, was utterly sublime, and considering that Montrachet is probably the finest white wine in the whole world it is not surprising that I preferred it to the Gewürztraminer.

As cameras, lights, microphones, power-packs and cables were being cleared away, Raymond, Gary and I sat enjoying the wines and discussing their relative merits. 'The Gewürztraminer is a clean, fresh, light wine with the perfume and flavour of summer flowers, and is good with many seafood dishes. And the Montrachet? It is smooth and fully rounded, it is the perfect wine for any occasion, any time of the year. It is satisfying like a beautiful woman.' One of Raymond's front of house men appeared, to remind him that he had a party of one hundred arriving for dinner in less than two hours and that he and Gary were needed in the kitchen. Gary took his leave, but Raymond seemed completely unfazed by the prospect of a hundred diners descending on his restaurant and took the time to write a dedication to me on the back of a menu. 'You are going to win this competition?' 'I am going to try my hardest to.' I replied. 'No, no, you will win, you have to win for me. Remember, Peter, only the very best is good enough at Le Manoir.' With that parting shot he shook my hand and was gone, back to the kitchen where he reigns supreme.

It was a wonderful day, the high spot of the whole competition, and a day that showed me just how great is the gulf between being a good amateur and the ultimate professional. Late that night, in the car on the way back to the studio, I mentioned to the producer about noticing that Raymond had forgotten the oyster when he demonstrated his dish to me. 'I know,' he replied, 'I was there when Raymond told John and Gregg about it. He thought it was amazing that you picked up on it, specially when you'd never seen the dish before and under the pressure we put you through.'

CHAPTER NINETEEN

SO YOU THINK THAT'S WORTH A MICHELIN STAR, DO YOU?

Some days prior to my experience at Le Manoir aux Quat' Saisons we finalists were informed that we would be required to produce a meal in the style and to the standard worthy of a Michelin star rating. I thought long and hard about this, worried that we had only been allotted an hour in which to prepare, cook and present our food. Raymond Blanc had asked me about my intentions for this challenge, and began to make some suggestions of his own until I told him that we were allowed only 60 minutes. 'Ridiculous,' he exclaimed, throwing both hands in the air. 'It's not possible to create a great dish, including mis en place, in only 60 minutes.'

This was if anything even more of a challenge than cooking for Raymond himself, as at least in his kitchen I had all the preparation done beforehand and the finest professional ovens and hotplates on which to cook. Still, there it was: one hour, one dish, and I knew there could be no playing safe at this stage in the game. The word going round was that we should not attempt to cook anything we had never cooked before, but I was convinced that this was the moment to really raise my game and establish an undeniable lead over the other two contestants. I devised a dish, and convinced myself that I would be able to pull it off within the time limit.

That night I lay in bed and 'cooked' the complete dish in my head. I did it in just under the hour. Then I had one final check through of the lists of ingredients and equipment, at which point I realised that I'd forgotten to include chestnuts on the list I'd handed in. These were vital ingredients, adding the final touch to my 'Christmas' dish. I had decided that as we had to present this meal on 9th December, it would be a great idea to cook the judges an 'alternative' Christmas lunch. It was to be pheasant stuffed with liver and wild mushrooms, potato rösti, spinach and Parmesan galette. This I would serve with baby onions and white grapes cooked in Sauternes, plus a mixture of smoked bacon, shallots, and chestnuts in a cream sauce. The whole thing was to be finished with a sherry and game jus. I knew it was wildly ambitious, but I was absolutely determined to make it work. Just before I fell asleep I made up my mind to leave extra early in the morning. I remembered seeing chestnuts for sale in a greengrocer's shop behind Baker Street tube station the day before, and I prayed that they would still have some in the morning. Luck was on my side and I met the shopkeeper at 6.30am to buy a pound of chestnuts.

Michelin starred dish to be completed in 60 minutes

Pheasant ballotine with liver and mushrooms

For two people

1 English hen pheasant, including giblets

100g wild mushrooms

2 shallots

2 chicken livers

A few sprigs of thyme

Salt and freshly ground black pepper

1 large Desiree or Maris Piper potato

Olive oil

2 handfuls baby spinach leaves

40g Parmesan cheese, freshly grated

10g Port Salut

A handful of baby onions

A handful seedless white grapes

1 glass Sauternes

20g unsalted butter

1 teaspoon caster sugar

2 or 3 rashers smoked streaky bacon

Handful of chestnuts

2 dessertspoons thick double cream

For the jus

Pheasant giblets plus 1 chicken neck

1 rasher smoked streaky bacon, rind removed

1 onion including skin

1 clove garlic

1 stick celery

1 carrot

Splash of sherry vinegar

Small glass dark sweet sherry

Teaspoon sugar

Redcurrant jelly

Hot water

Salt and freshly ground black pepper

Those of a nervous disposition should not attempt to do this in one hour.

1   You absolutely must begin by getting your sauce under way. Roughly chop the pheasant giblets and neck of chicken and put them in a hot pan with a splash of oil. Add the bacon, cut into lardons, and cook until well caramelised. Now add the roughly chopped, onion, carrot and garlic, including skins, plus the chopped celery. Again cook until the vegetables are well caramelised. Add a sprig of thyme and a good splash of sherry vinegar. Cook until the vinegar is completely evaporated, then add a generous glassful of sweet sherry. Cook to reduce by half, then pour over sufficient hot water to cover. Boil and simmer at the back of the stove, skimming off impurities as they rise to the surface.

2   Remove the wishbone from the pheasant and fillet out the two breasts. Remove the skin from the fillets and make a lengthways incision on the underside, halfway through the flesh. Now slide your knife sideways into the incision in both directions and open out the flaps like a pair of hinged doors. Season with salt and pepper.

3   Chop the mushrooms and shallots into very fine dice (brunoise) and sauté gently in butter. Slice the pheasant and chicken livers thinly and add to the sauté pan. Cook for 2 minutes, then remove from the heat, season with a little salt and pepper, and set aside.

4   Place a pheasant fillet on the end of a long piece of clingfilm and cover the centre with a generous amount of the duxelles and livers, then fold back the flaps of flesh and roll up tightly inside the clingfilm. Twist the ends to make a neat sausage shape and tie off with twine. Repeat

Pheasant ballotine with liver and mushrooms (cont)

for the second breast. These ballotines may now be gently poached in barely simmering water. To ensure that the ballotines remain submerged during cooking, place a saucepan of smaller diameter than the cooking pot on top of them in the water. (NB: The water must not be allowed to boil). They will take approximately 12 minutes to cook. Remove from the water and allow to cool slightly before snipping the clingfilm and sliding them out onto a plate.

5 Put the baby onions into hot water for a few minutes, then slide off their skins, Carefully trim off the bases but do not go too far up or the onions will collapse when cooked. Similarly, leave the pointed ends intact save for the brown tip. Melt some butter in a sauté pan, add the sugar and Sauternes, and when the sugar has dissolved put the onions into the pan and cover with greaseproof paper (cartouche). Simmer gently for 15 minutes, then add the grapes to the pan. The pan juices should become a thick syrup.

6 Cut through the outer skin of the chestnuts and boil in water for 10 minutes. Drain and remove the outer skin and the coarse inner skin. Place the chestnuts on a tray and pop them in a hot oven for 5-10 minutes. Finely chop a shallot and cut the bacon into fine strips (lardons) and cook in a little butter and oil. Add the chestnuts, roughly chopped, toss around in the pan, and set aside.

7 Peel and grate the potato, season with salt and pepper. Heat some oil in a pan and place two 5-6cm ring moulds in the pan. Put a spoonful of grated potato in each and press down. When the undersides are well browned, the moulds may be removed and the galettes turned over to cook the other sides. Remove and drain on kitchen paper.

8 Line a baking tray with baking parchment and place two 5-6cm ring moulds on top. Put a spoonful of freshly grated Parmesan into each, then a fine slice of Port Salut. Carefully lift off the rings and place the tray in a hot oven for about 3 minutes. Remove from the oven and set aside to cool. While these cheese galettes are warm they remain pliable and may be shaped if desired. Once they are cold they become hard and crisp.

9 Strain the jus through a sieve lined with 4 layers of dampened butter muslin, twisting the ends to get out every last drop of the precious liquid. Stir in a teaspoon of redcurrant jelly, taste for seasoning and add salt, pepper and sugar as necessary.

10 Wash and dry the spinach leaves and make up a vinaigrette with two parts olive oil to one part sherry vinegar plus a pinch each of salt, pepper and sugar.

11 Briefly sauté the ballotines in butter to just colour the outsides. Trim off the ends and cut each into three sections.

12 Place a potato galette in the middle of a warmed serving plate and surround with three sections of ballotine, the ends facing upwards to reveal the pale outer ring of meat with the dark filling in the middle.

13 Place the onions and grapes along with some of their syrup in the spaces between the sections of ballotine.

14 Stir some thick cream into the chestnut mixture and place a small teaspoon of this outside each section of ballotine.

15 Toss the spinach in the vinaigrette and use a ring mould to build a neat stack on top of the potato. Top this with a cheese galette and finish with a tiny quenelle of redcurrant jelly on top.

16 Finally, carefully spoon the jus around the meat and serve to tumultuous applause! Well, that's what I got from the judges, but what, I ask myself, ever happened to Escoffier's enduring edict to 'Keep it simple'?

Now that I sit here writing this I find it hard to believe that I actually did pull this dish off inside one hour. It scares me to think about it even now, but I remember standing back and looking at my completed dish as I took a swig of water, just as Gregg called '30 seconds, you've only got 30 seconds'.

I'd been so engrossed in what I was doing that I hadn't even looked at what the other two were up to. It turned out that Daksha chose to cook a fillet of red mullet on garlic mash with a sauce made of oranges flavoured with aniseed and saffron. This was a somewhat strange combination that didn't quite come off, and her attempt to present the judges with a European dish did not do justice to her mastery of the cuisine of Gujurat. The judges showed little mercy in their criticism of her dish; Gregg could not handle the odd combination of flavours, and the fact that she had overcooked her fish and broken the skin on the presentation side caused John to condemn it as 'scruffy' and 'careless'. I felt every verbal blow that landed on her. I had come to know her well enough to realise that she would be deeply wounded by their remarks. They asked her if she was proud of what she had cooked; fighting back the tears, she replied that her heart just wasn't in it. Of course it wasn't. In an attempt to give the judges what she thought they wanted Daksha turned her back on the food she knows and understands, and threw herself into a far less familiar cuisine. I still believe that she should have stayed with her own style. Atul Kochar has achieved a Michelin star for the outstanding quality of the Indian food he serves in a London restaurant, so why not Daksha Mistry?

John and Gregg turned their attentions to Dean. After a day spent working at Midsummer House Dean was determined to show what he had learnt from Chef Daniel Clifford. Somehow he had managed to 'borrow' from his mentor a huge state-of-the-art water bath with temperature regulators and goodness knows what other gadgetry. This was his secret weapon, the piece of equipment that he believed would put his dish way out in front. But any piece of equipment is only as good as the person who uses it, and the pork mousseline wrapped in sage and ham that was poached in it ended up delicious but overcooked. Dean is a lovely cook; he has a light touch and a natural talent. With a little more experience he will become a very fine chef, of that I have no doubt, but on that day he tried to pull off a dish that was beyond him and sadly it didn't quite work. Gregg seemed concerned with the 'abstract expressionist' presentation of the dish, where wild mushrooms and red wine sauce were splattered on the plate à la Jackson Pollack. The fundamental problem, however, was that just about any chef would need to cook this kind of food for a year or so before becoming a master of it. John told him that his meal was 'good, very good indeed', praise that was well deserved because Dean had come so far in such a short space of time.

As the judges approached my plate, for the first time in the competition I felt supremely confident. I have no doubt that messrs Fort, Spicer et al would have considered my dish 'pretentious' and I am not convinced that the Michelin inspectors would have given me a star for it, but I did know that I had definitely won the day. Gregg blurted out some rubbish about not liking the 'over constructed' presentation. I know he had to say something for the cameras, but at that moment his brain was not engaged with his mouth. He knows as well as anyone that today's fine dining dishes have to look as good as they taste. When he did taste the food, he was quite literally blown away by it. John also loved the dish: 'Hmmm, pheasant, mushrooms, liver, bacon, onions, grapes, Sauternes, chestnuts; all there, all on the money. You've given us the taste of Christmas on a plate. Very, very good'.

So that was Friday night, and the end of the competition was in sight. This time the questioning on camera went along the lines of: 'So you've saved the best for last? If this was your strategy, do you think you may have left it too late to catch up with the others after so many disasters?' Once again this was the kind of questioning designed to draw comments of bitter rivalry out of me. There hadn't been any disasters as far as I was concerned, and I wasn't having any of it. By this time I'd become quite an old hand at fending off such inflammatory questions. I replied that I didn't have a strategy, just a plan to take each day as it came, and that if I remained focused on the job in hand I just might get to the winning post ahead of the others.

CHAPTER TWENTY

LAS PALMAS, FOOD POISONING, AND QUARANTINE ONBOARD RMS QE2

'Bloody hell, I reckon we'd be safer to get out and walk.' Saturday 10th December. Dean and I had checked out of our accommodation, and the driver of the mini-cab hired to take us to Gatwick Airport was doing his level best to ensure that we did not arrive in one piece, if indeed we were going to arrive at all. To say that he was a bad driver would be a gross understatement. He crunched through gears, continuously took his eyes off the road, almost rammed into the rear of every car in front, swerved from lane to lane, carved up other drivers, and was totally oblivious of the trail of anger and confusion he left in his wake. His only method of braking entailed stamping on the brake pedal with all his might, which had the effect of sending Dean and me into a rib-crushing lunge against our seatbelt straps. The traffic was very heavy getting out of London and it seemed to take forever to get to the M23. We were running late, a fact that I was constantly reminded of by being rung every few minutes on my mobile phone by the crew, who were waiting at the airport. 'Tell the driver to get a bloody move on or we'll be late checking in' I was told, but believe me there was no need to give our suicidal driver any more encouragement. The same foot that fell heavily on the brake pedal was now doing its best to force the throttle through the bottom of the car. I could hear the engine valves bouncing, and could see the trail of smoke from the exhaust of the clapped out Toyota. God must have been with us, because we did eventually arrive at the Departures level of Gatwick's South Terminal. There was then further confusion over the price of the ride; I'd been given £50 in cash with which to pay him, the driver insisted that he had quoted £60. I made up the difference, asking for a receipt to add to my growing list of expenses that would be claimed back later. Poor guy, we had learned he couldn't drive; now we discovered he couldn't write either, at least not in English.

Having had our mettle well and truly tested, Dean and I met up with the rest of the crew and the judges and made our way towards the Departure security gates. One of the Airport's female officials looked at us and said: 'I know you lot, you're on the telly aren't you?' Not such an observant remark, considering our soundmen and cameramen were carrying their portable equipment with them. Looking at John Torode our self-appointed inquisitor remarked 'Course, you're that DIY bloke.' 'No

I'm bloody not,' replied John, 'I'm a bloody chef!' 'Oh yeah, you're that Super Cook programme, and that's 'im with the bald 'ed.' Neither John nor Gregg was amused, but the rest of us were by now convulsed with laughter.

Las Palmas looked lovely, and it felt lovely too as we stepped off the plane into 28°C. The London we had left behind was struggling to keep above freezing, so this was a very welcome change of climate. Unlike many of our previous adventures, this time we knew a little about what was in store for us. We knew for example that we had about 24 hours free time in the sunshine before going on board QE2 for the penultimate challenges of the whole contest. At this point there was a relaxed, almost holiday atmosphere among us, and everyone was looking forward to just chilling out for a little while. The crew and the judges had been working on the programme almost continuously for months on end, and we three finalists were into our sixth consecutive week of a heavy schedule of challenges on camera.

I went for a wander through the town and along the beach and the palm-lined promenade, thinking about the incredible journey I'd been on. Here I was just 400 miles north of the Tropic of Cancer, while only three weeks earlier I'd been 400 miles north of the Arctic Circle. Nobody would ever have guessed the magnitude of the dramas we'd been put through. Even viewed as a television programme, few would have grasped the level of commitment needed to survive such a marathon.

That evening we all met up for drinks in the hotel's cocktail bar, then walked to a seafood restaurant at the far end of the harbour. It was a balmy evening, the wine flowed almost as freely as the conversation, and great platters of seafood, salads and 'wrinkled potatoes' went down with ease. As night closed in and the local sounds mingled with the gentle lapping of waves against the rocks, we might have been excused for forgetting, just for a few hours, why we were there. The producer told us that we would not be boarding QE2 until the following afternoon, so as far as he was concerned we could do what we liked until then. Stay in bed, go shopping, go for a swim, anything we wanted; provided we were back at the hotel by 2pm Sunday.

I awoke very early next morning. It was beautifully sunny outside so I took myself off for a long walk along the shoreline. There in the harbour in front of me was the unmistakable profile of QE2. I'd never seen her in real life before, and although she's getting on for forty years old now she really is a magnificent sight. I am not exactly a nautical person, but I have to admit that the idea of setting sail on such a glorious ocean-going liner gave me quite a thrill.

I wandered back to the hotel to see what was going on and found my two fellow contestants in the foyer, deep in conversation with one of the VCR Directors. It seemed that once again someone had altered the rules and we, the pawns in the game, were expected to fall in line. Daksha was getting quite heated, and insisted that the producer had given us time out until 2.00pm. 'You need to be back here by twelve noon and that's all there is to it. Here's some money to buy yourselves some lunch. Bring back the change, and don't forget the receipt.' With a sigh and a shrug of the shoulders the three of us took ourselves off to the rasping cry of 'And don't be late or you'll be in serious trouble.' More of the 'kindergarten' treatment followed, but we ignored it and just kept walking.

Out in the sunshine Daksha calmed down a bit while Dean insisted that he wanted to go back to the hotel and 'Give that woman a dose of her own medicine'. This was a sentiment fully shared by both Daksha and me. With our recreation time curtailed we gave up any notion of going for a swim and settled for a coffee in an open-air café in the piazza. We took photographs of each other with QE2 in the background and took advantage of a quiet moment to phone home to our loved ones, all of whom were beginning to wonder if they might have lost us for good. At about 11am my mobile rang. 'You all need to have smart evening wear otherwise you won't be allowed in the public areas, bars or restaurants on board ship. Daksha needs a long dress and proper evening shoes, and you and Dean need black trousers, jacket, white shirt and tie and black leather shoes. Now, have you got things like that with you?' Of course we hadn't; we'd only packed what we'd been told to pack, chefs' whites and casual clothes for travelling. 'Well you'll have to go and buy them and you need to be back here at the hotel in one hour.' My reply went something like this: 'Well that's just brilliant. If you'd told us before we left the UK we could have packed accordingly. As it is, we're in a foreign land and none of us speaks the language, we don't have anything like enough local currency, it's Sunday, who knows if there will be any shops open, and you seriously expect us to be back in one hour?' 'Don't argue with me, you're wasting time; just go and do it.' 'So what do you suggest we do for money, always assuming we can find somewhere open?' 'Hasn't one of you got a credit card or something – just bring back the receipts and we'll give you the money.' As it happened I was the only one who had taken credit cards with me, the others didn't have so much as a wallet between them.

We spent half our 'lunch money' on a taxi that took us to the one big department store that was open on Sundays, and there, at break-neck speed, we dashed around and managed to buy all the clothes and shoes we needed. In total it came to the equivalent of about £350, which I though was pretty good considering how much we bought. Clutching our shopping bags and boxes we ran back to the street and spent the other half of our 'lunch money' on the taxi journey back to the hotel. We arrived with one minute to spare, only to discover that we wouldn't be boarding the ship for at least another two hours. Once more it felt as if everything had been done to cause us the maximum possible inconvenience and stress.

We'd checked out of our rooms by this time, but one had been kept on as a holding room for contestants, crew and a whole load of equipment, and here we waited in considerable discomfort for the call to board the ship. Eventually we all piled into people carriers for the short trip down to the harbour. Its not until you are standing on the quayside with QE2 towering over you that you gain a true impression of its gigantic proportions. I find it difficult to give meaning to a statistic of 70,000 tons weight, but when you learn that the ship is almost three hundred yards long and

175

that it carries nearly three thousand passengers and crew, you begin to grasp the magnitude of the leviathan.

In true TV filming style, we stood about on the quayside for an hour or more with nothing to do but watch passengers re-boarding after a few hours ashore in Las Palmas. I couldn't help noticing that everyone was required to cleanse their hands with antiseptic jelly before being allowed onto the gangways. Infections can spread like wildfire aboard ship, and clearly they weren't taking any chances. The director took us out to the far end of the jetty to get a good shot of us being introduced to the Captain. From that position we were beneath the vast bow of the ship that because of its dramatically acute angle looked like it might crash down on us at any moment. The kindly and softly spoken Captain came down to greet us, and after four or five takes we finally boarded QE2. Inside the purser's office I waited to be photographed and officially checked on board. On the wall there was a picture of the Captain, the twenty-second to serve aboard QE2 since her maiden voyage in 1969. *Captain N Bates, 18th September 2004.* The file inside my brain marked 'silly thoughts' immediately registered that other N Bates, as in Norman Bates of Bates Motel in Hitchcock's *Psycho.* That was the last thing I had to smile about aboard QE2, as within a few hours I had been struck down by the food poisoning I picked up in Las Palmas. That was on the night of Sunday 11th December, and I didn't emerge from the quarantine imposed by Dr. Hoffmann until we docked in Southampton on Thursday 15th. By then I'd lost almost a stone and a half, and the absolute final of MasterChef was only two days away.

On Thursday, just before I parted company with the producer, he asked me to be sure to dress smartly for the following day's photoshoot. When I arrived at the studio I was the only one of the finalists to be 'suited and booted'. Dean and Daksha had been told to come as they were. Thus Dean's image in grey granddad T-shirt and combat trousers supported how he had been packaged as 'the road digger from the school of hard knocks'. Daksha's plain black top was suitable attire for her image as ' the housewife', and as they had often erroneously referred to me as 'advertising hotshot' and 'advertising guru' (if only), my smart suit, shirt and tie played right into their hands.

The press photographs done, I went to check on my ingredients for the final three-course meal. After crashing out on QE2 and missing the two penultimate challenges I was sure that I would be too far behind the others to have even the remotest chance of winning. Nevertheless, I was determined to go out on a high note by cooking one of the finest meals of my life. They showed me the vegetables, dry goods and dairy products, then they showed me the Barbary duck and turbot; and then, to my horror, they produced a foil package of shelled scallops. I made a huge fuss, insisting that the scallops MUST be alive. They promised to bring live scallops into the studio for me next day.

CHAPTER TWENTY-ONE

SO THIS IS IT THEN

Saturday 17th December 9.00am, and I was on my third take of walking from the hotel where I'd been staying to the studio across the road. A round of the inevitable interviews followed, the same old questions coming back again and again. How did I feel to be entering the final day of the competition? Did I feel confident of pulling off my three courses within the two hours allotted? Did I still think that I could win the title? I gave them the answers I thought they wanted to hear, in the hope that they might then leave me alone to get on with the day.

It was now more than six months since I had walked into my audition, and since then I had been on the most remarkable journey of my life. Just being in the final with two other people out of the five thousand-plus who had originally applied was an incredible achievement. Quite apart from being ill on the QE2, I had already made up my mind that they would not give the title to a man of my age, and as a consequence now felt under no pressure whatsoever. For me, winning no longer mattered. I simply wanted to produce the best food I could.

At around midday one of the young women who take care of providing the ingredients came to give me the strangest piece of information. 'I'm very sorry,' she said, 'but it looks like somebody has stabbed your tomatoes! I'm just going out to buy some fresh ones for you'. I thought this was decidedly odd, but no matter if they were being replaced. The astute reader may well have already put two and two together, but for me it was only some time later that I saw the picture of John and Gregg on the BBC MasterChef website. There was Gregg with a bunch of carrot tops in his hand, and beside him stood John with one of my tomatoes stuck on the end of a chef's knife. Nice one John.

At last the time came for us to go into the studio kitchens and cook our final three dishes for the judges. The three of us had a last mutual hug, wished each other the very best, and went for it.

Masterchef final championship meal Saturday 17th December 2005
Three courses to be prepared in 2 hours

BRAISED FILLET OF TURBOT WITH FRESH LEAVES AND TOMATO BUTTER
TWO KINDS OF DUCK WITH L'ALIGOT, POTATO GALETTE,
CREAMED SAVOY CABBAGE AND RED WINE SAUCE WITH MUSHROOMS
MINI GÂTEAU PARIS-BREST

First course

Braised fillet of turbot with fresh leaves and tomato butter

Piece of turbot fillet 50g-60g
1 live scallop
A few leaves each of:
  Little gem lettuce
  Baby spinach
  Watercress
  Sorrel
  Chives
Stalk of lemongrass
Finely chopped shallot
Glass dry white wine, reduced to 1/4
Glass of Noilly Prat, reduced to 1/2
Salt and freshly ground white pepper
Unsalted butter
Dessert spoon whipped cream
A few drops of lemon juice

For the tomato butter
100g ripe tomatoes
15g unsalted butter, diced and chilled
Salt and freshly ground white pepper
Touch of caster sugar

Blitz the tomatoes in a processor, then pass the purée through a fine sieve and refrigerate.

Carefully skin the turbot fillet and trim to a neat shape.

Open the scallop and remove from shell. Reserve the white scallop meat, sliced in half horizontally, and the flange. Save the coral for another dish by freezing.

To make the braisage sweat the shallots in a little butter with a pinch of salt. Add the scallop flange and the turbot trimmings and sweat a little more without colouring. Add a teaspoon of crushed and chopped lemongrass, together with the reduced alcohols and a tablespoon of water. Simmer for two minutes, then allow to rest before passing through a fine chinois.

Brush the turbot with melted butter and season with salt and white pepper. Place the turbot on top of the braisage so that it is just raised above the surface of the liquid. Bring up to a boil, cover, and simmer for two minutes. Remove the turbot to a plate and keep warm.

Gently warm, but do not boil, the tomato purée. Remove from the heat and whisk in the diced butter. Season with salt and pepper and taste for sweetness. If necessary add a pinch of caster sugar and stir to dissolve.

Return the braisage to the heat and quickly poach the leaves in sequence: watercress, spinach, lettuce, chives and sorrel. Remove to a plate with a slotted spoon. With the braisage at the boil, poach the scallop discs for 10-15 seconds and immediately remove to a plate. Test the braisage for seasoning, adjust if necessary, and whisk in whipped cream.

Place the leaves in the centre of a warmed plate (or bowl) and carefully place the turbot on top. Add the two discs of scallop, then two or three drops of lemon juice before drizzling over a tablespoon of the bubbly braisage. Carefully spoon the tomato butter around the outside of the leaves and serve immediately.

Main course
Two kinds of duck with l'aligot, potato galette, creamed Savoy cabbage and red wine sauce with mushrooms

	For the stock	
Small Barbary duck	Duck neck and trimmings	Handful chestnut mushrooms
250ml rendered duck fat	2 carrots	Savoy cabbage
Coarse sea salt	1 onion	Crème fraîche
Black peppercorns	1 leek	2 medium Desiree
Juniper berries	2 sticks celery	or Maris Piper potatoes
Fresh thyme	Fresh thyme	2 cloves garlic
Bay leaf	Garlic	10g unsalted butter
Garlic	Red wine vinegar	25g grated Gruyère cheese
Unsalted butter	Large glass red wine	Salt and freshly ground black pepper
Olive oil	Small glass ruby port	
Runny honey		
Salt and freshly ground black pepper		
White wine vinegar		
Sprig fresh rosemary		

181

Remove the wishbone from the duck and cut away one whole leg and thigh and one whole breast fillet. Remove the thighbone and tidy up the edges of the breast fillet. Slash diagonally through the skin on the breast, then cover and set aside.

Roughly crush the peppercorns and juniper berries in a pestle and mortar and place in a dish along with a few leaves of thyme, a crushed bay leaf and a handful of coarse sea salt. Crush a clove of garlic to paste and rub this all over the duck leg. Now roll the leg in the dry marinade and press in well all over. Wrap the leg tightly in cling film and refrigerate (ideally the leg should stay in the fridge for 12 to 24 hours, but in test conditions it had a mere 20 minutes).

To make the stock for the sauce first chop up the neck and duck trimmings and fry these in a little olive oil until deep brown (almost burnt). Add roughly chopped onion and garlic (including skins) chopped carrot, celery, and leek, and continue cooking until the vegetables are well browned. Add a sprig of thyme then a dash of red wine vinegar and cook until the vinegar has completely evaporated. Add the wine and port and reduce to about half volume, then cover with hot water and leave to simmer at the back of the stove, skimming off impurities as necessary.

Wash the marinade off the duck leg, pat it dry, and place in a small ovenproof dish with enough duck fat to cover. Cook at 180°C for 80 minutes: when cooked, the leg is removed from the fat and flashed under a hot grill to crisp up the skin before serving.

The duck breast is simply cooked in a dry, non-stick pan. Start by placing the breast skin side down in a cold, dry pan. Place over the heat and cook without moving for 5 to 10 minutes: the fat will render out and provide its own cooking medium. When the skin side is well browned, season the flesh side with salt and pepper. Place a sprig of rosemary in the pan and put the duck breast flesh side down on top. Transfer the pan to the oven for about eight minutes spreading a little clear honey over the breast skin about half way through. Remove from the oven and allow to rest for 5 to 10 minutes before carving into thick diagonal slices for serving. The inside flesh should be pink (medium rare).

Two kinds of duck (cont)

Finely shred the cabbage, add a tablespoon of finely chopped carrot, and blanch in boiling water for two minutes then drain through a colander and set aside.

Boil one of the potatoes and two cloves of garlic, both unpeeled, for about 20 minutes. When the potato skin splits it is cooked. Peel the potato, squeeze the garlic out of its skin and pass them together through a mouli or potato ricer. Add the butter, salt, pepper, and grated cheese and beat well with a wooden spoon over a moderate heat until smooth and creamy.

Peel and finely grate the second potato into a bowl. Season with salt and pepper, squeeze out excess liquid, and form into a small neat galette. Fry in olive oil until crisp and golden on both sides.

To finish the cabbage, melt a little butter in a saucepan, add the blanched cabbage and carrot, season with salt and pepper, and stir-fry for a couple of minutes. Stir in a generous tablespoon of crème fraîche and cook for two more minutes before serving.

To finish the sauce, line a sieve with butter muslin, place another sieve over the top and pour the stock through into another saucepan. Press and rub the solids through the first sieve, discard the remains, and twist the muslin tightly to ensure all the goodness goes through. Gently reheat the sauce – if too thin add a few pea-sized pieces of beurre manié – and whisk in over the heat to reach the required consistency. Season to taste with salt and pepper.

Wipe and cut the mushrooms into quarters and sauté in a little butter before stirring them into the finished sauce.

Place a small mound of cabbage in one third of the plate and top with the duck confit. Place the potato galette in the second third and top with a quenelle of l'aligot. Pour some sauce into the last third and arrange the sliced duck breast on top. Spoon mushroom sauce around the breast.

Dessert

Mini gâteau Paris-Brest

For the choux pastry	For the crème pâtissière
65g plain flour	2 egg yolks
50g diced unsalted butter	40g caster sugar
150ml water	25g plain flour
2 eggs lightly beaten	Pinch of salt
A few drops concentrated vanilla extract	160ml milk
Tablespoon flaked almonds	1/2 teaspoon instant coffee
Icing sugar for dusting	A few drops of vanilla extract

Sift the flour onto a sheet of paper. Place the water and butter in a saucepan, heat until the butter has melted, then bring up to the boil. Remove from the heat and pour in the flour all at once. Beat with a wooden spoon until the dough leaves the sides of the pan in a ball. Return to the heat and stir continuously for two minutes until the dough glistens. Tip out into a bowl and allow to cool a little. Add the vanilla extract to the beaten eggs and beat into the dough a little at a time. The mixture should be very shiny, and just fall from the spoon.

Mini gâteau Paris-Brest (cont)

Line a baking sheet with non-stick baking paper. Scoop the dough into a piping bag fitted with a 12mm plain nozzle and pipe out a 150mm disc onto the baking paper. Add a drop of water and a tiny pinch of salt to the residue of beaten egg, then brush the top of the disc with the egg mix. Sprinkle generously with flaked almonds and bake in a pre-heated oven at 220°C for 10 minutes. Turn the heat down to 180 and continue cooking for a further 30 minutes. Remove from the oven and transfer to a wire rack. Immediately cut the disc in half horizontally to release all the steam. If the inside is still soft and doughy, return to the oven for a few more minutes to dry out. Leave in two halves to cool thoroughly.

Beat the egg yolks and sugar in a bowl until pale and fluffy, then stir in the flour. Flavour the milk with the coffee, salt and vanilla and bring to the boil. Whisk the hot milk into the egg mixture, then return the mix to the pan and whisk continuously over a moderate heat. If lumps form simply remove from the heat and whisk hard until the liquid is smooth again. Keep whisking until smooth and creamy throughout, then cook for two more minutes. Finally, scrape out into a bowl and leave to cool.

To finish the gâteau, place the bottom half of the pastry on a serving plate, pipe on the cream using a star tipped nozzle and set the upper half on top: the cream should 'squidge' out of the sides. Dust generously with icing sugar and serve.

184

* * *

The two hours passed quickly enough, but for the first time in the competition I didn't feel rushed, instead working methodically and enjoying what I was doing. The judges made it clear that they thought I'd taken on too much but I remained unfazed, and as the allotted time drew to a close I think they were genuinely surprised that I was ready and cleaning down the surfaces. When time was called I stood back, looked at my three plates of food, and was pleased. At that point I no longer cared about the judges' opinions. I had set a high standard for myself, and was satisfied that I had reached it.

I slipped into a kind of daze while the judging was going on. It felt as if I had spent months getting to the top of a mountain, and now that the summit had been reached I experienced a mixture of elation, relief, and a little sadness that the challenge was over. The judges told Dean that his bass was undercooked but his seafood bisque was divine. They said his venison wrapped in chicken mousse was not rare but raw, and I remember thinking that the concept of the dish was flawed. Chicken mousse was always going to cook long before a solid piece of red meat. Dean's dessert was a triumph, classic bread and butter pudding laced with toffee liqueur, sitting in a pool of beautiful crème à l'anglaise. Dean had been bold and adventurous; he had tried to create modern fine dining dishes that illustrated where he was going as a chef – I thought they'd probably give him the title.

I was next in line for the judges' scrutiny. My braised turbot with tomato butter sent them both into raptures, although not for the first time I noticed that Gregg is very adept at giving the producer alternative soundbites. He made both positive and negative comments, thus leaving the editors with the flexibility to show what they wanted. John was more committed, he just thought the dish was sublime. Both judges loved my two kinds of duck with two kinds of potato, but again Gregg made sure that the cameras and microphones recorded a negative remark. This time he commented that the duck leg was: 'a bit overcooked'. That, I would say, was a matter of opinion. In contrast to the rare, pan-roasted breast, the duck leg was intended to be 'well done', soft and falling off the bone within and crispy and well-caramelised outside. Again John remained nothing but positive and complimentary. Finally they tackled my gâteau Paris-Brest, a dish that both enjoyed so much they ate the lot, and caused Gregg to comment 'Cor, I'm being spoilt rotten'.

As John and Gregg made their way over to Daksha's workstation I was naturally pleased that they'd enjoyed my food and given me so much praise, but still reckoned that they'd give the title to Dean.

Just as in the Michelin test, I think Daksha lost her way with her final meal. She tried so hard to prove to the judges and the viewing public that she was not just a home cook from Gujurat, that she could tackle and master European dishes. The result was an eclectic meal, to say the least. Her main course of roast partridge and her dessert of lemon tart both required a high degree of professionalism in classic European cooking techniques, the very area in which she lacked experience. Her starter of samosas with minted cucumber raita was of course a hit, but I can't imagine ever wanting to eat highly spiced samosas as a prelude to roast partridge. Daksha had never before cooked a lemon tart, yet she tackled it with her irrepressible enthusiasm and brought it off triumphantly. Her partridge, however, was a total disaster. Lack of experience left the judges faced with a game bird that was completely raw. I looked back at Dean, he looked straight at me. We were both so sorry for Daksha. In her attempt to give the judges what she thought they wanted she had turned her back on the food she knows and loves, and as a result ruined her final meal in the competition. Any winner would want to win on merit, not because an opponent had failed.

Back out in the holding room, while the judges deliberated over their final decision, there were yet more of the incessant interviews for us to contend with. Dean seemed nervous and said that it would be a bitter blow to him to get that far and then lose. Daksha said she thought the raw bird had cost her the title, but that she was still proud to have reached the final. As for me; well, I thought that on cooking ability I should win, but being realistic I suspected that young Dean would be the popular TV winner.

One of the assistant directors told us that the previous year it had taken John and Gregg about three hours and a bitter argument before they reached the decision to give the title to Thomasina Miers. We settled in for a long wait, but within 30 minutes we heard a roar of laughter from behind the closed doors. Whatever else was going on in there they certainly weren't arguing about who should win this year. Ten minutes later there was a burst of activity – down came the acoustic

185

curtain from in front of the doors, cameramen and soundmen were rushing along the corridor, and in came the producer. 'That's it guys, the judges have made their decision. You will be going in to hear the result in five minutes.'

I had been unusually cool all day, but those words set my nerves jangling and my pulse racing. Of course the result mattered to me. Of course I wanted to win, that's what the previous seven months of my life had been all about.

'After what you guys have been through and the work you've put in, it's the toughest task in the world to pick one from the three.

Our winner ... our MasterChef ... is Peter.'

CHAPTER TWENTY TWO

AFTERTASTE

It is not possible to describe the emotions that accompanied the announcement of my win; they were too many and too profound. For me, it represented so much more than merely winning a TV reality show. It was an affirmation that I still have it in me to achieve. Over the previous couple of years trading in my erstwhile business had become so poor that I was forced to find an alternative means of earning a living. Gaining the title of MasterChef meant opening the door to a new career, and a potentially rewarding future. The scenes of me phoning my wife to tell her that I had won were absolutely genuine, as was her scream of delight in response that was heard by millions. Jacqueline my wife, Dean's wife, and Daksha's husband all came into the studio to join in the celebrations and commiserations, and in a truly magnanimous gesture Daksha told Jacqueline that she believed the right person had won. 'After all' she said, 'Peter has more food knowledge and ability than Dean and me put together'. Contrary to what viewers may have been led to believe we have remained close friends with Daksha and her family, and have enjoyed a Gujurati banquet cooked by her at her home in North London.

Once the glasses of champagne had gone down and the handshakes were over, all three of us finalists had to sink into oblivion for a full three months. The final programme in the series was not screened until 17th March, and we couldn't breathe a word about it until then. It was a strange time, knowing that I'd won a big national competition but not being able to tell anyone. Living in a small village I fortunately didn't have to lie to too many people, and the story I devised to get myself out of tricky conversations was that although the filming was over, no verdict would be made until the final programme was shown. I became so adept at reeling this one out that I almost came to believe it myself.

The screening of the first programme in the series was the cause of great excitement. Eight months after I first applied for an audition, there I was on national TV. I wasn't sure about how I came across – it was early days with a long way to go – but I remember thinking that what they'd chosen to show made me appear a little too sure of myself. Programme number five on 26th January was my next appearance, the one in which I won the quarter-final despite having failed to serve a sauce with my roast grouse. The fact that so much was made of that moment should have warned me that far worse was to come. There were then five more weeks of heats and quarter-finals to be gone through before the semi-finals even began.

Viewing the semi-finals of MasterChef shown in early March caused me, and those close to me, far more anxiety and emotional suffering than the editors could ever have imagined possible. The more I saw of myself, the less I recognised the man I was looking at. The whole series of programmes was completely devoid of humour, which certainly wasn't the case during filming. Not with Gregg treating us to an almost uninterrupted string of jokes, both blue and otherwise, that had the desired effect of defusing moments of heightened tension. Worse though was that even I didn't like what I saw of myself. The programmes had definitely been edited in such a way as to make viewers believe that I couldn't possibly become the winner. One night, up in the Arctic Circle, one of the crew had told me 'We always knew you'd make it this far'. Someone else said 'I don't know who will win, but you are the finest cook we've ever seen on this programme'. The slow, bungling and easily over-heated competitor I saw on television bore little resemblance to the person they were describing, and many people who know me well have commented that the man they saw was definitely not the Peter they know.

I recall telling my wife that the programmes during the finals week would have to turn this around, otherwise the judges' decision would appear ridiculous. The next programme was about the day at The Ritz, and I knew how well I'd done there and the praise I had received from Chef John Williams and the 'guests'; Brian Turner, Richard Shepherd, and the others. Surely, I thought, they couldn't cut that to make me look incapable. In the event the programme dwelt on my one little problem with the foie gras ravioli, and made a meal out of my trip upstairs to meet the diners. Remember 'absolute truth' number two about being in a TV programme?

Just like being a patient in hospital, you give up all rights to your own body for the duration of filming. You will be accompanied at all times. You will be told when to stand up and when to sit down, when to talk and when to be silent. What time to arrive and when you may leave – you are even told when you may use a lavatory and when you may not.

True to form, I was told when to leave the kitchen to go upstairs. I was told to wait outside the dining room door. I was told when to go in and where to stand when I got in there. I was told to answer any questions the guests may wish to ask of me, and I was told when to take my leave and return to the kitchen. But it didn't appear like that at all on television. Instead it looked like I swanned off upstairs to ingratiate myself with the guests, leaving the other two contestants in a state of panic in the kitchen. Daksha was shown doing a pretty good impersonation of a headless chicken, and Dean appeared resigned to the fact that he'd have to pick up the reins because I was upstairs. In themselves each of these things appears unimportant, but taken together they gave viewers a completely false version of what actually took place.

The next evening television viewers were treated to the fiasco that was outside catering for Silent Witness. Again young Dean was shown to be in control, every bit the frontrunner in the competition. At home we simply could not believe the evidence of our eyes. There were only three more programmes before I was to be announced as the winner, and still I was looking like a poor also-ran. Some of my best friends even rang up to offer their commiserations, as it was clear I wasn't going to win.

What followed was all very confusing. The actual sequence of events was that I spent the day after the location catering at Le Manoir with Raymond Blanc, followed by the studio challenge to cook a meal worthy of a Michelin star rating, then our journey to Las Palmas to join QE2. The editors must have decided that it would look bad if the winner was absent from the penultimate programme because of illness, so they switched the sequence and showed the QE2 episode first. I can't think why they bothered; all the previous programmes had been cut to downplay my chances of winning.

The programme on Thursday evening finally showed me doing well at Le Manoir and subsequently cooking the best meal in the studio, but not without a couple of digs. 'Will Peter hold up the whole lunchtime service at Le Manoir because he's too slow with his starter?' And yet again they showed my signature sequence: 'Where's your sauce, Peter?'

189

On the final day I had cooked my heart out, and there was really nothing negative to say about my performance. The way it was shown, however, still left a question or two unanswered. I asked the production company why they hadn't shown that Dean undercooked his bass as well as his venison, and was told that if they'd showed it like it was it would have been too obvious that I'd won. I also asked them why they'd kept showing: 'Take a bow Dean', followed by the applause from the Royal Marine Commandos that had been taken from another sequence altogether. They 'justified' this deliberate deception by explaining that it would have looked silly for Dean to be bowing to no one in the kitchen. What they didn't explain was why they had felt the need to splice and run it in the first place.

The result of these manipulations was that when the verdict was announced, many viewers felt cheated. They had gone along with what they'd been shown, and were convinced that they were correct in their judgement that Dean should have won the contest. Many of them vented their anger on the BBC website, while others phoned in to complain. Letters were sent to the Radio Times, and even Radio 2's Wogan show received calls from disgruntled viewers. The judges came in for all sorts of criticism and the Executive Producer of the programme went to the almost unprecedented length of posting a justification for their decision on the website. None of this made me feel particularly good about winning. Irrespective of these bad feelings, nothing could have prepared me for the morning after the final programme. On Saturday 18th March people I've never met before left me in no doubt that I had achieved something very special. In our local town of Lewes I was mobbed by well-wishers of all ages and types. The attention I attracted in the supermarket brought several aisles to a standstill, and so it went on everywhere I appeared. As days rolled into weeks the incidences of being recognised reduced in number, but I still meet strangers who recognise me and wish me well.

The 'Prize' for winning MasterChef Goes Large is the opportunity to work in a top London restaurant, but it is not a paid position. Arrangements had been made for me to work at Le Gavroche under Chef-Patron Michel Roux Jr, and for a man who loves food and cooking as much as I do that was the opportunity of a lifetime. I spoke to Michel soon after the programmes were televised, and we discussed the ways and means whereby I could accept and enjoy my prize whilst keeping in mind my need to earn a living. Chef Michel could not have been kinder or more accommodating. He also invited me to join him and his team at the 'Taste of London' food festival in Regent's Park in June 2006 for what proved to be five of the most exciting and frenetic days of my life. With something like fifty of the capital's top restaurateurs taking space at the festival, there was no shortage of celebrity faces at an event that attracted many thousands of visitors.

I guess I should have anticipated that Le Gavroche would be the main attraction, and that more people would want to sample Michel Roux's food than anyone else's. Le Gavroche served three quintessentially French – and utterly delicious – dishes: a terrine of foie gras, smoked chicken and green lentils wrapped in Parma ham and served with a truffle vinaigrette; a saucisson Lyonnaise en brioche with Madeira sauce; and finally daube de boeuf with gratin de pommes de terre Dauphinoise. Over the course of four exhausting days we served over six thousand dishes, but it was Le Gavroche's beef that was undoubtedly the dish of the whole event. Thanks to my involvement with Michel I got to meet many of this country's top chefs, all of whom descended upon us to sample his celebrated beef dish. The list of celebrity chefs reads like a who's who of British cooking: Gary Rhodes, Marcus Wareing, Angela Hartnett, Atul Kochar, Richard Corrigan, Aldo Zilli, Giorgio Locatelli – yes, even John Torode! – and all of them were highly complimentary to me when I was introduced by Michel. Michel Roux Jr is clearly a star among stars, and I confess to basking in a little of his reflected glory. The irony and indeed running joke of the whole event was that more visitors to the show wanted autographs and photographs of 'MasterChef' than of the real master chef, Michel. Michel thought this was hilarious, and insisted that I remain out front at the serving area as a crowd-pulling attraction. He certainly didn't need me to attract the crowds, but the suggestion was a selfless act of generosity on his part. It was a heady experience for me to be recognised and congratulated by so very many people, and it gave a feeling of genuine warmth that no amount of money could ever have bought.

Has winning MasterChef changed my life, as the programme initially promised? The short answer is not yet, but given time I am determined that it will. The phone was not blistering with heat the day after the final show, and the offers have not been pouring in through my door. I went out to the Mid West of America shortly after the result was announced and met with people who were unconditional in their enthusiasm for a 'winner'. They'd be prepared to back me too, if I decide to move out there and open a restaurant. It would be an enormous adventure, not to mention the realisation of a dream. With determination and persistence dreams can be realised; I'd proved that by winning the MasterChef competition. Now to achieve my ambition I have to prove it once more. One thing is for sure, it is certainly not too late to try.

CONVERSION TABLES

OVEN TEMPERATURES

°celcius	70	100	120	140	160	170	180	190	200	210	220	230	240
°fahrenheit	160	215	250	285	320	340	355	375	395	410	430	450	475
gas mark	0	1/4	1/2	1	3	4	4	5	6	6	7	8	9

GRAMS to OUNCES
(divide grams by 28.35)
The table below is rounded up or down for convenience

grams	5	10	25	50	75	100	125	150	200	250	500	750	1Kg
ounces	0.2	0.5	1	1.75	2.5	3.5	4.5	5	7	9	17.5	26.5	35

MILLILITRES to FLUID OUNCES
(divide millilitres by 29.57)
The table below is rounded up or down for convenience

millilitres	5	10	25	50	75	100	125	150	200	250	500	750	1Ltr
fluid ounces	0.2	0.5	1	1.75	2.5	3.5	4.25	5	7	8.5	17	25	34

CENTIMETRES - INCHES
Divide centimetres by 2.54